Oilmen and Other SCOUNDRELS

Oilmen and Other
SCOUNDRELS

· · · JAMES M. DAY · · ·

BARRICADE
BOOKS
FORT LEE, NEW JERSEY

Published by Barricade Books Inc.
185 Bridge Plaza North
Suite 308-A
Fort Lee, NJ 07024

www.barricadebooks.com

Library of Congress Cataloging-in-Publication Data

Day, James M.
        Oilmen and other scoundrels / James M. Day.
            p. cm.
        Includes bibliographical references.
        ISBN 1-56980-272-6 (hardcover)
        1. Petroleum industry and trade--United States--Biography. 2. Petroleum industry
and trade--United States--History. 3. Petroleum industry and trade--Corrupt practices--
United States--Case studies. I. Title.

HD9569.8.D39 2004
338.2'728'0973--dc22
                                                                        2004043724

First Printing
Manufactured in Canada

 Contents

 PREFACE

The oil industry has given us more than its share of scoundrels. Oil companies are at the top of everyone's hate list along with insurance companies, lawyers, politicians, and the new culprits—corporate executives who defraud investors and devastate their employees' retirement plans.

Oilmen are blamed for polluting the air, spilling black gunk, killing wildlife, and drilling in pristine wildernesses where it might disturb the sex life of caribou. They also have history's epitome of avarice they cannot live down—John D. Rockefeller, still reviled for his Standard Oil monopoly 100 years ago.

Who doesn't complain about high gasoline prices and the really, really, really high gasoline prices during a so-called "energy crisis"? Economists claim the demand for gasoline is "inelastic"—drivers will pay almost any price to drive to work and the 7-Eleven for a loaf of bread or a six-pack of Bud. To make matters worse, oil companies throw the prices in our face by posting them in two-foot-high letters at their gasoline station and adding a teeny "9/10¢" in the hope you won't notice or think it's trivial. That might sound insignificant unless you realize that Americans buy 360 million gallons of gas every day, and the 9/10¢ adds $3.25 million to their corporate pockets every day. (In case you don't have a calculator handy, that amounts to $1.2 billion a year.)

From its infancy, the oil industry has been notorious for cutthroat competition, price fixing, environmental degradation, and greed unlike any other industry. Pennsylvania's Oil Regions were the cradle of the petroleum industry in the 1860s and gave birth to its ills and greed. The Rule of Capture was conceived by greed. Oil and gas migrate beneath the surface and pay no heed to man's artificial boundaries, and the archaic legal rule induced the landowners and oilmen to drill and capture the oil before their neighbors could. Too much oil was produced, and prices fell from $30 to 10¢ a barrel within two years of Col. Edwin L. Drake's discovery in 1859, sowing the seeds of chaos and price fixing for Rockefeller reap. But Rockefeller couldn't do it alone. He manipulated greedy railroads and bribed greedy politicians to succeed. *Oilmen and Other Scoundrels* is about greed.

Oil is big business controlled by "Big Oil." It is not for the faint of heart and is far more complex than the public and bureaucrat regulators realize. ExxonMobil and many other oil companies take in and spend more money than many Third World nations. Few industries are as capital intensive. It spends billions each year exploring for oil, billions refining it into products, and more billions transporting it to your local gasoline station or for the manufacture of nylons, plastics, medicine, and other petroleum products. Offshore drilling platforms can cost in excess of $1 billion, and an offshore federal lease might cost $100,000 million without any guarantee oil or gas will be found. In 1983 Standard Oil of Ohio drilled a $2-billion dry hole in Alaska. It's no wonder oil companies spend millions on lobbying and political contributions.

The U.S. Department of the Interior, as manager of our public lands, collects billions in oil and gas royalties every year. The value of federal oil lands led to the infamous Teapot Dome scandal in the 1920s that dwarfed the news media's frenzy over Enron's corruption and collapse. Secretary of the Interior Albert B. Fall was convicted and went to jail for accepting a bribe of $100,000 in 1922, but the oilman who bribed Fall was acquitted. In 2002, $100,000 would be the equivalent of $1,075,000. As greed is about money, Appendix A is provided to show what the seemingly high or low prices of oil or how much the scoundrels bribed politicians years ago would be worth in 2002.

Oilmen and Other Scoundrels is not an attack on the oil industry or oilmen. I have known many honest oilmen who made valuable contributions to society and the nation. As a lawyer, I represented oil and gas companies for more than thirty years. (Okay, several were guilty.) I also served in the U.S. Department of the Interior and represented environmental groups. So I've seen all sides. In 1980 I formed a company to drill for oil and gas, so I was one of them and have been called "a damn oilman." For two decades, I have taught Oil and Gas Law and the Regulation of Energy at the Washington College of Law, the American University.

I accept all credit and blame for my irreverent opinions and attempt to add humor. However, some recognition must be given to John Cleese of *Monty Python* fame. I never told him, but during an attempt to write a serious tract I could entice my students to read, I realized it was dull and dry, like most tomes disgorged by historians. So the manuscript gathered dust. Years later, I saw Mr. Cleese on an educational TV channel. I decided if he could add irreverent humor to the slaughter, rape, pillaging, and devastation during the Crusades, I could do the same in a history of oil and oilmen.

Some credit or censure for my irreverence should also be given to the biographers who whitewashed the corruption of Rockefeller and other oilmen who attempted to atone for their sins by making contributions to charities. Rockefeller's unscrupulous tactics ruined honest businessmen in his quest to control the oil industry, and his giving millions to charities and establishing universities cannot change the facts or make his Standard Oil the "angel of mercy" he claimed it to be.

In researching the lives of Rockefeller, H. L. Hunt, Armand Hammer, and other scoundrels, I spread four or five books on my desk in an attempt to dig out the facts. More often than not, comparing the writings exposed academic apologists with a grant to write a biography of the impeccable life of an industrialist, a public relations hack paid to embellish the deeds of a rugged individualist, or a muckraker set out to expose the warts of a robber baron. Rockefeller and Hammer paid biographers, and Hunt gave interviews on the condition "mentions of him be favorable." Newspaper and other media coverage of the times and now are also often guilty of bias and sensationalism. The cherished "freedom of the press" is too often claimed when the scoundrels slant the news with impunity. Reading about the same event from several tomes reminded me of the often-portrayed comic strip character with an angel and devil on each shoulder whispering what he should do.

As few biographers were familiar with petroleum economics and technology and failed to show the results of overproduction, price

9

gouging and undercutting, kickbacks, bribes, and monopolies, dry petroleum and economic treatises were poured over. To make the economics and complex shenanigans understandable (how to squeeze competitors out of business and flimflam the government, investors, and the public), I included a few charts and maps, tossed in a smidgeon of petroleum economic analysis, and dug into court cases to explain the skullduggery. For those needing to incite their prurient interest, I added a little sex and adultery.

During my writing, I accumulated a debt of gratitude to members of Washington Independent Writers of Arlington, Virginia, including Mary Bird, Leo Solomon, and Penny Paugh for their critiques of my drafts.

As you sip a libation while reading (I personally prefer a single malt Scotch), note how few things have changed in the 140-odd years of petroleum history. There was financial hanky-panky in the corporation that financed Col. Edwin L. Drake's first oil well in 1859 and in Kenneth Lay's Enron conglomerate in 2001. Another similarity is neither were oilmen. Drake was a railroad conductor, and Lay is a Ph.D. economist.

James M. Day
Arlington, Virginia
February 2004

PART I
EARLY OILMEN

AMERICA'S MOST INFAMOUS OILMAN

John Wilkes Booth, President Abraham Lincoln's assassin and an actor, organized the Dramatic Oil Company in the early 1860s. The company struck oil, but Booth was swindled out of his investment. He never made a penny from the well and was shot a few months later.

CHAPTER ONE
THE FIRST OILMEN

ANCIENT OIL HISTORY

God commanded Noah to build an ark and "pitch it within and without with pitch." *Genesis* 5:14. The use of oil dates back over 4,000 years. In the fifth century B.C., the Greek historian Herodotus recorded Persians digging pits for salt near oil seeps. Understanding physics, they stuck a pole in the ground, attached a horizontal beam for a lever, and lowered a goatskin bag into the hole. Then they scooped up the slime and poured it into clay vats. The smelly stuff separated into brine to make salt, heavy asphalt for caulking and building, and oil for lamps and medicine.

The Greeks marveled at Babylonians laying building bricks sealed with pitch they dubbed *asphaltos,* literally "not to fall," what we call asphalt. They also derived *naphtha* from the Babylonian *naptu,* "that which flares." The Greeks added saltpeter and created "Greek Fire," the first military flamethrower.

It came as no surprise to the Persians when the Anglo-Persian Oil Company (now British Petroleum or BP) discovered oil in Maidan-i-Napti in 1908. The area had been called the "Plain of Oil" for as long as man could recall.

Throughout Persia and Mesopotamia (Iran and Iraq for those not up on history), oil seeps were common, and mothers gave their children hell for tracking the smelly gunk in the house. However, the men found uses for the black ooze—lamps, pouring burning oil over the walls on their attackers, boiling miscreants alive for their crimes, balms for burns, and cures for diarrhea and camel mange.

13

"Petroleum" comes from the Latin *petra*, "rock," and *oleum*, "oil." But the early Middle Eastern and Mediterranean civilizations were not the only ones using the black goo. The Aztecs around Tampico, Mexico, traded it throughout the Aztec Empire to make torches and as a toothpaste and chewing gum, *tzicle* or "chicle." Centuries later, crude oil seeping into streams and washing up on the beaches drew oil companies to the Gulf of Mexico.

THE EARLY AMERICANS

Centuries later, Western civilizations still hadn't figured out new uses for the glop that was more of a nuisance than a valuable product. Sir Francis Drake anchored off the coast of California to gather tar from seeps and caulk his ship in the sixteenth century, long before the Environmental Protection Agency and California proclaimed that oil was too nasty to drill for along California's pristine shores.

American Indians weren't considered civilized, but they had caulked their canoes, soothed burns, and made fire arrows with the glop long before the Europeans trespassed on their lands. In the eighteenth century, the Seneca Indians of western Pennsylvania sold "Seneca Oil" as a cure for the civilized whites' ailments—toothaches, rheumatism, headaches, indigestion, and dropsy. The white men learned that oil lubricated their machinery, railroads, and wagon wheels, which helped them settle the West and steal the Indians' lands.

By the early 1800s, settlers in Kentucky and West Virginia were peddling oil as a medicine or cure-all elixir. But little had changed since Herodotus recorded the work of the Persians. Drilling was still in search of salt. Oil was a minor by-product and screwed up salt production. In 1829 an American Medical Oil Company salt well in Burkesville, Kentucky, spewed thousands of barrels of oil that ran into the Cumberland River. America's first gusher and oil spill disaster caught fire and sent a river of flame fifty miles downstream, destroying vegetation for more than a decade.

Around 1830, the practice of digging holes to extract salt or brine gave way to the fifteen-hundred-year-old Chinese method of boring that reached depths of 3,000 feet. A heavy steel chisel was attached to the end of a rope tied to the top of a "spring pole" that was nothing more than a tall flexible tree stripped of its branches. The base of the spring pole was held down by large boulders and cradled on a yoke made from stout branches. The top of the pole was suspended over the hole, and a rope with the chisel tied on the end was dropped in the hole. Tied to the top of the rope were two or three ropes with loops similar to a stirrup into which men could insert a foot. The spring pole raised the chisel when the men released the pressure and dropped it when they stepped down. Called "kicking it down," it looked like a bunch of farmers who forgot to bring their leotards to an aerobics session.

Another method borrowed from the Chinese looked like a seesaw. Men walked the length of a beam to the end where a cable and drill were suspended over the hole to produce a downward stroke, then walked back to raise the drill. The beam of a modern oil pump is still called the "walking beam." The primitive methods were later replaced by steam engines and diesel motors.

Around 1839, Samuel M. Kier drilled a salt well in Tarentum, Pennsylvania, and found it plagued with oil. He solved the problem by dumping the oil run in the Pennsylvania Canal that led to the Allegheny River, a practice the Environmental Protection Agency would raise hell about today. When his wife became ill a few years later, he noticed that the oil he was dumping in the canal smelled and tasted like the American Medical Oil Company's medicine prescribed by his wife's doctor. Soon Kier was selling half-pint bottles of "Rock Oil" for $1 and sales were averaging 30,000 bottles a year. His advertisements claimed Kier's Rock Oil not only cured corns, cholera, and coughs, but after three doses, the lame had been known to walk and the blind to see.

Today the Food and Drug Administration would charge Kier with fraudulent and misleading advertising, and Madison Avenue might award him a prize for the corniest advertising jingle:

> The healthful balm, from Nature's secret spring,
> The bloom of health and life to man will bring;
> As from her depths the magic fluid flows,
> To calm our sufferings and assuage our woes.

Kier's well bottomed at 465 feet, and he had more oil than he could market as a medicine, driving the entrepreneur to buy a five-barrel a day still to refine the crude oil into lubricants and kerosine for lamps.

The First Oilmen

An apocryphal tale is that George A. Bissell saw an advertisement for Kier's Rock Oil in a druggist's window in 1856 and was fascinated by the picture of the well and oil being lifted from more than 400 feet. Bissell, a Dartmouth graduate who had taught Latin and Greek, was fluent in French, Spanish, German, and Portuguese, read and wrote Hebrew and Sanskrit, and had been a journalist and lawyer. The well-read gentleman believed, if Kier could drill for salt, he could drill for oil. While visiting his alma mater's chemistry lab in 1854, he had noticed a jar of rock oil and became intrigued with its similarities to coal oil being sold as an illuminant. If substantial amounts of oil could be found, immense profits were possible. Whale oil for burning in lamps was selling for $2.50 a gallon ($55 today), and the lower-priced coal oil stunk up the house and often exploded, killing people and burning down buildings. Camphene, distilled from turpentine, wasn't much better and was hard to keep lit.

Bissell organized the Pennsylvania Rock Oil Company of Connecticut. To attract investors, the company retained Benjamin Silliman Jr. to analyze the rock oil's properties as an illuminant and lubricant. Silliman was the head of Yale's prestigious chemistry department and wrote a glowing analysis of rock oil's commercial potential. The venture's first hitch arose when the company couldn't scrape up $526.08 ($11,436.45 in 2002) to pay for Silliman's report. Silliman refused to release the study until Bissell finally coughed up the money one year later. The records are scant on the corporation's finances, but it is known the $5,000 they paid for the lease on a Pennsylvania farm to drill for oil was capitalized on the books at $25,000, and several investors paid for their shares in worthless securities.[1] (The Securities and Exchange Commission frowns upon such accounting practices today, although the SEC's record of catching crooks like Enron is not great.)

The company named Silliman president for promotional reasons, but he did very little. Like most academics, he preferred the classroom and laboratory and knew or cared little about business. Silliman was replaced by James M. Townsend, a New Haven banker and a true

---

[1] Five thousand dollars in 1859 is the equivalent of $108,595 in 2002. As the costs, prices, and bribes mentioned might appear small during the past 140-odd years, Appendix A is provided to show the equivalent values in 2002.

16

believer in rock oil's potential. As the investors and officers were educated gentlemen, they needed someone to do the actual dirty work of
finding the oil in the backwoods of Pennsylvania. Townsend selected
Edwin L. Drake, a former railroad conductor, as the ideal candidate.
Drake was unemployed, would work for $1,000 a year, and had a rail-
road pass permitting him to travel free.

Drake's lack of technical experience proved no hindrance.
Townsend instructed him to stop on his way in Syracuse, New York,
to see what a salt well looked like. From Syracuse, Drake took a train
to Erie, Pennsylvania, and rode the last forty miles by a stage that ran
twice a week to Titusville (population 125). To his surprise, he was
greeted as "Colonel." Townsend had sent his mail in advance
addressed to Col. E. L. Drake to impress the hicks.

Drake trenched for oil near a seep on Oil Creek, which sounded
like a good place to look for oil, but failed to gather more than ten gallons a day, far less than Bissell and Townsend believed necessary to
make humongous profits. In May 1858, he traveled to Tarentum, a
100-mile journey by carriage and riverboat, to hire a driller. Warnings
that salt drillers were a hard-drinking, unreliable lot, Drake insisted
his man be a teetotaler. It took him weeks to find a sober driller, who
wouldn't be available until mid-August, before he returned to
Titusville to erect a derrick and install a steam engine to power the
drill. A wooden structure towering 100 feet over the country landscape brought dozens of volunteers to help erect "Drake's Folly."
When September rolled around and the driller still hadn't arrived,
Drake journeyed back to Tarentum, but couldn't find the driller or a
replacement, forcing him to suspend work for the winter.

Back in New Haven, cash was low, and the investors were having
second thoughts about the venture. Townsend scrounged up $1,000
for Drake's expenses and notified the former railroad conductor he
had been elected a member of the board of directors and president of
the new, solvent corporation, the Seneca Oil Company.

The spring of 1859 looked brighter. Drake found a salt driller,
William "Uncle Billy" A. Smith. Uncle Billy was also a blacksmith and
one of those handy fellows who could fix most anything. And the price
was right—$2.50 a day and he would throw in his two sons to help.

Drake's insistence they drill next to Oil Creek invited water to seep
into the hole. Attempts to hold back the water and mud in the thirty-
two feet of soil above the bedrock ended with cave-ins and flooding. A

pump Uncle Billy devised lost ground to the water and mud and forced the workers to wade through a knee-deep quagmire. In a last desperate attempt, Uncle Billy drove a three-inch pipe into the bedrock with a battering ram powered by a windlass that allowed drilling by steam power through the pipe at up to three feet a day, one-half the normal salt-drilling rate because of the low-powered steam engine.

Uncle Billy's and Drake's struggles took months. The New Haven stockholders, tired of reading reports of water, mud, and excuses for the lack of progress, cut off funding in midsummer. Townsend paid the costs out of his pocket until the last week in August when his personal funds and faith ran low. Reluctantly, he sent Drake a money order to cover his expenses and a letter instructing him to cease business and return to New Haven.

On Saturday, August 27, 1859, Uncle Billy stopped drilling at sixty-nine feet. The drill had slipped into a crevice, dropped six inches, and jammed. With nothing to do in Titusville on a Sunday, Uncle Billy checked the well. On top of the water, he thought he saw oil a few feet below the derrick floor. He crafted a ladle from a tin rainspout, lowered it into the hole, and confirmed the first oil well strike in America.

Drake arrived Monday to find a crowd of well-wishers (no pun intended) and Uncle Billy and his sons filling wash basins, tubs, and whiskey and beer barrels with oil. Drake installed a pump to increase production. He couldn't keep an accurate record of how much oil the well produced because he was too busy scavenging barrels to store the oil.

George Bissell rushed to Titusville and spent hundreds of thousands of dollars buying oil leases around Oil Creek. He became extremely wealthy and donated money to build a gymnasium at his alma mater, where he first saw a bottle of rock oil in the chemistry lab. Townsend also became rich, but complained he didn't receive the credit for taking the greatest financial risk. The banker also wondered where Bissell suddenly found the cash to buy oil leases.

The story of the first oil well is like a tale out of pulp fiction. If Townsend's letter had arrived a day earlier, drilling would have stopped and no one would have heard of the former Connecticut railroad conductor, "Col." Edwin L. Drake.

Hundreds of fortunes were to be made, lost, squandered, and stolen in the area called the "Oil Regions." But what happened to Drake?

COL. EDWIN L. DRAKE

While Seneca Oil Company investors were leasing lands and adding to their wealth, their dutiful agent managed the well. Thirty-nine days after his discovery, the derrick and oil storage caught fire and were destroyed. Drake never claimed to be an oilman nor did he drill another oil well. In 1860 he was elected a justice of the peace and worked for a New York oil buyer. Three years later, he moved to New York and became a partner in a Wall Street brokerage firm. By 1866, he lost his $20,000 savings earned from the Seneca Oil Company speculating in oil stocks.

Drake lived in poverty and bad health the rest of his life. In 1873 the commonwealth of Pennsylvania granted him a pension of $1,500 a year in recognition of the economic prosperity he brought the state. He died in obscurity in 1880.

CHAPTER TWO
SEEDS OF CHAOS

THE OIL REGIONS

Drake's 1859 oil strike drew thousands to western Pennsylvania's Oil Regions. America's first oilmen didn't realize what they were about to face. Boom towns colorfully named Oil City, Pithole, and Oleopolis rose up along Oil Creek and Allegheny River tributaries. By the end of 1860, seventy-five wells produced oil and 400 dry holes scarred the landscape along Oil Creek. Before the decade ended, 1,186 wells would hit oil and 4,374 would earn the stigma "dusters."

Unlike California's Forty-niners a decade earlier, where the early gold seekers panned streambeds and built crude wooden sluices to seek their fortune in nuggets and tiny flakes, drilling for oil cost between $1,000 and $2,000. Wells 500 feet deep or more might cost in excess of $10,000. California land was *free* for the taking. Pennsylvania oil prospectors faced hardy Scotch-Irish and German farmers demanding payment for the right to explore for oil on their land. Early leases granting a one-tenth royalty soon ballooned to one-quarter or one-third of the oil produced delivered in barrels. Today the standard minimum oil and gas royalty is one-eighth.

U.S. MINING LAWS

The 40,000 forty-niners of the California gold rush were trespassers on the public lands in 1849.[2] So were 10,000 "forty-eighters," who beat them there in 1848 to claim the first gold strikes. Gold was discovered in January 1848. However, the Treaty of Guadalupe Hidalgo acquiring California from Mexico wasn't signed until February 2 and wasn't ratified by the Senate until May 30, 1848. Congress admitted California as a state on September 9, 1850, but never bothered to establish a territorial government or protect the federal domain. President James Polk, whose platform included whipping Mexico and taking its land, kept his 1844 campaign promise not to run for reelection in 1848.

Presidents John Tyler, Millard Fillmore, Franklin Pierce, and James Buchanan, all known for not doing anything, did nothing about trespassers taking the nation's minerals. During the Civil War, Lincoln couldn't spare the troops. Andrew Johnson, busy fighting impeachment, didn't stop the Lode Law of 1866 that gave away lode-mining claims *free*. Under Ulysses Grant's giveaway administration, Congress passed the Placer Act of 1870 and General Mining Law of 1872 providing for the trivial payment of $5 an acre for lode claims and $2.50 an acre on placer claims.

Congressional acquiescence in federal oil lands falling into the hands of oil companies forced President William Howard Taft to issue an executive order withdrawing 3,041,000 acres of western oil lands from mining claims in 1909. In 1912 Taft began setting aside the lands as Naval Oil Reserves for the navy, which was converting its fleet from coal to oil. But that didn't stop attempts to grab the Naval Oil Reserves, as revealed in Part Three.

The nation's public oil lands were sold for pittances until the passage of the Mineral Leasing Act of 1920 that required the federal government to collect oil royalties. You can still file a mining claim for minerals on much of the federal lands under the archaic General Mining Law of 1872 at $2.50 to $5 an acre.

From the beginning, the oil industry was plagued with problems that distinguished it from other industries and still dominate it today. Crude oil is a flammable, fugacious liquid that must be produced from the earth, transported, refined into a product, and marketed. By definition, an integrated oil company is one that engages in all four phases, from exploration to filling up your Ford at the pump.

---

[2] *United States v. Gear,* 42 U.S. (How.) 120 (1845). Case citations are provided for dull lawyers who thrive on dry legal authority.

MAP 2:1
OIL REGIONS OF THE 1860S & 1870S

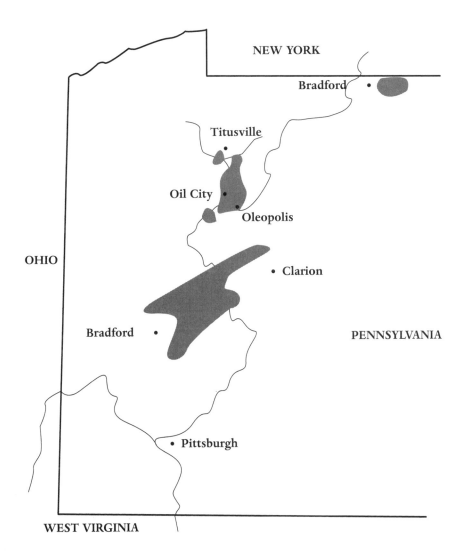

The Rule of Capture

Before you run to the dictionary, oil's fugacious characteristic means it is fleeting and tries to escape. The term is derived from the same Latin stem for fugitive. Crude oil and its sister hydrocarbon, natural gas, migrate in the bowels of the earth. Trapped under pressure for millions of years, they escape along the path of least resistance and pay no heed to man's surface boundaries. Thus an oil or gas well can drain oil and gas from neighboring lands.

If you give three children one soda to share and each a straw, the child who sucks the fastest gets the most. The same principle applies to men and oil. State courts universally adopted the Rule of Capture based on English water law: No one owns oil or gas until it is reduced to his possession. In a suit against a gas company that maliciously drilled near the plaintiff's boundary to steal his oil and gas, the Pennsylvania Supreme Court ruled in 1907:

> [E]very landowner or his lessee may locate his wells wherever he pleases, regardless of the interests of others. *** He may crowd the adjoining farms so as to enable him to draw the oil and gas from them. What can the neighbor do? Nothing, only go and do likewise. He must protect his own oil and gas. He knows it is wild and will run away if it finds an opening and it is his business to keep it at home.[3]

The Rule of Capture induced landowners to demand that the oilmen drill as soon as possible or pay a penalty for fear of losing the oil under their land and to capture as much oil as possible before his neighbor could. The failure to drill in a timely fashion is still grounds for an automatic termination of an oil and gas lease today. More wells were drilled than necessary to recover the oil. As there was no use for natural gas, it was flared. Decades passed before oilmen learned that producing oil too fast and wasting gas depleted the natural energy in the oil field that raised the oil to the surface, leaving three-quarters of the oil in the ground. Conservation laws slowly evolved to ban the flaring of gas and drilling near boundaries or more wells than neces-

---

[3] *Bernard v. Monongahela Gas Co.*, 216 Pa. 362, 65 A. 801, 802 (1907). An earlier similar battle against a tentacle of the Standard Oil octopus is found in *Kelly v. Ohio Oil Co.*, 57 Ohio 317, 49 N.E. 399 (1897)

sary to recover the oil under one's land. In a nutshell, the laws allowed landowners the opportunity to recover their fair share of the oil and gas beneath their land under the doctrine of "correlative rights" and barred *physical waste.*

The next battle was over *economic waste*—producing more oil or gas than can be sold at a profit. It still haunts us and is faced in Part Five.

BARRELS

In order to capture the oil, the oilmen had to put it in something. Barrels were an obvious choice, but no one made barrels to store oil. Barrels came in all sizes, and purchasers insisted the size be uniform so the oil could be measured. As the United States had no size standards, oilmen turned to England. King Edward IV had standardized barrel sizes to prevent "divers deceits" in 1482. The Oil Regions Petroleum Producers Association formally adopted the English 42-gallon herring barrel in 1872. Herring barrels were larger than the standard English 36-gallon beer barrel. (Pay no attention to the wags who claim the use of beer barrels might have created a beer shortage or made the beer taste bad.)

Although petroleum is seldom shipped in barrels today, it is measured worldwide by 42-gallon barrels (American, not British imperial gallons) until it is sold at retail in gallons or liters. Environmentalists and the press are the exceptions and prefer to quote in gallons. Doesn't it sound worse to claim the *Exxon Valdez* spilled 11 million gallons than 260 thousand barrels?

Petroleum is measured at 60°F (15.6°C) because it expands with temperature rises and contracts at lower temperatures. However, early oilmen didn't have the means to measure temperature variances. Because many barrels were made of green wood due to the unquenchable demand and the saltwater found in all crude oils tended to dissolve the glues, most barrels leaked. A deduction of 25¢ a barrel was charged rail shippers until 1866 when the practice evolved to deduct two gallons per barrel as a "leakage allowance."

Prior to Drake's 1859 discovery, barrels cost 50¢, but the price tripled by the spring of 1860. Over the next decade, prices varied between $2 and $4, plus $1 for cooperage. During the 1860s and 1870s, barrels often cost more than the crude oil they contained.

Barrels were also used to store oil at the wellhead. In 1860 Frank

25

Tarbell built large rectangular wooden vats, in defiance of the laws of physics and common sense, that leaked in the corners. Cylindrical wooden tanks supported by steel bands were built that also leaked. Steel tanks eventually displaced wooden tanks.

With the increase in barrel costs, oilmen refused to deliver the landowner's royalty oil in barrels. Landowners welcomed the change. The logistics of shipping oil to market was a headache and the cost exorbitant. *Scientific American* estimated the transportation and handling costs to New York City at $8 a barrel in 1862.

TRANSPORTATION

Shipping oil took many forms from the Oil Regions during the early years. It was commonly declared: "You can't get there from here!" Crude oil not only had to be shipped from the backwoods to a refinery, the refinery had to transport its products, primarily kerosine for lamps, to distant East Coast markets. During 1860-61, the nearest railhead lay twenty to forty miles north from the wells.

Teamsters drove two-horse teams to haul five to seven barrels weighing roughly 315 pounds each by wagons over narrow, muddy roads during the spring and fall rainy seasons and ice and snow of the winter to the railhead. The going rate ranged from $2 to $3 a barrel based on distance, weather, and what the traffic would bear and reached $5 during bad weather. Accidents caused losses some claim were as high as 20 percent. (An exaggeration?)

The alternative to the railroads in the early years was by water 135 miles from where Oil Creek entered the Allegheny River to Pittsburgh. The drawback was the river froze over during the winter and dropped too low for navigation in the dry summers. Teamsters still had to cart the barrels to a wharf. The river freight was generally below $1 a barrel, but the risks were high. In December 1862, an ice floe broke loose and crushed 200 boats, resulting in a loss of 30,000 barrels of crude. The following spring, a fire destroyed more than fifty boats and 8,000 barrels of crude and burned a bridge over the Allegheny River. Capt. Jacob Vandergrift of Pittsburgh, one of the first bulk handlers of crude oil on the Allegheny, built a fleet of shallow-draft vessels. He later expanded into producing, refining, and pipelines and joined forces with the most infamous oil scoundrel, John D. Rockefeller, whose skullduggery is disclosed in Part Two.

Railroads took a brief wait-and-see attitude to the fledgling oil industry. Would it be a boom and bust after the oil ran out? Would the Erie Canal capture shipments to New York? There was also the problem of the transfer of bulk shipments between the varying track gauges. The railroads were also slow to build tank cars and would find that Rockefeller was their false friend and manipulated them after acquiring the majority of the petroleum tank cars.

The fledgling pipeline industry had to overcome poor cast-iron pipe, pump vibration causing leaking joints, and teamsters tearing up the lines in the dead of night to eliminate the new competition. Samuel Van Syckle completed the first crude-oil pipeline in October 1865 between Pithole and the Oil Creek Railroad, an unbelievable distance of five miles, using wrought-iron pipe and lap-welding, burying it underground and hiring enough guards to prevent the teamsters from ripping it up. Van Syckle's pipeline made a profit charging $1 a barrel compared to the teamsters' rate of $2 to $3.

As technology improved, pipelines would battle railroads for supremacy. Until 1878, the railroads' influence over the Pennsylvania legislature kept the pipelines from obtaining rights-of-way to thwart the competition that would evolve into a cheaper and more efficient carrier of crude oil and petroleum liquids.

OIL PRICES AND PRODUCTION

Early oil price and production statistics range from contradictory to nonexistent. Keeping in mind Mark Twain's admonition, "There are three kinds of lies: lies, damn lies, and statistics,"[4] many historians believe the best data source for the era is *Derrick's Hand-Book of Petroleum: A Complete Chronological and Statistical Review of Petroleum Developments from 1859 to 1898, Vol. I.* Another excellent data source is J. T. Henry's *The Early and Later History of Petroleum, with Authentic Facts in Regard to its Development in Western Pennsylvania.* (Apparently, Mr. Henry agreed that some published facts are not authentic.)

Estimates of 1860 crude-oil production run the gamut between 200,000 and 500,000 barrels. The guesstimates soared to 2.1 million barrels for 1861 and 3 million in 1862 with the oil discoveries in Ohio and West Virginia. The combination of a crude-oil surplus, low

---

[4] Mark Twain admitted in his autobiography that he stole the phrase from Benjamin Disraeli.

prices, and flush production[5] tapering off lowered 1863 production to 2.6 million barrels. Robert E. Lee's invasion of Pennsylvania drove many to shut down their wells and run for cover until after the battle of Gettysburg. A lull in drilling and finding new oil dropped 1864 production to slightly more than 2 million barrels.

Crude-oil price statistics are no better, but show the effect of overproduction that Scotsman Adam Smith warned about in his 1776 treatise on capitalism, *The Wealth of Nations*. Drake's well in August of 1859 had buyers at $30 a barrel, which some attribute to the novelty of the first production. The price soon leveled at $20 until January 1860 when it slipped to $18.50. In March it dropped to $12, then fell to $8.50 in July. By October 1860, it sank as low as $4.

According to *Derrick's Hand-Book*, 1861 saw price fluctuations early in the year up to $10, before plunging to $2 in the summer. The economic question was simple: What could be done with all the damn oil? The price fell to 10¢ a barrel! The infant petroleum industry was about to collapse if something didn't happen.

The South fired on Fort Sumpter! Camphene made from turpentine extracted from the South's pine forests was no longer available, and whaling was curtailed, creating a shortage of lamp fuel. As usual during wars, there was also inflation. Prices crept to more than $1 a barrel in 1862 and averaged around $3.50 in 1863. By the end of 1864, the price was in the neighborhood of $12 after peaking in July at $13.75, and averaged slightly more than $8 for the year. After the war ended, prices slumped and closed out in 1865 below $7. To help pay the Union's Civil War debts, Congress levied a $1-per-barrel tax on crude oil to add to the oilmen's woes in May 1865. The tax was repealed the following May, but too late to help the price of crude oil from sinking below $1.50.

God created economists to make weathermen look accurate. But it doesn't take an economist to figure out that wars, recessions, overproduction, and shortages affect prices. The 1973 Arab embargo after the Yom Kippur War (Ramadan War if you are a Muslim Arab) created a worldwide shortage and skyrocketing prices. Today, the Organization of Petroleum Exporting Countries periodically cuts production in an

---

[5] Flush production refers to the oil rising to the surface without pumps or other forms of extrinsic energy.

attempt to raise crude-oil prices to *their target level*. Fortunately, they all cheat and can't control their maverick member, Iraq.

The effects of war, recessions, and overproduction are evident in Chart 2:1. But be careful of yearly average prices of crude oil. Oil prices fluctuated wildly during a year. Today the New York Mercantile Exchange crude-oil prices might bounce up or down more than $1 a barrel on a single day. One should heed Mark Twain when analyzing averages. Remember, when computing the average American's wealth, it includes Bill Gates and a guy who flips hamburgers at McDonald's. But riches are what drew the average man to the oil fields. A good example was J. W. Sherman.

J. W. Sherman Well

Sherman arrived in Oil Creek in 1862 with little cash and had to drill using a spring-pole powered by the legs of two men. After hitting a promising show of oil, the drill couldn't penetrate a layer of hard sandstone. He traded a 1/16 share of the well for a horse to power the drill, but the horse died a week later. Sherman traded another 1/16 for a secondhand steam engine. With no money to buy coal, he traded another 1/16 for $80 and a shotgun. The following week, he brought in a gusher that earned $1.7 million over the next two years, equal to $25 million today.

The farmer who traded Sherman the old nag that died for a 1/16 interest earned $106,250, the equivalent of more than $1.5 million today.

REFINERS

Not surprisingly, lamp oil distilled from coal was called coal oil, a form of kerosine. The short-lived coal-oil industry began in America around 1855. The best estimate by Abraham Gesner, a pioneer in the industry, was there were fifty-six coal-oil distillers and probably a dozen or more that he didn't know about in 1860. Gesner also noted that fifteen small crude-oil refineries were distilling kerosine.[6] "Small" meant from two or three barrels a day capacity up to twenty. Today, there are refineries capable of running more than 400,000 barrels a day. One has to wonder what was done with the estimated 200,000 to

---

[6] Gesner is credited with first calling the refined product "kerosene" from the Greek *keros* for wax and *ene* because it resembled camphene, a lamp illuminant. The oil industry generally spells it kerosine.

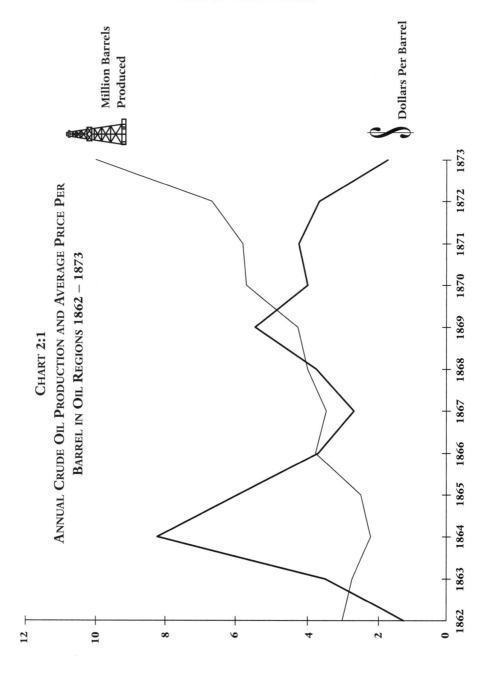

CHART 2:1
Annual Crude Oil Production and Average Price Per
Barrel in Oil Regions 1862 – 1873

Million Barrels
Produced

Dollars Per Barrel

500,000 barrels of crude oil produced during 1860 or the accuracy of the estimates. But the few number of refineries might explain why crude-oil prices dropped faster than a brick. During 1861, refineries sprouted like weeds and reached close to fifty in Erie, Pittsburgh, and the Oil Regions, several with a capacity of 100 barrels a day.

Thomas A. Gale's *The Wonder of the 19th Century! Rock Oil, in Pennsylvania and Elsewhere,* published in 1860, may explain the small businessman's rush to riches. Gale touted that for a mere $200, a man could build a five-barrels-a-day still to refine rock oil into kerosene. A $1,500 investment would build a refinery capable of producing up to thirty barrels a day. For $4,000, you could go big time and erect a 100-barrel-a-day refinery. Not only did comparable coal-oil refineries cost up to $100,000 to construct, they were more expensive to run. Coal-oil refineries had no choice but to shift to crude oil.

Estimates of the number of crude-oil refineries at the close of 1863 were as high as 300, but no one really knows. Nor are there accurate figures of refinery capacity or production because of the confusion between the volumes of crude run and what was actually distilled from the crude. Yields of kerosine ranged between 50 to 60 percent, and waste was rampant. *The American Petroleum Industry: The Age of Illumination 1859–1899* reports that annual refinery throughput capacity (actual crude run through the stills) grew from more than 500,000 barrels in 1862 to more than 2 million in 1865 and reached 3.2 million in 1866.

The best figures *The Age of Illumination* could possibly generate for the 1864-65 refinery capacity and location had to be extrapolated from six publications, as America didn't have the Department of Energy's statisticians trying to keep track of the petroleum industry. But alas, the hodgepodge conflicts with its text as to the refinery daily capacity in the major areas. Pennsylvania's refining centers were Pittsburgh (4,500 barrels), Oil Regions (2,160 barrels), Philadelphia (500 barrels), and who knows what was going on around Erie. The New York-New Jersey area had a capacity of 3,100 barrels, Cleveland 800 barrels, followed by Boston with 500 barrels, and Baltimore squeezing out 20 barrels.

Regardless of the conflicting "authentic" and semiauthentic data and anecdotal evidence, it is clear that the petroleum-refining industry was expanding. *The Age of Illumination* listed the major areas' refin-

ing capacity at 11,680 barrels a day in 1864-65 and 47,600 by 1872-73...
a fourfold increase in a decade.

THE SEEDS OF CHAOS SPROUTED CONFUSION

Statistics can be boring. The only reason to include dry numbers is to
make a point. Facts and figures show the oil industry was young, inefficient, and disorganized, but growing in an era thirsty for oil and ripe
for swallowing by a pious bookkeeper with a penchant for efficiency
and insatiable greed for money. John D. Rockefeller epitomized the
era of unscrupulous robber barons. He believed rugged individualism
was a thing of the past and the combination (monopoly) was the sal-
vation of American industry. When squeezing a refiner out of business or buying out a competitor, he claimed Standard Oil was "an
angel of mercy" by "replacing turmoil with stability."

BOOMS, BURNS, & BUSTS

There are no statistics on the saloons and brothels that flourished in
the Oil Regions. A typical historical comment is "Every other shop
was a saloon." Nor are there statistics on fatalities and fires. The
boomtowns of Pleasantville and Fagundas City burned to the ground.
After Oil Creek caught fire for the umpteenth time in 1863, the
Pennsylvania legislature banned the dumping of oil in the waterways.
Many claim the law was the first petroleum environmental legislation.

The first recorded major oil disaster occurred at Oil Creek on
April 17, 1861, when a gusher blew oil sixty feet in the air at 3,000 barrels a day. Henry Rouse, the operator, attempted to stem the flow, but
he and eighteen men were killed when the gases ignited. The fire
burned for three days before being smothered with soil and, believe it
or not, horse manure. Few paid attention to the minor newspaper
item reporting the disaster. The headlines blazed that the South had
fired on Fort Sumter and President Lincoln had called up 75,000
troops. But the 3,000-barrel-a-day gusher was good news to oilmen. It
proved there was plenty of oil and they wouldn't have to rely on
pumps to suck it out at a rate of ten or twenty barrels a day.[7]

As in any boom, con men scurried to the area faster than cockroaches. Speculators called "dump men" built the first independent

---

[7] There is always a Chicken Little in every neighborhood. In 1874, the Pennsylvania state
geologist predicted the state would run out of oil in four years.

storage tanks and purchased crude oil for resale to refiners, brokers, and wholesalers, often at distressed prices, and set crude-oil prices for the Oil Regions. The first oil exchange was organized in Oil City in 1869. Soon oil exchanges opened in Titusville, Pittsburgh, and New York to set market prices.

The nation became captivated by oil stocks. By 1865, more than 500 oil-stock corporations had been formed with a total capital in excess of $350 million ($3.8 billion today). Stocks not worth the paper they were printed on flooded the stock exchanges, and oil leases were sold in fractions down to 1/512 for the "little man" by con men and promoters on the streets and in saloons.

In the Oil Regions' era of boom and bust, Pithole City was a typical boomtown that went bust.

PITHOLE CITY

Pithole City got its start after a wildcatter took the advice of a dowser with a witch hazel twig and hit a 600-barrel-a-day gusher in January 1865. Two men bought a small farm and laid out a town that was to reach a population of 15,000. Within months, it overflowed with whorehouses, saloons, flophouses, hotels, banks, stores, and proof it was civilized—an opera house. By September, Pithole was producing 6,000 barrels a day. During 1865, it spewed 900,000 barrels—one-third of the crude oil produced in the Oil Regions.

The output slumped below 4,000 barrels a day in January 1866 and piddled to a stop in September 1867 because of wasteful practices, such as flaring the gas and wells drilled on one-half-acre lots. By then everyone had ventured off to the new boomtowns of Shamburg and Pleasantville.

A plot in Pithole City that sold for $2 million in 1865 was auctioned off in 1878 for $4.37.

PART II
ROCKEFELLER & STANDARD OIL

"Down with all tyrants! God damn Standard Oil!"
   —Eugene O'Neill, *Moon for the Misbegotten*
   (1952)

Mother's warning to children in the Oil Regions:
"Rockefeller will get you if you don't mind."
   —*Saturday Evening Post* (September 21, 1911)

"There was a man sent from God whose name was John . . ."
   —Beginning of a hymn sung by University of
   Chicago students after learning Rockefeller
   contributed $3 million to the university (1895)

CHAPTER THREE
BOOKKEEPER TO OIL BARON

**Warning: Reading About Rockefeller and Standard Oil
Could Be a Hazard on the Way to Finding the Truth**

Rockefeller and Standard Oil are not mentioned in Henry Demarest Lloyd's *Wealth Against Commonwealth* published in 1894, but everyone knew who was the "Millionaire Socialist" referred to in his attack on capitalism and the oil combination. The *Nation* said it was an example of "rhetorical blunder of overstatement" and "five hundred pages of the wildest rant." Still it was well received by the impossible-to-define intellectuals intrigued with populism and communism and the general public that despised the industry trusts.

The best-known exposé is Ida Minerva Tarbell's *The History of the Standard Oil Company*, a eighteen-part series published in *McClure's* magazine during 1902 and 1904 and reprinted by the Macmillan Company in 1904. Tarbell was the six-foot-one queen of writers bent on exposing corporate and government corruption who President Theodore Roosevelt baptized "muckrakers." She also had a sharp axe to swing. Raised in the Oil Regions, her father, Frank Tarbell, made those rectangular oil storage vats that leaked and was one of the many independent oilmen Rockefeller squeezed out of business. He was also one of the vigilantes who sabotaged Standard Oil's storage tanks in 1872. Her brother, William, was a founder and officer of the Pure Oil Company that challenged Standard Oil's monopoly. William testified against Standard Oil in the 1906 antitrust case and edited her drafts.

The bitter old maid delivered a coup de grâce in two brutal articles in the July and August 1905 issues of *McClure's*. In "John D.

Rockefeller, A Character Study," she wrote he was "the victim of a money-passion which blinds him to every other consideration in life" and viciously attacked his physical appearance. It is no wonder Rockefeller called her "Miss Tar Barrel." It could have been worse, her writing was in the magazine style of the times and too often today— full of sensational anecdotes to shock the reader and lacking hard facts. Many "factual" accounts are vague, unsubstantiated, and show little understanding of the petroleum industry or economics even though she was given access to Standard Oil's records. If she had better analyzed the records and 242 pages of material in the appendices to her 554-page invective, she could have crucified Rockefeller and Standard Oil. In a sop to the appearance of fairness, she devoted one chapter entitled "The Legitimate Greatness of the Standard Oil Company."

On the flip side, there were the defenders of Rockefeller and Standard Oil. Columbia professor and twice a Pulitzer Prize winner Allan Nevins wrote two treatises that by their titles warn of bias: *John D. Rockefeller, The Heroic Age of American Enterprise* (1940) and *Study in Power: John D. Rockefeller, Industrialist and Philanthropist* (1953).

The mass of statistics and anecdotes range from enlightening to meaningless in *The American Petroleum Industry: The Age of Illumination—1859-1899*. It is often more of a history of Standard Oil and its contribution to efficiency and order than a history of the petroleum industry. (Yes, Standard Oil gave meaning to "economies of scale," but at the price of fraud and ruin of those in its path.) Its sequel, *The Age of Energy—1899-1959*, stated Standard Oil was merely an "alleged monopoly." The bias wasn't a surprise. One of the authors had been a public relations flack for Standard Oil of Indiana and an employee of the American Petroleum Institute, which funded the study. Nevertheless, scholars will find it a useful source.

Standard Oil bought publications and hired an advertising agency to pay 3¢ a line for favorable articles in newspapers. U.S. Senator Johnson Newlon Camden of West Virginia wrote an article supporting Standard Oil in the influential *North American Review*. The public was not aware that Camden had secretly sold his refinery to Standard Oil, concealed that his purchases of other oil companies were for Standard Oil, and that he was a Standard Oil shareholder. Camden also greased the Congress and state legislatures with cash and pamphlets. For $40,000 spread around the Maryland legislature, he obtained an exclusive pipeline charter that eliminated Standard Oil's pipeline competition in the state.

THE BAPTIST BOOKKEEPER'S BLOODLINES

Today's psychiatrists would love to peer into the head of the boy raised by a pious mother and a father deserving the chapter title "The Flimflam Man" in *Titan,* Ron Chernow's excellent Rockefeller biography. John Davison Rockefeller was born on July 8, 1839, to William "Big Bill" Avery Rockefeller and Eliza Davison and bore the name of his mother's sober Baptist Scotch-Irish father. The Rockefellers were hillbillies and fond of booze, and Big Bill had a passion for young women. In a tiny crowded house in upstate New York, he alternated having three children with Eliza and two with their housekeeper. John had to know that his father had been twice indicted for the rape of local women.

Big Bill regarded country folk ripe for plucking. His principal occupation was a traveling "botanic doctor." Disappearing for months offered the "cancer specialist" the opportunity to adopt the name Dr. William Levingston and marry Margaret Allen in 1855. The bigamist moved his Rockefeller family from upstate New York to Cleveland, far from Margaret, and started spending even less time as a Rockefeller.

Two traits the father passed to his son were the love of money and crafty dealing. Apologists claim his forcing John to earn money for his mother and four brothers and sisters after Big Bill had two families to support was part of his business education. John's hopes of becoming a Baptist minister were dashed when his father told him he wouldn't pay for college. He left school at sixteen, one month before graduation, and took a job as an assistant bookkeeper at $300 a year.

After three-and-one-half years and pay increases to $600 a year, John managed to save $800 and still give 5 percent of his earnings to his Baptist church. (Nineteen-year-old Baptists, who don't drink, smoke, dance, play cards, or chase women, can save more money than most of the guys.) When his employer denied his demand for a $200 raise because he was doing the work of two accountants, he quit. John joined Maurice B. Clark, an Englishman nine years his senior, in a partnership to buy and sell produce. The young man's problem of raising $2,000 for his share of the capital was solved by borrowing $1,000 from his father at 10-percent interest, more than double the going interest rate.

At the end of the first year, Clark and Rockefeller netted $4,400. Clark managed the buying and selling, and Rockefeller kept the books and assured they collected every penny due. To purchase large produce shipments, John often borrowed money from his father at exorbitant rates, making the young man a sharper businessman with an eye to cutting frills and waste. By 1862, Clark and Rockefeller's profits reached $17,000, and the Civil War promised greater profits. At twenty-two, the fervent abolitionist, hired a substitute to avoid serving in the Union Army.

THE OIL BUSINESS

Samuel Andrews, an Englishman who attended the Baptist church with Rockefeller and had distilled the first kerosine from crude oil in Cleveland, approached Clark and Rockefeller for financial backing of his ideas to improve kerosine yield and quality. Tales vary who first agreed to invest $4,000 in the venture, but Rockefeller's animosity toward both men was apparent after the refinery firm was named Andrews, Clark & Company in 1863. In the oil venture's pecking order, Clark regarded Rockefeller as the junior-bookkeeping partner, and Rockefeller considered Andrews a bullheaded mechanic with no business sense. However, there was no doubt that Andrews was instrumental in their producing the best and lowest-cost kerosine in Cleveland.

Rockefeller cringed at the chaos in the Oil Regions on his first trip to Titusville to purchase crude oil and decided that crude-oil production was too disorderly for his methodical way of doing business. He concentrated on refining and marketing and left much of the produce commission business to Clark. Always eyeing every detail, he selected an ideal site with access to Lake Erie and the railroad for their Excelsior Oil Works and devised methods to undercut the competition from Cleveland's fifty refineries, most of which were overgrown teakettles.

In 1865 Clark refused to go along with Rockefeller's insistence they borrow to expand the refinery that was now their major business. Clark hastily agreed to an auction of each other's interest. Unknown to Clark, Rockefeller had already lined up the financing to buy Clark's refining interest and leave him with the produce business. By borrowing $72,500, Rockefeller took control of a 500-barrel-a day-refinery—Cleveland's largest and most efficient.

The twenty-six-year-old bookkeeper still needed money to expand. His reputation for timely paying of debts enabled him to borrow the funds. The new refinery was named the Standard Works, the first indication he possessed marketing insights. *Standard* represented quality, distinguishing it from many competitors who blended unmarketable gasoline in the kerosine, which often exploded, burning buildings and killing thousands every year.

Rockefeller's aversion to shoddy suppliers charging what the market would bear added to his profits. He eliminated barrel manufacturers charging $2.50 a barrel by buying a cooperage firm and made barrels for less than a $1. This not only assured him of a cheaper barrel supply that was often the margin of profit, it guaranteed they were properly made of cured oak that didn't leak, thereby cutting his transportation losses. His finishing touch was to paint them blue. Before the decade ended, Standard's blue barrels would be known worldwide.

The introverted bookkeeper brought his brother, William, into the business to manage the New York and export sales and put the Standard Works under William Rockefeller & Company. William was not only an astute businessman and supersalesman, he possessed something John could never achieve, charm and the ability to make friends easily.

In need of cash for further expansion, Rockefeller found another ideal partner. Henry M. Flagler, a visionary with extensive business experience, had married into the family of Steven V. Harkness, a multimillionaire. Harkness's directorship in banks and railroads opened doors to hundreds of businesses. Impressed by Rockefeller's plans, Harkness took stock in the company rather than extend a loan. Flagler remained Rockefeller's right arm for many years and still found time to buy cheap land, drain swamps, and build railroads and resorts for his real estate venture to turn mosquito-infested Florida into the Sunshine State.

On January 10, 1870, the Standard Oil Company of Ohio was organized with a capital of $1 million and elected John D. Rockefeller⊗, president; William Rockefeller⊗, vice president; and

Henry Flagler⊗, secretary/treasurer. Its 10,000 shares of common stock were divided: 2,667 to John D. Rockefeller, 1,334 to Steven Harkness⊗, 1,333 each to William Rockefeller, Samuel Andrews, and Henry Flagler, and 1,000 to the Rockefeller, Andrews, Flagler & Company and Oliver B. Jennings⊗, William's wealthy brother-in-law.

Samuel Andrews, a minority shareholder, was considered a mere refinery technician and not a businessman. Rockefeller shunted him aside and hired Ambrose McGregor to run the Standard Works.[8] The hard-nosed Scot was a brutal businessman and efficient refinery operator. One of his assignments was to evaluate and oversee refineries Standard Oil was to take over.

Rockefeller's Standard Oil, with its unheard-of-refining capacity of 1,500 barrels a day, was the biggest predator in America's ocean of oil. As it grew, it would devour crude oil producers, refiners, pipelines, railroads, marketers, and petroleum-product manufacturers until no one could compete with the giant octopus.

At Standard Oil's organization meeting, Rockefeller added an incentive for his sharklike partners—no one, including Rockefeller, were to be paid salaries. Their income was to be solely from dividends and the increased value of their stock.

DIVISIONS AND SELF-INTERESTS

The petroleum industry, divided between the crude-oil producers, refiners, and marketers, and split further by location, fought like stepsisters battling over an inheritance. As the major markets lay in the populated East Coast and its ports for export, the railroads controlled the fourth segment of the oil industry—transportation. Pipeline technology had yet to develop the capability to deliver over long distances and only served as gathering lines from the wells to the railheads.

Pennsylvania's railroads were run by robber barons through their major railroads and alliances with connecting lines—Jay Gould's and

---

[8] After a dispute over dividends Rockefeller wanted to plow back for expansion, Andrews said he wanted out of the business. Rockefeller asked him to name his price. Andrews said $1 million. The following day, Rockefeller handed him a check for $1 million and sold Andrews's shares on behalf of the company to William H. Vanderbilt, son of New York Central Railroad president, Cornelius Vanderbilt, for $1.3 million. The squeeze not only netted Standard Oil a quick $300,000 profit, it would earn the company trainloads of profits on shipping its oil and kickbacks from the railroads on the shipments of its competitors' oil.

Jim Fisk's Erie, Tom Scott's Pennsylvania, and Cornelius Vanderbilt's New York Central. The small Philadelphia and Erie Railroad had no firm associations with the connecting lines to the refining centers. All railroads secretly offered rebates off the publicized rates to the few large producers and refiners, a common practice justified on the basis of volume discounts. Rail routes connecting the major refining centers of Pittsburgh, Cleveland, New York/New Jersey, and Philadelphia with the Oil Regions crude oil and East Coast in 1863 are shown in Map 3:1.[9]

At first blush, Pittsburgh appears to have had an edge over the other refining centers except for the Oil Regions because of its proximity to the crude-oil production. However, the Pennsylvania Railroad's sole control of the lines to the East Coast eliminated competition from the Erie and New York Central. The same was true of Philadelphia, and both suffered high rail rates.

Cleveland, although served by all three lines and with access to the Erie Canal except when closed during the winter, lay farthest from the East Coast markets and ports for export. It's only edge was access to Chicago and scattered small western markets. Another disadvantage was the crude oil had to be shipped from the Oil Regions west to Cleveland before the refined products were shipped east to New York, burdening Cleveland with 780 freight miles compared to Oil Regions refineries near the wells with distances of 450 to 500 miles.

Another major cost factor was refinery inefficiency. The early refineries only yielded 60-percent to 70-percent product, principally kerosine, unlike modern refineries that crack the petroleum molecules and yield in excess of 100 percent by volume. The rule of thumb was 1.4 barrels of crude yielded one barrel of refined product, handicapping Cleveland with another disadvantage to Oil Regions refineries. To the railroads' consternation, the Oil Regions refiners' advantage was too good—they weren't shipping crude oil, but refined product in volumes 29 percent less than crude oil, which translated to 29-percent less rail traffic. The same was true from Pittsburgh. This would be Standard Oil of Ohio's ace up its sleeve to take the pot from the Oil Regions refiners and get a better deal from the railroads.

As far as Rockefeller was concerned, there were two other players

---

[9] The Baltimore and Ohio Railroad to the south served the smaller West Virginia oil fields and wasn't a factor until it ran a line to Pittsburgh in 1875.

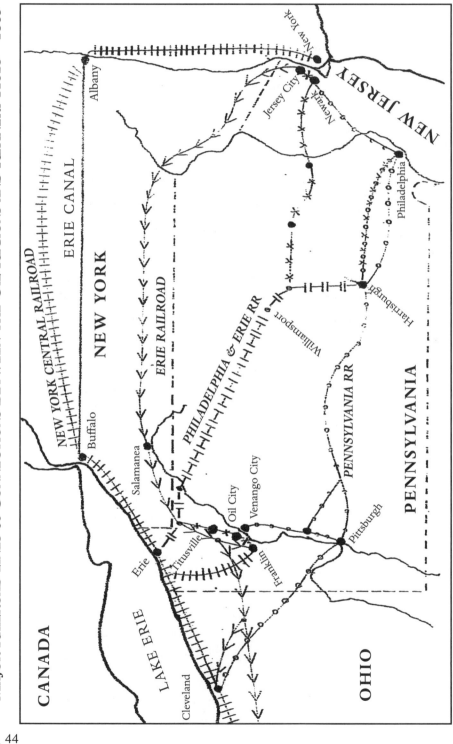

Map 3:1

Major Railroad Lines & Connections Between the Oil Regions and Refinery Hubs—1863

at the table—the other refiners and the producers. And there were too many of both. During 1871-72, there was more than 12 million barrels of annual refining capacity, but crude runs of only 5.2 million barrels in 1871 and 5.7 million in 1872. With more than one-half of the refinery capacity idle, refiners often bid up the price of crude.

CHART 3:1 MAJOR REFINING CENTERS & CAPACITY—1872-73

Refinery Centers	Number Refineries	Barrel Capacity Per Day
Cleveland*	27	12,500
New York/New Jersey	15	10,000
Pittsburgh	22	10,000
Oil Regions	27	9,200
Philadelphia	12	2,000
Other Centers**	16+	3,900
Totals	119	47,600

*The number of Cleveland refineries dropped significantly during 1872 and 1873, as noted below. **Minor refining centers included Erie, Buffalo, Baltimore, and Boston. Source: *The American Petroleum Industry: the Age of Illumination—1859-1899.*

The weakest oil industry link was the crude producers, reported to be more than one thousand. All were trying to strike it rich by producing as much as possible under the rule of capture. Rockefeller concluded there were roughly 2,000 producing wells, and the numerous wildcatters were disorganized and most vulnerable.

THE SOUTH IMPROVEMENT COMPANY

Rockefeller and Flagler were not satisfied with the rebates from the railroads. They sweetened the deal by selling Standard Oil shares to Cornelius Vanderbilt of the New York Central and Peter H. Watson, president of the Lake Shore Railroad connecting the New York Central to Cleveland and the Oil Regions.

Standard Oil increased its marketing power by secretly purchasing J. A. Bostwick & Company, New York's largest oil dealer and marketer with wharves, barges, and a refinery. Like Rockefeller, Jabez Abel Bostwick⊗ was a devout Baptist and no-nonsense businessman. As a kerosine and crude-oil purchaser, he also influenced New York prices. With Standard Oil shares that Bostwick accepted for his business locked in his safe, he secretly played the role of an independent marketer in the eyes of Standard Oil's competitors and independent producers.

Standard Oil's executive committee of teetotalers celebrated New Year's Day in 1872 by resolving to buy out its refining competition in Cleveland and other key locations and raising its capital from $1 million to $2.5 million. After sleeping on it, they raised the capital to $3.5 million the following morning and agreed to a scheme proposed by Tom Scott of the Pennsylvania Railroad.

Scott, one of Lincoln's assistant secretaries of war and renowned for keeping the Union's railroads operating during the Civil War, bought the Pennsylvania legislature with bribes and free transportation. The Pennsylvania lawmakers granted a charter to the South Improvement Company (SIC) permitting it to do most anything, including the right to own stock in other corporations. In most states, including New York and Ohio, such holding companies were barred by statute.

Scott's proposal was simple. The railroads would divide the oil freight: 45 percent for the Pennsylvania and 27.5 percent each for the Erie and New York Central and stop cutting each other's throats and prices. The SIC, with Peter H. Watson as president, assured the railroads received their share of the traffic in return for the refiner members collecting rebates of up to 50 percent. Nonmember refiners' and producers' rates would be increased, in some cases doubled, and the SIC members would receive a secret 50-percent "drawback" *on all oil shipped by nonmembers.*

The scheme would make the railroads greater profits and drive nonmember refiners out of business. Allan Nevins, Rockefeller's academic apologist biographer, had to admit, "Of all devices for the extinction of competitors, this was the cruelest and most deadly conceived." The collusion becomes more insidious when the refiners' stock ownership is analyzed. Of SIC's 2,000 shares, Cleveland *appeared* to hold 720 shares (Standard Oil officials 540 and Oliver H. Payne☻ 180). The remaining shares were held by Pittsburgh 525 (mainly controlled by William. G. Warden☻), Philadelphia 475, New York 180, and Peter Watson 100. New York's interest was held by Jabez Bostwick, Standard Oil's secret partner, and Oliver Payne in Cleveland had agreed to jump in bed with Standard Oil. Obviously missing from the conspiracy were the Oil Regions refiners the SIC members and railroads planned to squeeze out of business.

The news in the Oil Regions in February 1872 that freight rates were doubling except for members of the SIC was a declaration of war, and they wouldn't find out about the drawbacks until later. It united the refiners and producers at a meeting of 3,000 jammed into the Titusville Opera House. The producers vowed to sell only to Oil Regions refiners until the discriminatory freight rates were reduced.

Rockefeller was castigated in the Oil Regions by John D. Archbold⊗, a young hard-drinking, poker-playing refiner, who vowed to fight the "Great Anaconda." Archbold was also a producer and officer of the Petroleum Producers's Union leading the boycott of the SIC refiners. At his side in lobbying the Pennsylvania legislature to annul the SIC's charter and gathering a ninety-three-foot petition to Congress to demand an investigation was the rough-and-tumble Jacob J. Vandergrift⊗, a refiner, producer, and bulk crude-oil and kerosine steamboat shipper to Pittsburgh.

When the local refiners and producers tore up railroad tracks and dumped oil from the cars, Samuel C. T. Dodd☺, an attorney for the Oil Regions' refiners, warned there wouldn't be one mile of railroad track left in Venango County if the rates weren't reduced.

The producers' boycott worked, even though many desperate or greedy producers sold crude to SIC members. In March crude shipments to Cleveland dropped 80 percent and Pittsburgh deliveries fell 40 percent. Standard Oil felt the brunt and was forced to lay off 90 percent of its refinery employees.

New York refiner Henry H. "Hell Hound" Rogers⊗ demanded that Scott give New York refiners the same rebates and drawbacks. By the end of March, the railroads capitulated and canceled their agreement with the SIC. On April 2, 1872, the Pennsylvania legislature was forced to revoke the SIC's charter. But Tom Scott still held sufficient power and handed out enough money to bribe the lawmakers when it came to passing a free pipeline bill granting the pipelines the right of eminent domain for rights of way. He lobbied a compromise restricting the law to the eight oil producing counties that excluded Allegheny County and left Pittsburgh still under the Pennsylvania Railroad's tariffs.

Rockefeller wired the crude producers and blamed the entire fiasco on the railroads. He swore he never meant to depress crude-oil prices and didn't receive a single rebate. But Rockefeller had been busy, as the refiners, producers, and railroads would find out.

BY NOW READERS SHOULD BE ASKING:
WHAT'S THAT GLOOMY ☹ AFTER NAMES MEAN?

The ☹ identifies *Oilmen and Other Scoundrels* who eventually joined Rockefeller's conspiracy. This is not merely the author's opinion. The Supreme Court of the United States (the "Supremes") listed them as conspirators in its 1911 landmark case ordering the dissolution of the Standard Oil Trust. However, only seven were named as individual defendants: John D. and William Rockefeller, Henry M. Flagler, Henry H. Rogers, John D. Archbold, Charles M. Pratt, and Oliver H. Payne. *Standard Oil Company of New Jersey v. United States*, 221 U.S. 221, 34 (1911).

Samuel C. T. Dodd was awarded a ☺ for his services as attorney for Standard Oil between 1881 and 1905 and devising the Standard Oil Trust after years of suing the railroads and Standard Oil.

Dodd came to Rockefeller's attention in 1878 when Dodd was representing two refiners in a case against the United Pipe Lines Company owned on paper by his client, Jacob J. Vandergrift. Vandergrift admitted to Dodd that Standard Oil actually owned United Pipe Lines and he was merely a front.

Rockefeller asked Dodd at a contentious point during the settlement negotiations: "Do you often act for both sides in a case?"

Dodd replied: "Not often…but I am always ready to do so when both sides want an honest lawyer."

They settled the case, and Dodd went to work for Standard Oil. As the Supremes didn't name him as a conspirator, he couldn't be awarded a ☹. However, as in the case of many oil company lawyers who devise devious schemes, he deserves a sneaky smile ☺.[10]

---

[10] Please, no nasty letters from lawyers. The author admits to representing oil companies as a lawyer for thirty years.

CHAPTER FOUR
THE OCTOPUS SPREADS ITS TENTACLES

THE CLEVELAND MASSACRE

While everyone was bashing the South Improvement Company, Rockefeller gobbled up his local competitors. By the time the Pennsylvania legislature revoked the SIC's charter, he had bought twenty-one of the twenty-six competing refineries in Cleveland. His line was the same to all: Your inefficient company will go bankrupt. You cannot continue under the railroad rates and SIC's volume discounts. Your only way out is to sell your company. Your choice is cash or Standard Oil shares. I recommend you take stock, it will become very valuable.

Rockefeller was right. Standard Oil's stock soared and it never failed to pay sizable dividends. But it was a going-out-of-business buyout of a refinery's fixed assets based on Ambrose McGregor's niggardly appraisal that didn't include a penny for goodwill. The thirty-two-year-old former bookkeeper gained great satisfaction in not budging from the offering price to his former employer who had refused to give him a $200 raise in 1859. There are numerous lurid tales of coercion during the take-my-price-or-go-bankrupt negotiations. Tarbell wrote a tearjerker about the blind "Widow Backus" paid a pittance for her husband's refinery. In truth, Rockefeller paid her more than she had offered to sell it to another refiner two years earlier. As in the case of most competing refineries purchased, her husband's refinery was dismantled and sold for scrap.

The only refiner Rockefeller thought overpaid was Col. Oliver H. Payne, who moved into the sanctity of Standard Oil of Ohio's headquarters. Payne was wealthy, a war hero, and his father, Henry B. Payne, was a political power in Ohio. Republican Rockefeller knew that Henry was a Democrat, but he would come in handy to push Standard Oil causes as a United States senator.

THE TREATY OF TITUSVILLE

In May 1872, Rockefeller listened to the "Pittsburgh Plan" proposed by William G. Warden, a major player in the SIC with substantial refinery interests in Pittsburgh and Philadelphia, and Charles Lockhart⊗, a tight-fisted, taciturn Scot who only bought ten SIC shares, but owned seven refineries that made up one-half of Pittsburgh's capacity. Lockhart's refinery engineering advances permitted him to operate as efficiently as Standard Oil. (Rockefeller's kind of guy.) Although the Pittsburgh Plan was designed to save the Pittsburgh and Philadelphia refiners from the Pennsylvania Railroad's high rates, it needed the Cleveland, Oil Regions, and East Coast refiners' backing. The plot called for organizing a refiners' association to purchase crude oil, allocate refining quotas, fix prices, negotiate uniform railroad rates as a bloc, and become pals with the producers, who needed their guidance for their own good.

WAS THE PITTSBURGH PLAN ILLEGAL?

Monopolies were illegal in England long before the Pilgrims landed and brought the common law, but the federal government didn't do anything about them until the passage of the Sherman Antitrust Act in 1890 prohibiting " . . . every contract, combination in the form of trust or otherwise, or conspiracy, in restraint of commerce . . ." However, in 1895 the Supremes ruled it didn't apply to manufacturing. Standard Oil and the other trusts had better lawyers and had paid off members of Congress for the nifty loophole.

The Sherman Act finally got teeth in it with the passage of the Clayton Act in 1914, which forbade rebates, price discrimination, price cutting to restrain trade, and ownership of stock in competing companies.

Venturing to Titusville, where Rockefeller had been branded the "Mephistopheles of Cleveland" a few months earlier, had to take the WASP's version of chutzpah. Rockefeller and Flagler went with the Pittsburgh refiners, not that they were crazy about uniform rates that might work to Cleveland's disadvantage. No one knows what went on behind closed doors or in Rockefeller's head, but he convinced Jacob J. Vandergrift, one of the SIC's wiliest Oil Regions adversaries, and two sharp New York refiners and former antagonists, Henry H. Rogers and Charles Pratt ⊗, to secretly join the Standard Oil conspiracy.

The cozy National Refiners' Association (NRA) was organized in August 1872 with Rockefeller, president; Vandergrift, vice president; and Pratt, treasurer. (The records are vague as to the NRA's secretary. Possibly, the NRA didn't want a record of what the rascals were doing.)

The producers organized the Petroleum Producers' Association (PPA) to deal with the NRA. As Rockefeller expected, the PPA couldn't restrain hundreds of independents from violating PPA production quotas, even with some of their more exuberant members dynamiting uncooperative producers' storage tanks. To offer an incentive, the PPA formed the Petroleum Producers' Agency to raise $1 million to buy crude oil at a fairy-tale price of $5 a barrel for resale to the NRA.

Rockefeller agreed to $4 a barrel, with an escalator based on the current kerosine price in New York. Each 1¢ kerosine price increase would raise the price of crude 25¢ until it reached $5. Of course, he conditioned the crude-oil price on the PPA maintaining the production quotas. On December 19, 1872, an agreement was signed by the PPA and NRA that the press touted as the "Treaty of Titusville."

The agreement should have been called the "Trick or Treaty." The PPA's first trick was to make the surplus holding down the crude-oil price at $3.25 a barrel disappear. The PPA was forced to concede $3.25 was as high as it could obtain at the start. Rockefeller played his trump card in mid-January when the deluge of crude drove the price down to $2. He canceled the agreement.

Rockefeller knew the producers weren't entirely to blame. Nonmember refiners had increased their output to take advantage of the NRA quotas. He called the agreement "a rope of sand" and followed the advice of a plaque on Flagler's desk: *Do unto others as they would do unto you—and do it first.* He dissolved the NRA and presented his plan to eliminate the need for untrustworthy cooperation to the Standard Oil board—we must control every element of the petroleum industry.

ROCKEFELLER'S PLAN

One thing Rockefeller couldn't control was the financial panic that started on Black Thursday, September 19, 1873. The investment house of Jay Cooke & Company failed, and the country fell into a depression that would drag on until 1878. However, Standard Oil had staying power. Since its inception in 1870, it had grown to where it was refining more than one-third of the nation's petroleum products. It had sufficient capital, highly efficient refineries, barrel-manufacturing facilities, and an aggressive marketing organization led by William Rockefeller and Jabez Bostwick.

With the railroads weakened by the depression, Standard Oil's capability to guarantee minimum daily shipments of sixty tank cars and its ownership of more than a thousand tank cars gave it the power to demand greater rebates and drawbacks. Its large volumes doomed to failure the "railroad-pipeline pool" formed to fix rates for oil to the East Coast. Rockefeller started investing in gathering pipelines, the railroad's link to the oil wells, with the purchase of a one-quarter interest in Jay Gould's Allegheny Transportation Company and a one-third interest in Jacob Vandergrift's United Pipe Line Company. Vandergrift, smelling Rockefeller's plan, took Standard Oil stock for his Imperial Refining Company, the largest refinery in the Oil Regions, and climbed on the bandwagon. Through Jabez Bostwick's formation of the American Transfer System, Standard Oil acquired other pipelines in the Oil Regions. *And it was all done secretly.*

Two other grabs tightened the noose. The New York Central leased Bostwick its New York City oil docks. As part of a deal to ship one-half of Standard Oil's shipments to the East Coast, the Erie leased its Weehawken, New Jersey, oil terminal to Standard Oil. The operations made more than money. They provided control of two major railroad facilities on the East Coast and knowledge of its competition's sales. A financially weak Erie became wedded to Standard Oil when Flagler leased it more than 500 Standard Oil tank cars and charged a mileage rate.

Behind the scenes, Standard Oil acquired the biggest, best, and brightest of the refiners, both cohorts in the South Improvement Company scam and former foes. By 1874, Rockefeller had recruited William G. Warden and his Atlantic Refining Company, the largest in Philadelphia, and Charles Lockhart of Lockhart, Frew & Company, with one-half of Pittsburgh's capacity. The following year, he drew his former enemy, John D. Archbold, into the fold. Then Rockefeller traveled to the oil fields around Parkersburg, West Virginia, and secretly acquired controlling interest in the largest West Virginia refinery and put the partners, Johnson Newlon Camden⊗ and W. P. Thompson⊗, in charge of Camden Consolidated Oil Company.

The refiners joining the Standard Oil web kept it secret for years, although many suspected they were tentacles of the octopus. Following Rockefeller's "Cleveland massacre" plan, they secretly bought competing refineries. John D. Archbold set the record by swallowing twenty-seven refineries in one year—the same year he reached the age of twenty-seven. It is little wonder that Rockefeller groomed the young firebrand to take over Standard Oil, although Archbold had to swear off his hard-drinking during his climb to the top.

Camden and Thompson not only bought West Virginia refineries, in Camden's words, he "starved them out." He made a deal with the Baltimore and Ohio (B&O) to ship 50,000 barrels a month at a rate far below what the Pittsburgh refiners obtained from the B&O. And no one knew of the 10¢ per barrel drawback on *all oil* the B&O shipped from Pittsburgh, including the oil it picked up from the Columbia Conduit Company, a pipeline competing with Standard Oil's pipelines. The B&O didn't find out until it was too late that it was dealing with a Standard Oil front.

Rockefeller's cohorts were brutal. Manufacturers of lubricants and petroleum products that Standard Oil wanted to acquire or force out of business faced tank-car shortages. Standard Oil, the owner of most of the tank cars on the New York Central and Erie, dictated to the railroads which refinery competitors could use their cars. Secret ownership or control of pipelines gave Standard Oil the ability to delay or refuse competitors' deliveries and charge them premium rates. Barrel manufacturers were told not to supply Pittsburgh refiners if they wanted Standard Oil's business.

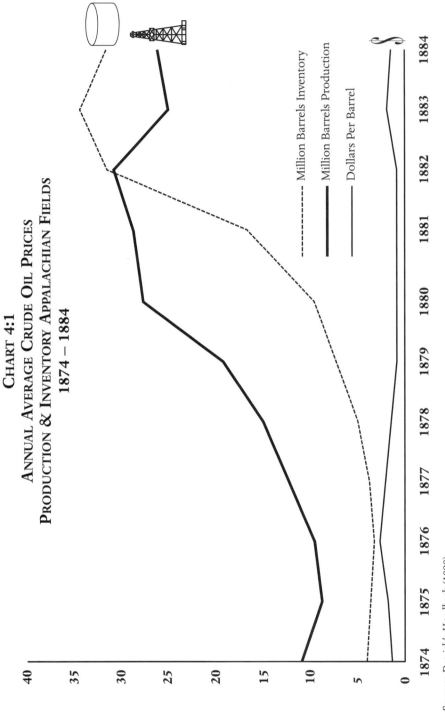

CHART 4:1
ANNUAL AVERAGE CRUDE OIL PRICES
PRODUCTION & INVENTORY APPALACHIAN FIELDS
1874 – 1884

- - - - Million Barrels Inventory

——— Million Barrels Production

——— Dollars Per Barrel

Source: *Derrick's Handbook* (1898)

THE PENNSYLVANIA RAILROAD'S LAST STAND

Rockefeller tolerated the Pennsylvania Railroad's subsidiary, the Empire Transportation Company, organized in 1865 as a gathering pipeline from the wells to its railheads. But when Empire purchased refineries in New York and Philadelphia in 1876, he ordered that no Standard Oil shipments be given to the Pennsylvania. Archbold piously complained that the Pennsylvania was a common carrier and was discriminating against Standard in favor of Empire's refineries. Of course, Standard Oil's pipelines were common carriers, but no one knew of its ownership.

Daniel O'Day, the manager of Standard Oil's American Transfer Company blessed with Irish charm and iron fists, expanded its pipelines in the Oil Regions and the new Bradford oil field and built more storage tanks. The Bradford field oil strike a few miles south of the New York border was gushing so much oil they had to store more than one-third of the production and the price kept dropping. Standard Oil took advantage of the surplus by buying oil at fire-sale prices and putting it in storage. Purchasing crude oil below $1 per barrel also undercut its refinery competition.

Standard Oil's idle refining capacity blossomed into an asset. It shut down its Pittsburgh refineries and ordered its other refineries to take up the slack and undersell Empire in its markets. The Erie and New York Central cut their rates to turn the screws on their competitor and received additional Standard Oil tank cars to carry the Pennsylvania's former oil freight.

Scott asked for a war he couldn't win, even if Rockefeller played fair. His railroad lost two-thirds of its oil revenues overnight because he didn't know the extent of his enemy's refinery ownership. Meanwhile, Standard Oil continued to reap huge revenues in areas Empire couldn't serve and cut prices below its costs in Empire's markets. Unable to determine the white hats from the black hats, the Pennsylvania carried secretly owned Standard Oil kerosine at a loss.

The Pennsylvania's shareholders began to question Scott's motives. Empire was a subsidiary and a substantial amount of its shares were held by the Pennsylvania's management, including Scott. The depression added to the loss of other freight. Scott laid off workers, cut wages by 20 percent, and increased train lengths and workmen's hours, but continued paying quarterly dividends on nonexistent earnings. (Enron wasn't the first to think of this type of chicanery.)

At the same time Standard Oil was earning huge profits, it squeezed the rates it paid the Erie, B&O, and New York Central. Soon the three lines had to lay off workers and cut wages, and a general railroad strike erupted. Riots broke out, and hundreds of tank and freight cars and railroad buildings went up in flames. The governor of Pennsylvania ordered the militia to Pittsburgh. When the militia fired on the rioters, the mob drove the troops into the railroad roundhouse and ran burning oil tank cars into it. The militia narrowly escaped when President Rutherford B. Hayes sent federal troops to quell the riot. But the troops didn't arrive until after the strikers had run out of buildings and railroad cars to destroy and caused damage in the millions.

Scott surrendered to Rockefeller in October 1877. Rockefeller appeared generous. He still needed the Pennsylvania to carry his freight . . . at least for a while. Standard Oil loaned the Pennsylvania $1.65 million and purchased Empire's refinery operations for $500,000, which was a fair price and a partial washout on its loan. Standard Oil's subsidiary, United Pipe Line, bought Empire's 500 miles of pipelines. To ensure a stranglehold over the B&O, it purchased the Columbia Conduit Company, the pipeline to the B&O's Pittsburgh terminal, along with its two refineries. The total cash for the Empire buyout reached a colossal $3.4 million. Rockefeller had to borrow $1.25 million within twenty-four hours to close the deal. It was hectic, but he did it through his powerful bank connections. As expected, Tom Scott put cash in his pocket from the sale of Empire's assets.

The revised railroad pooling arrangement divided *all* Pennsylvania oil freight: the Pennsylvania 47 percent, the Erie and New York Central 21 percent each and the B&O 11 percent. Standard Oil received a 10-percent "commission" (read drawback) on *all* oil freight. Four months later, Daniel O'Day informed the Pennsylvania the drawback was a minimum of 20¢ a barrel to keep it in line with the other railroads. The result was a published rail and pipeline crude-oil tariff from the Oil Regions to New York of $1.70 a barrel that only cost Standard Oil $1.06. Standard Oil was also earning a profit from its pipelines in the range of 10¢ a barrel. As the 1878 average price of crude oil was around $1.20 and dipped as low as 70¢ a barrel, the transportation costs of Standard Oil's competitors exceeded the crude-oil price. Standard Oil's kerosine had a better deal at 80¢ a barrel after it forced the railroads to meet the total price of an independent pipeline in the north and the Erie Canal's rate.

Standard Oil evolved bigger and more powerful. In 1878 it declared a $60 dividend on its closely held $100-par-value stock—a 60-percent return. Rockefeller's combine celebrated owning or controlling interest in 90 percent of the nation's refining.

PIPELINES—THE FINAL LOOP IN THE NOOSE

Another desperate attempt by the independents to break the stranglehold of the railroads and Standard Oil was the formation of the Tidewater Pipe Company in November 1878. Unable to obtain a corporate charter from a Pennsylvania legislature bought and paid for by Tom Scott, it was organized as a limited liability partnership. Without the power of imminent domain, its plan for a pipeline from Oil Creek to Baltimore vanished like smoke in the wind after J. N. Camden bribed the Maryland legislature to grant a secret Standard Oil subsidiary an exclusive pipeline charter.

Tidewater made a pact with the former Philadelphia & Erie Railroad, now the Philadelphia & Reading Railroad (Reading), to build a 110-mile pipeline from Coryville in the Bradford oil field to Williamsport. Williamsport was a misnomer—it was on the Susquehanna River that wasn't navigable in the winter when the river froze or during dry summers when the water was low. The Reading, battling the Pennsylvania for anthracite coal freight, contributed $250,000 of Tidewater's initial capital on the condition it wouldn't build the pipeline east of Williamsport for eight years, which allowed the Reading to carry Tidewater's oil to Philadelphia and New York.

Daniel O'Day threw roadblocks in Tidewater's path by buying strips of land along Tidewater's route to block its progress and threatening pipe manufacturers with the loss of Standard Oil's business if they sold pipe to the upstart. He also began construction of pipelines from the Oil Regions and Bradford to Buffalo, Cleveland, Philadelphia, and Bayonne.

Henry Flagler and J. N. Camden forced the railroads to cut rates in areas where Tidewater would compete, bought out refiners Tidewater planned to serve, and bribed state legislatures to impede legislation for pipeline right-of-way bills. Flagler failed in New York because of the lobbying by Buffalo and the ailing Erie Canal interests. But Standard Oil didn't need eminent domain authority. It obtained a right of way along the Erie's tracks for a pipeline to Bayonne in return for a guarantee of continuing oil freight on its line. Similar rights of way were cajoled out of the Pennsylvania, Lake Shore, and Tidewater's almost insolvent ally, the Reading, which then had to allow Tidewater to build its pipeline to Bayonne.

Within two years, Standard Oil's National Transit Company subsidiary would link its pipelines to Cleveland, Buffalo, Pittsburgh, Philadelphia, and Bayonne, primarily on railroad rights of way. By 1881, National Transit controlled 3,000 miles of oil-field gathering lines and pipelines to refinery centers and an estimated 40 million barrels of crude-oil and refined-product storage capacity.

By the time the Pennsylvania legislature passed a free pipeline bill granting rights of way and preventing mergers of competing pipelines, Tidewater's pipeline had reached Bayonne. But it was too late. Tidewater had lost any chance to serve Standard Oil's refinery competition and couldn't compete. It couldn't even merge with Standard Oil. Several historians with little or no economic understanding claim that Tidewater "sold out" and colluded with Standard Oil, but it was inevitable. Tidewater was forced into an agreement granting Standard Oil 88.5 percent of the pipeline traffic from the Oil Regions and Bradford and being satisfied with 11.5 percent. The alternative was bankruptcy.

Standard Oil's venture into pipelines and the construction of massive storage facilities gave it sway over crude-oil prices. Its United Pipe Line Company that gathered crude oil at the wells periodically announced its storage tanks were full and it could only take crude oil that had been sold. United called them "Immediate Shipment Orders." Producers called them [expletives deleted] when forced to sell their crude oil at rock-bottom prices or shut in their wells.

Reports of the times disagree on whether United Pipe Line's storage tanks were actually full or committed under contract, but all agree that there was far more oil being produced than consumed and the principal purchaser in the oil fields was J. A. Bostwick & Company, Standard Oil's secret agent. On occasion, United Pipe Line pulled the we-don't-have-enough-tank-cars-to-take-your crude-oil ploy. The distressed sales were below the local oil exchanges quotes, ranging from a few pennies to 25¢ a barrel. With crude-oil prices hovering below $1 a barrel, a 25¢ cut was brutal. Bostwick's offers well below the exchanges' quotes would eventually make the Pennsylvania and New York oil exchanges' prices meaningless and force them to close. Standard Oil's ability to dictate crude-oil prices was another strangling tentacle of the octopus.[11]

Standard Oil's ownership of the pipelines to the East Coast tolled the eventual death knell to the railroad's crude-oil freight. Pipelines were cheaper, reduced the handling and storage, and were more efficient. Today only 3 percent of crude oil is shipped by rail.

With the control of refining, transportation, and storage, Standard Oil had de facto control over crude-oil and kerosine prices. What was next in Rockefeller's plan to dominate the oil industry? Or as Rockefeller claimed from behind his desk at 26 Broadway in New York: "Bring it stability."

> "The American Beauty rose can be produced in all its splendor only by sacrificing the early buds that grow up around it."
>
> —John D. Rockefeller (1905)

---

[11] No hard data on actual crude-oil prices during the period is available, making it impossible to determine the accuracy of a nebulous "average price" or the payments for distressed sales.

CHAPTER FIVE
THE BIGGER, THE BETTER, & THE BADDEST

LEGAL SKIRMISHES

Standard Oil faced lawyers and state governments riled by irate consumers, producers, and refiners in 1879. In April, a Clarion County, Pennsylvania, grand jury indicted Standard Oil for common law restraint of trade by monopoly, extorting railroad rates, and manipulating prices. Also indicted were several Standard Oil officers, including the usual suspects: John D. Rockefeller, William Rockefeller, Daniel O'Day ☹, Jabez A. Bostwick, Charles Lockhart, Henry M. Flagler, John D. Archbold, Jacob Vandergrift, William G. Warden, and George W. Girty. ☹ [12]

In August the commonwealth of Pennsylvania filed *quo warranto* proceedings against Standard Oil's United Pipe Line subsidiary for failure to act as a common carrier and injunctions against the Pennsylvania, Lake Shore, and Atlantic & Great Western Railroads for discriminatory prices and rebates granted Standard Oil. *Quo warranto* is archaic Latin legalese for an action to cancel United Pipe Line's corporate charter.

Not one to leave anything to chance, Rockefeller put some of the best lawyers who had sued him on Standard Oil's payroll. Nor did he trust politicians. He extracted commitments from Governor Henry M. Hoyt of Pennsylvania not to subpoena him and Governor Lucius

---

[12] O'Day was not mentioned in the Supremes' 1911 breakup of Standard Oil, but the scoundrel deserves a ☹ in this case. According to Ida Tarbell, the only source who mentioned George Girty, he was Standard Oil's cashier. Men who handle the kind of money Standard Oil handed out must have been in on the skulduggery.

Robinson of New York to not allow Pennsylvania to extradite him in case Hoyt weaseled on his promise. Tom Scott, Pennsylvania Railroad president, slipped word to Governor Hoyt not to press the case. (Who said political contributions don't influence politicians?)

Standard Oil withdrew its immediate shipments ploy to squeeze cheap crude oil out of the crude-oil producers and swore not to take rebates or drawbacks and that its United Pipe Line subsidiary would not discriminate against its competition. It sounded good, but the producers and refiners had heard the promises before. Standard Oil's out-of-state witnesses could not be subpoenaed, and the cumbersome combined court cases involving the *quo warranto* action and the tedious legal process of the era dragged until it was settled. The restraint-of-trade case was settled in 1880 by Standard Oil denying it did anything wrong and promising never to do it again.

It was an obscure New York assemblyman, Alonzo B. Hepburn, holding public hearings in July, who publicly disclosed Standard Oil's and the railroads' collusion and made the biggest headlines. Weeks of testimony detailed the railroads' rebates, drawbacks, and preferential dealings with Standard Oil. As expected, there was the usual perjury and finger pointing when the railroad and Standard Oil officials took the stand. And there was the normal press bias. Ida Tarbell wrote that the Pennsylvania Railroad's president, Tom Scott, and vice president, A. J. Cassatt, weren't greedy bad guys: "[T]hey were already weary of Standard, and would cease their illegal practices gladly if they could."

NEWS CLIPS

"There never has existed in the United States a corporation as soulless, so grasping, so utterly destitute of the sense of commercial responsibility and so damaging to the commercial prosperity of the country than the Standard Oil Company." *Oil, Paint & Drug Reporter,* September 3, 1879, page 224.

The *Oil, Paint & Drug Reporter* merged with a trade journal backed by Standard Oil in 1883 and started singing a different tune about the small refiners. "[T]hey lacked the brains, capital and energy . . . When they fail, they . . . resort to all manner of persecution [of Standard Oil]." *Oil, Paint & Drug Reporter,* May 2, 1888, page 6.

The Standard Oil Trust

The year 1879 also raised an issue the Standard Oil Company of Ohio had ignored. Its charter barred ownership of corporations outside of Ohio. The fast and dirty method of evading the antiquated law that prevented the efficient operation of an interstate business was to appoint three employees as trustees of the stock in subsidiaries operating out of state. This worked until Pennsylvania sued to collect taxes on Standard Oil's property outside Pennsylvania. Although the court cut the tax bill from $3 million to $3,200, it made the Standard Oil hierarchy nervous. Other states were prying into its affairs, and there were dozens of secretly controlled corporations they didn't want revealed.

The answer was the Standard Oil Trust Agreement devised by their attorney, Samuel C. T. Dodd, under Henry M. Flagler's guidance. It was executed secretly on January 2, 1882, by Standard of Ohio's forty-one shareholders and three trustees holding stock in forty companies. But control still lay with the Cleveland Mafia of John and William Rockefeller, Steven Harkness, Henry Flagler, and Oliver Payne.

The trust included Standard of Ohio and forty other companies, fourteen of which were wholly owned. The trust certificates gave the tight-fisted and tight-lipped men meeting in Suite 1400 at 26 Broadway full control over their domain and plans to extend their monopoly. Soon the Standard Oil Company of Ohio would be joined by siblings: Standard Oil of New York … New Jersey … Indiana … Kentucky … Louisiana … Pennsylvania … Illinois … California … Iowa … Minnesota. Of course, there were secretly controlled bastards in the family that couldn't bare the hallowed or hated Standard Oil name. But Standard Oil's troubles weren't over, and the trust's life was relatively short.

In 1890 Ohio brought a *quo warranto* proceeding against Standard of Ohio alleging the trust was a sham and still a monopoly controlled by the same evil men at 26 Broadway. The Ohio Supreme Court agreed, but instead of cancelling its corporate charter, it merely ordered Standard of Ohio to sever connections with the trust in March 1892. Before the state of New York could file a similar case against Standard of New York, Samuel Dodd announced that the trust would be dissolved.

63

By 1892, it was no simple task. The trust now held interests in more than ninety companies, and the number of certificate holders had reached 1,600, many of whom were former owners of small companies Standard Oil had gobbled up. The two-step process began with the twenty larger companies buying out the small refining and marketing companies until there were only twenty companies. The trust certificates were then traded for stock of the twenty corporations on a pro-rata basis. In the end, Rockefeller still held more than 26 percent of each of the twenty corporations. And with his pals at 26 Broadway, they still held the majority of shares.

But there was a problem. Trust certificate holders were issued scrip that were not entitled to dividends for share fractions if the certificate did not make up a full share. This callous squeezing of the small trust certificate holders, many of whom had been forced out of business and accepted shares in Standard of Ohio for their companies, caused complaints and refusals to trade in their certificates. In 1897 a dissatisfied former refiner turned his scrip over to the attorney general of Ohio as evidence Standard of Ohio had evaded the 1892 court order and was still in violation of the state's antitrust laws and in contempt of the court's order. The case dragged on after Standard Oil refused to turn over its records when ordered by the court and it claimed some of their books had been "accidently burned." The case was dismissed by the Ohio Supreme Court for lack of evidence. Wayne Henderson and Scott Benjamin in *Standard Oil: The First 125 Years*, a slick glorification of Standard Oil, admitted "The Rockefeller influences in courts in Standard's home state brought the lawsuit to a stalemate and the action was terminated in 1902." [13]

Soon after the filing of the 1897 case and while swearing the web of twenty companies were independent, the men at 26 Broadway consolidated their holdings in Standard Oil of New Jersey under a recent New Jersey statute permitting corporations to own stock in

---

[13] One has to muse about the competence and complaisance of the Ohio attorney general's office or whether the Ohio judges had been paid off by the Rockefeller crowd. Simple math disclosed Rockefeller's interests in the twenty companies was based on his holding 256,584 of the total 972,500 trust certificates (26.41 percent). The complaining refiner's scrip were diminished to as little as a 50/9725 fraction (a 100:1 ratio, as evidenced by the 972,500 total trust certificates) on its face proving the circumvention of the 1882 court order. *The Age of Illumination* points out it would have required 194½ trust shares valued at $66,000 to obtain a full share in each of the twenty companies, a sizable amount in 1897 and equal to $1,435,000 today.

foreign (out-of-state) corporations. Today it would be called a holding company. Standard of New Jersey merely exchanged its shares for those of the twenty affiliates and the new companies it acquired. By 1901, it controlled all but three of the forty-one companies and was bigger and badder.

STRETCHING ITS TENTACLES

During the flurry of lawsuits, Standard Oil continued to expand. Its acquisitions were not merely grabs of refineries, pipelines, marketing outlets, terminals, and lubricant manufacturers. It gained patents for the manufacturing of cans, vital for marketing kerosine and lubricants, and formulas for lubricants to solidify its monopoly. The purchase of controlling interest of the Chesebrough Manufacturing Company in 1881 gave it chemical and medicinal patents, the most famous being the trade-marked Vaseline petroleum jelly.[14]

The takeover of the scores of refining and marketing companies would require a book by itself. Noteworthy are Vacuum Oil Company, a manufacturer of superior lubricants merged with Standard of New York (now Mobil) in 1879; Continental Oil Company, a major western marketer acquired in 1884 (now Conoco-Phillips and a subsidiary of Dupont); and Ohio Oil Company, a crude-oil producer purchased in 1889 (now Marathon Oil and a subsidiary of USX). However, Waters-Pierce & Company deserves description for no other reason than Henry Clay Pierce had been as vicious as Rockefeller since he took over his father-in-law's business in 1871 at the age of twenty-two.

Waters-Pierce built the first refinery west of the Mississippi River and marketed in Texas, which enforced its antitrust laws prohibiting out-of-state corporations from doing business in Texas. It also operated in Mexico, where it gouged profits three times those in the United States and evaded Mexican taxes. Standard Oil secretly acquired a 40-percent interest in Waters-Pierce in 1878 and control with an additional 20 percent in 1886. With Standard Oil's backing, Waters-Pierce seized 90 percent of the Texas market through rebates and selling below cost to drive out competition. Professor Jacqueline Lang

---

[14] After the 1911 dissolution of Standard Oil of New Jersey, the company evolved into Chesebrough-Ponds, a major manufacturer of soaps, lotions, beauty aids, hair spray, deodorants, and a myriad of other products found on the shelves of drugstores and supermarkets.

Weaver of the University of Houston Law Center wrote, "Standard Oil's early practices in Texas can only be described as sordid."

Believe it or not, in those days Texas was against anything big. Texas brought an antitrust suit and canceled Waters-Pierce's corporate charter in 1898. Texas's only disappointment was it couldn't extradite and jail Rockefeller. Undaunted, Pierce bribed an official for a new charter and formed a new corporation without bothering to change its name. In 1907 Texas revoked its charter a second time, fined it $1,623,000, and jailed the Waters-Pierce officers it could find. In 1909 Texas hunted down three more secretly controlled Standard Oil companies and tossed them out of the Lone Star State.

The discovery of the Lima, Ohio, oil field in 1885 was the first major oil field found outside Pennsylvania. It was also Rockefeller's first uncharacteristic gamble in crude-oil production. He bluffed his fellow board members by threatening to go it alone if they didn't approve. Lima sour crude oil was called "skunk oil" due to its high sulfur content and rank smell. Sulfur also made it highly corrosive. When refined into kerosine, it continued to reek and leave a film on lamps housewives complained of having to clean every day. Another drawback was it couldn't be refined into as high a percentage of kerosine as the lighter and sweeter Pennsylvania crude oils. (High sulfur crude oil is referred to as sour, and low sulfur is called sweet.)

Daniel O'Day struck the Lima oil field like a school of piranha. By 1888, he had signed up 85 percent of the field's production, stored more than 40 million barrels of crude oil, and built gathering lines to the Ohio Oil Company's refinery, which it took over in 1889 when Ohio Oil realized Standard Oil controlled the crude oil and pipelines. At least the price of the smelly sour gunk was right—15¢ a barrel. Pennsylvania sweet crude oil was selling for between 75¢ and 90¢ a barrel.

Rockefeller hired Herman Frasch, a German chemist, to eliminate the sulfur and dreadful stench. What became known as the Frasch Process eventually made millions annually in patent licenses alone. By the time Frasch solved the problem in 1888, O'Day had constructed a pipeline from the Lima field to the world's largest refinery in Whiting, Indiana.[15] With the Pennsylvania oil production declin-

---

[15] Standard Oil's plan to build the refinery next to the railroad in Chicago was stopped by the town fathers who objected to the horrible odor. To avoid objections, a refinery was built in Whiting, Indiana, a few miles across the state line. The workers refused to admit what they were building behind a high fence until the refinery was completed.

Map 5:1

Standard Oil Marketing Territories—1899

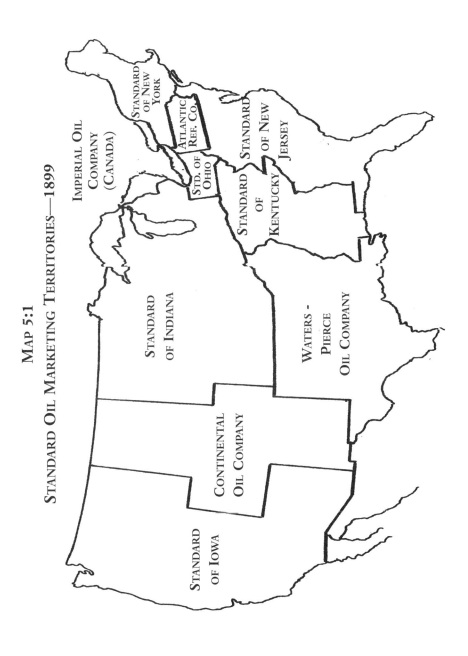

ing, the Lima field became the nation's largest crude-oil producer in the 1890s, and Standard Oil would produce one-third of the nation's crude oil by 1898.

Marketing became the key, not only in the United States, but in Europe. The Anglo-American Petroleum Company was organized in England in 1888. Soon subsidiary companies in Germany and France followed. Standard moved into Canada in 1898 with the purchase of the Imperial Oil Company, a refiner and producer that would grab 60 percent of the Canadian market. Waters-Pierce expanded its operation in Mexico with the construction of a refinery in Tampico.

In 1890 Standard Oil's Domestic Trading Committee met at 26 Broadway to consolidate their many outlets and divided the nation into nine marketing territories. (See Map 5:1.) Standard of Minnesota, which covered Minnesota and North Dakota, was placed under Standard of Indiana. Standard of Illinois was split under Standard of Indiana and Standard of Kentucky. Standard of Iowa, which covered the far west and had nothing to do with Iowa more than a thousand miles away, was replaced by Standard of California in 1906.

Under autonomous regional umbrellas, Standard Oil continued to take over marketing companies. In areas where the Standard Oil name was despised or to avoid state antitrust actions, the companies were acquired and operated secretly. The ability to deliver wholesale and retail cheaply and efficiently eliminated the small jobbers, often hardware and general store operators. With its corporate integration capable of producing cans, barrels, rail tank cars, horse-drawn tank wagons, tank storage terminals, and lubricants, it was a formidable machine. Even so, the tactics were always the same—Standard Oil cut prices below cost and drove their competition out of business. Their avarice was to be part of their undoing. Also, there was something they couldn't control and didn't believe possible.

WESTERN OIL?

On hearing that oil had been discovered in Oklahoma in 1885, John D. Archbold of Standard Oil scoffed, "Are you crazy, Man? Why, I'll drink every gallon of oil produced west of the Mississippi!"

In 1901 on a spindly-treed dome aptly called Spindletop outside Beaumont, Texas, a gusher spewed oil like no one had ever seen before—forty thousand barrels a day. And Standard Oil was nowhere to be seen. The wildcat well was financed by the Andrew W. and Richard Mellon, Pittsburgh bankers, who bought out the wildcatters and turned the discovery over to their nephew, William L. Mellon.

William had dabbled in the Pennsylvania oil fields and was hesitant about going up against Standard Oil after being forced to sell the Mellon's Crescent Pipeline Company to it in 1893. He offered to sell their interests to Standard Oil. Instead, a Standard Oil director gave him the green light. "After the way Mr. Rockefeller has been treated by the state of Texas, he'll never put another dime in Texas." (He lied. Standard Oil was secretly operating in Texas through at least four subsidiaries.)

Actually, William had little to worry about. James Guffey, one of the wildcatters, had sold a fifteen-acre lease to ex-Governor Jim Hogg and his cronies in the Texas legislature. Guffey explained the sale to Hogg for $310,000 ($270,000 borrowed). "Northern men were not well respected in Texas . . . Governor Hogg was a power down there, and I wanted him on my side." William organized the Mellon interests as the Gulf Oil Company.

Jim Hogg, the 350-pound former Texas governor and attorney general, is renowned for establishing the Texas Railroad Commission (which regulates everything in Texas, including oil), passing and enforcing antitrust legislation to expel out-of-state corporations from Texas, and naming his daughter "Ima."

Hogg and his partner and former Texas Senate floor leader, James M. Swayne, despised corporations to the extent they refused to incorporate and called their venture the "Hogg-Swayne Syndicate." To pay off their purchase price debt, they sold plots as small as 1/24 acre for $50,000. Hogg admitted he knew little about the oil business and against his better judgment swapped a few acres for stock in the Texas Fuel Company owned by "Buckskin Joe" Cullinan that later became Texaco.

Another oilman who arrived at Spindletop after he was forced to sell his gas business in Pittsburgh to Standard Oil and squeezed out of the Lima field was J. Edgar Pew. Pew, free from Rockefeller's clutches, went into the storage, tanker, and refinery business. He purchased cheap Spindletop oil (sometimes as low as 3¢ a barrel) for shipment by tanker to Pennsylvania where he built one of the world's largest refineries. As Pew would have made a terrible company name, he selected the biggest thing in the heavens and named it the Sun Oil Company.

Spindletop, many called it "Swindletop" because of the infamous stock swindles that made more money than oil in the early years, was the womb of Standard Oil's first real competition—Gulf, Texaco, and Sun. Standard Oil was legally shut out of Texas, the state that would become synonymous with oil wells and oil millionaires, until it acquired Humble Oil in 1919. There was little the men at 26 Broadway could do about the new oil discoveries in Oklahoma, Texas, and California that would relegate the Appalachian and Lima fields to less than 10 percent of the nation's crude-oil production by 1920. All were west of the Mississippi and produced a hell of a lot more oil than Standard Oil's John D. Archbold could drink.

TRUSTBUSTERS AND BLUSTERS

The states could not rely on an inert Congress influenced by Standard Oil and the whisky, tobacco, salt, sugar, and steel trusts, to name a few, and the powerful interstate combines were impossible to regulate under state antitrust laws.

John Pierpont Morgan, the most infamous "robber baron," ruled the United States Steel trust with his purchase of Rockefeller's Mesabi iron ore field and later ran the farm equipment trust under International Harvester. Best known was his "money trust" created by merging 112 banks and brokerage houses under J. P. Morgan & Company, National Bank of New York, and National City Bank of New York. The banks became a money store for Standard Oil and provided John and William Rockefeller's children and grandchildren with banks to run. William's two sons married the daughters of James Stillman, the head of National City Bank, now part of Citigroup that includes Traveler's Insurance and SolomonSmithBarney. David, John's grandson, became chairman of Chase Manhattan Bank that later merged to form J. P Morgan Chase & Company (Citigroup and J. P. Morgan Chase were Enron's bankers.)

Other than Standard Oil, the most despised and obvious trust in the public's eyes was Morgan's vast web of railroad holdings. It was also common knowledge that Rockefeller and Stillman money was behind many major railroads, including the Union Pacific and the New York Central that granted favorable rates to Standard Oil. Farmers across the country were the first to form powerful voting blocs through the Granges, the popular name for the Patrons of Husbandry, to elect populist representatives.[16] Their protest against high railroad tariffs helped force the passage of the Interstate Commerce Act in 1887 to regulate railroads.

The Interstate Commerce Act required "just and reasonable" rates approved by the Interstate Commerce Commission (ICC) and prohibited rebates, drawbacks and discriminatory prices, and preferences. However, railroad and Standard Oil lobbyists punctured holes in the Act a first-year law student could find. It wasn't until the Elkins Act of 1903 mandating fixed rates did it afford a scintilla of protection against discriminatory rates. Even then appeals of ICC's rates dragged cases through the courts for years. Standard Oil thumbed its nose at the prohibition against rebates and chuckled at the same weight-based rate for oil shipped in barrels and tank cars. The small independents were charged for the weight of the barrels, and Standard Oil owned 80 percent of the railroad tank cars and seldom shipped oil in barrels.

Rockefeller was chagrined when Senator John T. Sherman, a Republican from his home base in Ohio, sponsored the Sherman Antitrust Act of 1890. He had only contributed $600 to Sherman's Senate campaign. No amount of money could buy another sponsor, Senator John Reagan, a Democrat from Texas, where Northern-controlled railroads and Standard Oil were fought with a passion second only to defending the Alamo, and a sponsor of the Interstate Commerce Act.

The Sherman Antitrust Act prohibited "every contract, combination in form of trust or otherwise, or conspiracy, in restraint of commerce between the several States." Penalties included criminal prosecution, confiscation of property used in the conspiracy, and treble damages. But after two years of debate and undermining by the likes

---

16 That is "populist" with a small p, not the Populists who supported the People's Party and advocated public ownership of railroads. Every law student studies the Supremes decision in *Munn v. Illinois*, 94 U.S. 113 (1877), *ad nauseam*. The most famous of the "Grange Cases" upheld a state's authority to regulate grain elevator rates and later formed the basis of regulating public utilities and business "affected with the public interest."

of Johnson N. Camden, Democrat from West Virginia and a Standard Oil shareholder, and Henry B. Payne, Democrat from Ohio and father of Standard Oil's treasurer, Oliver H. Payne, there were loopholes big enough to drive a railroad tank car through. The highly vaunted law did not cover manufacturing, such as refining and crude-oil production.[17] It was not until the passage of the Clayton Act of 1914, restricting the ownership of stock and interlocking directors in competing businesses was the antitrust law given teeth.

In the words of Senator Henry Cabot Lodge, Republican of Massachusetts, the Hepburn Act of 1906 amended the Interstate Commerce Act: "[T]o bring the pipelines of the Standard Oil Company within the jurisdiction of the Interstate Commerce Commission."[18] Lodge proposed to include natural gas pipelines in the bill, but Senator Joseph B. Foraker, Republican of Ohio on Standard Oil's payroll (read bribe) to pass out cash to Senate buddies, rallied opposition, and Lodge was forced to cede he didn't have the votes. Natural gas, oil's sister often emerging from the same well, would not be regulated until the passage of the Natural Gas Act of 1938.

Standard Oil owned or controlled 90 percent of the pipelines and effectively stymied enforcement of the Hepburn Act for decades. It terminated many of its pipelines at state borders or only transported its own oil to avoid being involved in interstate commerce or classified as a common carrier. Its pipelines that could not avoid common carrier status insisted on minimum shipments of 100,000 barrels. If a small refiner or crude producer didn't have the quantity or the storage capacity, tough luck. The ICC was so busy regulating railroads, it didn't get around to investigating the oil pipeline industry until 1911. The ICC finally proposed its first pipeline tariffs in 1912—six years after President Theodore Roosevelt, the "Trustbuster," signed the Hepburn Act into law.

More disturbing than the Hepburn Act to Standard Oil was the basis for the legislation, a 500-page report prepared by the Bureau of

---

[17] *United States v. E.C. Knight Co.*, 156 U.S. 1 (1895), held the Sherman Antitrust Act did not cover manufacturing. *In Champlain Refining Company v. Oklahoma Corp. Coms.*, 286 U.S. 210, 235 (1932), the Supremes confirmed crude-oil "production is essentially a mining operation, and therefore is not a part of interstate commerce, even though the product obtained is intended to be and in fact is immediately shipped in such commerce."

[18] *Congressional Record.* 59th Cong., 1st sess., 1906. 6366.

Corporations (the forerunner of the Federal Trade Commission), under the direction of James R. Garfield, son of former President James A. Garfield. The report detailed Standard Oil's continued receipt of rebates and price discrimination. It was all Teddy Roosevelt needed to order the Department of Justice to prosecute Standard Oil. Release of the report also generated state antitrust suits in eleven states, including no less than a half-dozen cases in Ohio.

The first of seven federal cases was brought against Standard Oil of Indiana for taking illegal rebates. Judge Kenasaw Mountain Landis was an arrogant recently appointed U.S. District Court judge and a grandstander for the press. He insisted Rockefeller take the stand over the objection of the U.S. attorney prosecuting the case and the attorney general for fear Rockefeller would be granted immunity from prosecution in the federal antitrust case. Rockefeller snatched the subpoena and immunity faster than a fox in a chicken coop. Then the sly old fox testified he had retired from active management in Standard Oil in 1895 and claimed he could barely recall what Standard Oil of New Jersey did other than operate a refinery in New Jersey.

The press and public believed he was "a sweet bumbling old man" incapable of the evil deeds. Landis should have looked up the headline in the *World* the last time Rockefeller testified: "Rockefeller Imitates a Clam." To sweeten his reputation a week before Landis's decision, Rockefeller announced his $32-million donation to a negro educational fund that Senator Nelson Aldrich, Republican of Rhode Island and John D. Rockefeller Jr.'s father-in-law, had introduced in Congress to incorporate.

After having been made a fool of by Rockefeller, Landis bullied Standard Oil's lawyers and denied their attempts to present a proper defense. On August 3, 1907, before a packed courtroom Landis assessed the largest fine against a corporation in American history at the time: $29,240,000—$20,000 for each of the 1,462 tank car cargoes alleged to have received rebates.

COMMENTS ON THE LANDIS DECISION

Rockefeller heard about the fine while playing golf and replied, "Judge Landis will be dead a long time before this fine is paid," then continued to play one of the best rounds of golf in his life.

Mark Twain said it reminded him of a bride's comment after her wedding night. "I expected it, but didn't expect it would be so big."

A U.S. Circuit Court of Appeals reversed the decision in 1908 and ruled Judge Landis had abused his judicial discretion. On retrial, Standard Oil was found not guilty. Landis left the bench after the infamous Black Sox baseball scandal to become the first baseball commissioner, which allowed him to bully baseball players and insist everyone still call him "Judge."

Historians debate (some revel in proffering academic opinions, others by spewing cherished bias) whether the Wall Street Panic of 1907 was caused by Judge Landis's decision. It wasn't the primary cause, but was undoubtedly one of the many reasons in the era of rampant stock speculation. Standard Oil's shares dropped from $500 to $420 the week after the decision.

The U.S. Treasury loaned J. P. Morgan $25 million to prop up the banks and stock market. Morgan and Rockefeller, who personally despised each other, worked together to aid the government and themselves by earning commissions during their public-spirited endeavor. Rockefeller astounded the nation by announcing he would contribute half his worth to defend America's credit, starting with $10 million he had laying around in the National City Bank. His admirers praised Rockefeller's generosity. His detractors claim he did it because of the federal antitrust case filed to dissolve Standard Oil of New Jersey.

CAMPAIGN CONTRIBUTIONS

Standard Oil's John Archbold and Henry Rogers contributed $100,000 to President Theodore Roosevelt's campaign in 1904. After writing a letter and ordering the money returned, he was told the money had been spent and couldn't be returned. Teddy replied, "Well, the letter will look well in the record, anyhow."

CHAPTER SIX
THE BUSTED TRUST

THE SUPREMES RULE

Standard Oil of New Jersey, seventy affiliated corporations, and seven individuals were charged with forming and engaging in illegal combinations in restraint of trade under the Sherman Antitrust Act in November 1906. The trial in the U.S. Circuit Court for the Eastern District of Missouri dragged on for fifteen months, during which 444 witnesses paraded before the court and 1,374 exhibits were introduced.

Charges were dismissed against sixteen natural gas companies, most of whom would monopolize gas sales in areas until the passage of the Public Utility Holding Company Act of 1935 and the Natural Gas Act of 1938.[19] Ten affiliates were dismissed because they had been liquidated, primarily through incestuous marriages with other siblings. Two examples are John D. Archbold's Acme Oil Company and Johnson N. Camden's Camden Consolidated Oil Company, absorbed into Standard Oil subsidiaries after they had served their purpose of secretly buying out competing refiners. Seven were dismissed for lack of evidence of stock control, including Tidewater Pipe Line Company, which had been ignominiously drawn into the Standard Oil web to avert bankruptcy. Four subsidiaries found guilty by the circuit court were claimed liquidated before the case was decided by the Supremes.[20]

---

[19] Standard Oil's natural gas monopolies of pipelines and local distribution companies are omitted by most historians. The divestiture left Standard of New Jersey with an interstate gas transmission network and five major gas distributors.

[20] Two of the subsidiaries falsely claimed liquidated were Security Oil Company and Corsicana Refining Company, whose charters were revoked by the state of Texas in 1909. Texas also revoked the charter of Standard Oil subsidiary Navarro Refining Company, which the federal government didn't charge in the case.

The circuit court found the remaining thirty-four companies in violation of the antitrust laws in November 1909, and the case was appealed to the Supreme Court.[21] The Supremes had to grant a second oral argument owing to the deaths of two justices. On May 15, 1911, the Supremes upheld the circuit court and ordered Standard of New Jersey and thirty-three subsidiaries dissolved into separate corporations within six months. The rambling decision by Chief Justice Edward D. White, sitting in the seat by the grace of President Taft's desire to appoint a Southern Catholic Democrat to increase his reelection chances, was as boring as the 12,000 pages of transcript. Taft lost the 1912 election, and the Sherman Antitrust Act lost one of its claws. White insisted adding the "rule of reason" in his decision that boiled down to only restraints of trade that are unreasonable were covered. Associate Justice John Marshall Harlan concurred in Standard Oil's guilt, but dissented from what he called Chief Justice White's "judicial legislation" that corporations could restrain trade as long as they were reasonable about it.

THE DISSOLUTION—WHAT'S THE BIG DEAL?

The busted trust merely reversed the creation of Standard of New Jersey. Its stock and that of its subsidiaries was divided among its shareholders. With its stock value reported at $666 million, there were those who swore Standard Oil bore the sign of the devil. Rockefeller still held 26.4 percent of the whole, and his cohorts maintained their same pro-rata interests. *And their shares skyrocketed two to four times in value within three years.*[22]

The intended crippling blow was to bar the individuals and companies from conspiring and conducting business as a unit. But it failed to stop them from meeting at 26 Broadway for many years where Standard of New Jersey's president John D. Archbold and Standard of New York's president Henry C. Folger continued to maintain their

---

[21] *United States v. Standard Oil Co. of New Jersey*, 173 F. 177 (C.C.E.D.M. 1909). Judge Sanborn's opinion is far more lucid than Chief Justice White's verbose meandering and clearly sets out Standard Oil's predatory actions with a minimum of legal mumbo jumbo.

[22] Kevin Phillips in *Wealth and Democracy* estimated the wealth of six of the seven Standard Oil individuals indicted in the dissolution case in his list of the thirty wealthiest Americans in 1914: John D. Rockefeller, $1 billion; Oliver Payne, $100-$150 million; Henry Rogers, $100 million; William Rockefeller, $100 million; Henry Flagler, $75 million; and Charles Harkness, $75 million. The seventh, Charles Pratt, had died.

corporate headquarters. Behind closed doors the Standard Oil moguls divided the marketing territories remarkably similar to the assignments made in the 1890s shown in Map 5:1. Standard of New Jersey retained the mid-Atlantic region, Standard of New York kept New York and New England, Standard of Indiana held onto the Midwest, Standard of California maintained its hold on the far West, and Continental held onto the Rocky Mountain region. Atlantic, Standard of Ohio, and Standard of Kentucky also kept their areas. The scoundrels even had the nerve to assign Waters-Pierce Missouri and Texas after its corporate charters had been canceled by both states. As an agreement to split marketing territories was a violation of the antitrust laws and Supreme's decision, it didn't take long for the siblings to encroach on each other's territories.

Their biggest problem was the loss of integration and control they had enjoyed. They no longer commanded 90 percent of the nation's refining and 32 percent of the crude-oil production they held in the 1890s. New oil discoveries and the likes of Gulf, Texaco, and Sun and hordes of small independents reduced its share of crude production to less than 15 percent and refining dominance to 65 percent.

Most Standard Oil companies were primarily engaged in one facet of the industry. Standard of California was the only integrated subsidiary to emerge from the dissolution. Only six possessed crude-oil production, and just ten owned refining capacity. Ten merely operated pipelines. Continental, Standard of Kentucky, and Standard of Nebraska were solely marketers. Although Standard of New Jersey retained 43 percent of the combination, including a tremendous refining capacity, it owned little crude-oil production. Standard of Ohio and Standard of New York owned no crude oil, and Ohio Oil had no refining capacity. Deprived of the ability to operate as an integrated oil company with production, refining, pipelines, and marketing, the individual companies had to deal with each other and outside companies, acquire competitors as they did in the past, *or reunite with their sister companies after things cooled off.*

Standard Oil executives moved quickly in Texas through stock and partnership ownership hocus-pocus. Security Oil Company (owned by Standard Oil's English subsidiary Anglo-American Company to buy and ship oil from the Texas Gulf) and Corsicana Refining Company, a Texas partnership (owned by Henry C. Folger, president of Standard of New York, and Calvin N. Payne, son of Standard Oil's treasurer, Oliver Payne), claimed they were liquidated and did not appeal to the Supreme Court. Navarro Refining Company of Corsicana, Texas, a Standard Oil subsidiary that evaded the dissolution decision, and Security Oil were taken over by Magnolia Petroleum Company in 1911. Magnolia, formed in part by the assets of Corsicana Refining, was 88 percent owned by Henry C. Folger and John D. Archbold, president of Standard of New Jersey. Texas filed an antitrust suit against Magnolia Oil in 1913 and tied up Folger's and Archbold's stock. When Texas finally relaxed its antitrust laws in 1918, Standard of New York purchased their shares in Magnolia Oil. Thus the Supremes' order and the dissolution was circumvented from the start.

WHERE ARE THE STANDARD OIL COMPANIES TODAY?

Chart 6:1—Standard Oil of New Jersey Dissolution of 1911 and Reunification & Major Mergers as of 2002 shows the status of twenty-three of thirty-four siblings named in the dissolution that merged back with their sisters, acquired major competitors, and melded into five corporations. Current trade names are listed so the reader can express his or her brand loyalty at the pump or be reminded of their ancestral sins. Standard Oil companies are listed in bold. The years they merged and the value of recent mergers are in parentheses. Buckeye Pipeline, of which few consumers have heard, is large enough to be traded on the New York Stock Exchange. The incestuous twenty-three married siblings and formed five families, including BP Amoco, the British oil giant described in Part Four. Chart 6:1 is necessarily incomplete, as it would require a book by itself to describe all their acquisitions and mergers.

Standard of New Jersey, now Exxon, reunited with Standard of New York, now Mobil, via a $86.4-billion merger in 1998. Imperial Oil Company, Canada's largest integrated oil company, was beyond the jurisdiction of U.S. courts and remained part of Standard of New Jersey. The reasons it was allowed to hold on to Standard of Louisiana and Standard of Pennsylvania was not explained. It was also left with Gilbert and Barker, the nation's largest manufacturer of service-station equipment. (Check the pump the next time you fill up. Chances are it was made by Gilbarco.)

CHART 6:1 STANDARD OIL OF NEW JERSEY DISSOLUTION OF 1911 AND REUNIFICATION & MAJOR MERGERS AS OF 2002

Standard Oil of New Jersey (Exxon) included Standard Oil of Louisiana, Standard Oil of Pennsylvania, Carter Oil (Western production), Imperial Oil (Canada), and Gilbert & Barker (gasoline pumps)

    Humble Oil (1919)

    Anglo-American Oil (1930)

    Colonial Oil (1931)

    Tidewater (1935)

Standard Oil of New York (Mobil) (1998—$86.4 billion)

    Magnolia (1918—a former Standard Oil company)

    General Petroleum (1926)

    Vacuum Oil (1931)

EXXON-MOBIL

Standard Oil of Indiana (Amoco) (BP-2000—$55.0 billion)

    Midwest Oil Co. (1921)

    Pan-American (1933)

    Standard Oil of Nebraska (1939)

    Standard Oil of Kansas (1948)

Standard Oil of Ohio (Sohio) (BP-1987)

    Solar Oil (1931)

Atlantic Refining (Arco) (BP-2000—$33.7 billion)

    Richfield (1966)

    Sinclair (1970)

        Waters-Pierce (1930)

        Prairie Oil & Gas (1932)

BP AMOCO

Standard Oil of California (Chevron)

    Standard Oil of Kentucky (1961)

    Gulf (1984)

    Texaco (2001—$43.0 billion)

        Getty (1987)

CHEVRON

South Penn Oil (Merged with Zapata Oil to form **Pennzoil**-1963)

    Eureka Pipeline (1947)

    South West Pennsylvania Pipeline (1952)

    National Transit (1965)

    Quaker State (1998)

PENNZOIL-QUAKER STATE

Buckeye Pipeline

    Indiana Pipeline (1942)

    Northern Pipeline (1942)

    New York Transit (1964)

BUCKEYE

In 1930 Standard of New Jersey and its siblings, Standards of Ohio, California, Indiana, and Kentucky formed the Atlas Corporation to manufacture and market tires, batteries, and automobile accessories, known in the trade as TBA, through their service stations. In 1948 the Supreme Court ruled that Standard of California's contracts with gasoline stations barring them from marketing other TBA brands violated the antitrust laws and banned the practice.[23] Standard of California's defense that "everyone was doing it" was rejected—everyone had to stop forcing leased or privately owned gasoline stations to purchase only their TBAs.

Chart 6:2—Standard Oil of New Jersey Dissolution of 1911. The Other Nine. Where Are They Now? shows the status of the remaining eleven except two (possibly four) that went out of business.[24] Two, Chesebrough-Ponds and Union Tank, are not connected with former Standard Oil siblings. Ohio Oil, now Marathon Oil and part of USX, merged with Ashland Oil, which had taken over three Standard Oil siblings. Marathon is currently the seventh largest U.S. petroleum company. Like its sisters, Continental Oil, now Conoco, it was infected with a merger mania not unlike Standard Oil's "Angel of Mercy," although it did not merge with its incestuous sisters. Since its merger with Phillips Oil in 2002, Conoco is firmly entrenched as the third largest U.S. oil company, having more than three times the assets and five times the oil reserves as the fourth largest. Arguably, Marathon should have been included in Chart 6:1 to bring the total of Standard Oil siblings to twenty-seven out of thirty remaining siblings that have reunited into six megacorporations. Three former Standard Oil companies rank one, two, three in assets, oil reserves, and oil production in the United States and dwarf their competitors. (See Chart 6:3.)

As this was written, Pennzoil, the current name of South Penn Oil Company that evolved from the dissolution to swallow three of its siblings and merge with Zapata Oil in 1963 (see Chart 6:1), is being purchased by Shell Oil, a wholly owned member of the Royal

---

[23] *Standard Oil Co. of California v. United States*, 337 U.S. 293 (1948).

[24] The Crescent Pipeline Company Rockefeller purchased to avoid tangling with the Mellons and vice versa went under during the Great Depression. Swan and Finch Company, a small lubricant manufacturer, went out of business during the 1960s. Henderson & Benjamin, *Standard Oil: The First 125 Years*, page 126. According to Anderson, *Fundamentals of the Petroleum Industry*, page 27, Washington Oil went out of business in 1976. Borne Chemical did not pop up on Internet searches of chemical companies in 2003.

CHART 6:2 STANDARD OIL OF NEW JERSEY DISSOLUTION OF 1911
THE OTHER NINE. WHERE ARE THEY NOW?

Ohio Oil Co.—Changed its name to Marathon Oil in 1934. In 1981 it merged with Morgan's U.S. Steel (renamed USX). Marathon generates 90 percent of USX's income. In 1998 it merged with Ashland Oil Co., which had acquired Standard Oil siblings **Cumberland Pipe Line** (1932) and **Southern Pipe Line** (1949). **Galena-Signal Oil Co.** merged with Valvoline in 1932 before they were taken over by Ashland in 1963. Marathon is now the seventh largest U.S. oil company.

Continental Oil Co.—Now Conoco-Phillips and a subsidiary of Dupont. In 1917 it was acquired by the Marland Oil Co., an independent oil company that made the mistake of bringing in Morgan banks as investors and was taken over by Morgan interests in 1928. In 1982, after hostile takeover attempts by Mobil and Seagram's, a Canadian whiskey company, Dupont was chosen as its white knight. Conoco merged with Phillips Oil Co. in 2002 to become the third largest U.S. oil company.

Chesebrough Mfg. Co.—Now Chesebrough-Ponds.

Union Tank Co.—Now part of the Marmon Group.

Borne, Scrymser & Co.—Now Borne Chemical Co.?

Washington Oil Co.—Survives in Pennsylvania?

Dutch/Shell Group, two companies that combined in 1907 to form a 60-percent Dutch and 40-percent British "group" with worldwide shareholders. (See Chapter 10.) Digging back in history, one will find that Pennzoil purchased Wolf's Head Refining Company in 1963, which was once the Pennsylvania Railroad's Empire Transportation Company and purchased by Standard Oil after the "Empire War" in 1879. Although not top secret, like Standard Oil of old, Pennzoil didn't advertise it was really the Pennzoil-Quaker State Company, the largest independent lubricants company in the world, which permits Pennzoil and Quaker State oil to appear as competitors on television to market their fine Pennsylvania motor oil.

ARE PETROLEUM COMPANY MERGERS BAD?

According to the Democratic majority staff of the Senate Permanent Subcommittee on Investigations in 2002, oil industry mergers concentrated refining, storage facilities, and pipeline ownership, which resulted in control to limit supplies and competition.[25] Although the report failed to prove its contention beyond a reasonable doubt, it set out the criteria for market dominance, which any economist knows is an oligopoly and affords control. Senator Carl Levin, Democrat of Michigan and subcommittee chairman, was concerned about oil company dominance in Michigan. (No surprise there.) While most Midwesterners think of the Wolverines as the University of Michigan football team, a Big Ten powerhouse, few know that the Wolverine Pipeline Company delivers petroleum products to the Midwest, who owns it or that it dominates the market. According to the report, the pipeline is owned by major oil refiners or their subsidiaries that dominate the marketing in the area, which shouldn't come as a surprise: **Exxon-Mobil** (36.17 percent), Unocal (31.4 percent), **Chevron-Texaco** (17.2 percent), CITGO (9.5 percent), and **Marathon-Ashland** (5.63 percent).

The number of publicly traded U.S. oil and gas corporations is dwindling. The *Oil & Gas Journal* list of 200 (*OGJ/200*), which has listed the top 200 United States oil and gas companies for decades, had the shorten it to 176 in 2001 because of mergers and acquisitions, some of which resulted in takeovers by foreign companies, such as BP and Shell.

---

[25] *Gas Prices: How Are They Really Set?* Report prepared by the majority staff of the Permanent Subcommittee on Investigations. Hearings on April 30 and May 2, 2002.

Mergers, acquisitions, spinoffs, numerous subsidiaries, and joint ventures can inflict migraine headaches on anyone attempting to track petroleum corporations. For example, in January 1999, the upstream part of Pennzoil changed its name to PennzEnergy and five months later merged it with Devon Energy Company, then took the latter's name to form the ninth largest oil and gas company on the *OGJ/200*.

BP Amoco plans to drop "Amoco" from its name, pull down the Amoco signs at gasoline stations, and put up a bright green BP logo. To show American drivers the British company is thinking of America's environment, it flooded America with TV and billboard ads extolling its solar, wind, hydrogen, and clean-burning natural gas business and its future "Beyond petroleum."[26]

Since the $86.4 billion Exxon-Mobil megamerger in 1998, petroleum companies have justified the necessity for mergers due to the low cost of petroleum, worldwide competition, and the need to cut costs, even when the price of crude oil was more than $30 a barrel. A comparison of Chart 6:3—Ten Largest U.S. Petroleum Companies—2001 and Chart 6:4—Twenty Largest Non-U.S. Petroleum Companies — 2001 gives their argument some credence. The state-owned oil companies of many nations have oil reserves far in excess of not only American companies, but the entire United States. (See Chart 17:1— Estimated Principal World Oil Reserves & Production—2002.) Noteworthy are Russia's privately held oil companies, Lukoil, with more oil reserves than Exxon-Mobil, and Yukos, not far behind.

The cost savings of mergers mean the elimination of duplicate overhead, tens of thousands of jobs, and marketing, which includes cutting advertising and gasoline stations. This has resulted in a drastic drop in choices of gasoline brands and small independent marketers being forced out of business. The U.S. Department of Energy's Energy Information Administration (DOE/EIA) reported that the number of gasoline stations in the U.S. dropped from 210,120 in 1990 to 175,942 in 2001, a loss of 16.3 percent in ten years. The drop was caused mainly by the selling of stations and mergers among the major gasoline marketers, as shown in Chart 6:5   Six Leading U.S.

---

[26] Three weeks later, Harry Shimp, BP Solar president announced 160 job cuts at its Virginia solar-panel plant and the elimination of 100 jobs at a BP Solar plant in California. *Washington Post* (October 25, 2002).

Gasoline Marketers—1990 & 2000. The six top gasoline marketers increased their market share of outlets from 29.8 percent in 1990 to 53.8 percent in 2001, which supports the Democrat staff report. But, as most megamergers took place under a Democrat-controlled Federal Trade Commission and Department of Justice, the fact wasn't mentioned.

Another telling point is the prominence of the international Seven Sisters (described in Chapter 12) in U.S. gasoline marketing. Only Citgo, a subsidiary of Petroleos de Venezuela S.A. (the Venezuelan state oil company) cannot trace its roots back to the Seven Sisters or Standard Oil.

The question of whether there is real competition or collusion in gasoline marketing is too complex for this irreverent history of scoundrels and must be left in the hands of the Department of Justice and the Federal Trade Commission. The DOE/EIA noted that merchandise chains, like Wal-Mart and Costco, have grabbed almost 5 percent of the gasoline market. As far as the author is concerned, there will not be real competition until the gasoline stations start handing out maps, glasses, and other freebies, as they did decades ago, to entice him to fill up at gasoline stations. Until then, they are all scoundrels.

THE SCOUNDRELS

One must make up their own mind if Rockefeller and his confederates were scoundrels. Rockefeller gave hundreds of millions to charities and universities, including the Rockefeller Foundation, one of the largest charitable and educational foundations in the world. And don't forget he was famous for handing out dimes to the poor. Charles Pratt founded the Pratt Institute, and Henry C. Folger (the Phi Beta Kappa of the Standard Oil cutthroats) founded the Folger Shakespeare Library. Henry H. "Hell Hound" Rogers gave millions away, helped Mark Twain out of bankruptcy, financed the education and a lifetime annuity for blind and deaf Helen Keller, and set up a fund for Col. Edwin Drake's widow. Mark Twain said of Rogers: "He is not only the best friend I ever had, but he is the best man I have known . . . He's a pirate all right, but he owns up to it and enjoys being a pirate. That's the reason I like him."

Even Ida Tarbell's exposé, *The History of the Standard Oil Company,* had a few (very few) nice things to say in her chapter "The Legitimate

CHART 6:3—TEN LARGEST U.S. PETROLEUM COMPANIES—2001
RANKED BY ASSETS AND OIL (LIQUIDS) RESERVES & PRODUCTION

Company	Assets		Oil (Liquids)			
	$1,000,000		Reserves		Production	
			1,000,000 bbl.			
Exxon-Mobil	1	143,174	1	11,491	1	899
Chevron-Texaco	2	77,572	2	8,824	2	714
Phillips	3	35,217	3	3,660	3	226
Conoco	4	27,094	4	2,142	4	158
Occidental	5	17,850	6	1,037	5	112
Anadarko	6	16,771	5	1,132	7	85
Marathon	7	16,129	13	570	8	77
Amerada-Hess	8	15,369	7	984	6	111
Devon Energy	9	13,184	9	707	12	52
Kerr-McGee	10	10,961	8	841	9	72
Unocal	12	10,425	10	693	10	61

CHART 6:4—TWENTY LARGEST NON-U.S. PETROLEUM COMPANIES—
2001 RANKED BY LIQUID RESERVES

Company (Nation)	Reserves (1,000,000 bbl.)
1 Saudi Arabia Oil Co.	259,000
2 Iraq National Oil Co.	112,500
3 National Iranian Oil Co.	99,060
4 Kuwait Petroleum Co.	96,500
5 Abu Dhabi National Oil Co.	92,200
6 Petroleos de Venezuela SA	77,783
7 National Oil Co. (Libya)	29,500
8 Petroleos Mexicanos	25,425
9 Nigerian National Pet. Corp.	24,000
10 Qatar General Pet. Co.	15,207
11 OAO Lukoil (Russia)	14,243
Exxon-Mobil	*11,491*
12 PetroChina Co. Ltd.	10,959
13 OAO Yukos (Russia)	9,630
14 Royal Dutch/Shell (UK/Neth.)	9,469
15 Sonatrach (Algeria)	9,200
Chevron-Texaco	*8,824*
16 Petroleo Brasilero SA (Brazil)	7,749
17 BP PLC (UK)	7,217
18 TotalFinaElf (France)	6,961
19 Petroleum Dev. Oman LLC	5,525
20 Sonangol (Angola)	5,412

Source: *Oil & Gas Journal* (September 9, 2002)

Chart 6:5
Six Leading U.S. Gasoline Marketers—1990 & 2000

Rank	1993	Outlets	2001	Outlets
1	Texaco	14,151	Shell	22,000
2	Citgo	12,531	BP	17,500
3	Exxon	9,450	Conoco/Phillips	17,400
4	Amoco	9,370	Exxon-Mobil	16,800
5	Shell	8,533	Citgo	13,666
6	Chevron	8,525	Chevron-Texaco	8,055

Source: *National Petroleum News;* Energy Information Administration, *Wall Street Journal* (November 30, 2001).

Greatness of the Standard Oil Company." Americans often glorify scoundrels (Jesse James is a folk hero) and are fascinated by wealth. I watched the Public Broadcasting System's WETA TV two-part series, *The Rockefellers,* on May 15, 2002, foolishly expecting a depiction of Rockefeller's avaricious business tactics from left-leaning PBS. Instead, a good part of the four hours was devoted to repeated references to the Rockefellers' benevolence—the creation of the Teton National Forest, reconstructing Williamsburg, and building the Museum of Modern Art and a snooty church on Riverside Drive in New York. I should have recalled that WETA's president, Sharon Percy Rockefeller, is married to John D. Rockefeller IV, Democrat senator from West Virginia. No one should expect Mrs. Rockefeller to admit on television, "My husband's great-grandfather was a ruthless bastard."

It is customary for an author to conclude a part or chapter with a summary. This part ends with the type of distorted Standard Oil public relations garbage you should not allow your children to read from *Standard Oil: The First 125 Years*:

> In retrospect, the breakup of Standard served mainly to strengthen the ability of the government to intrude into corporate affairs. Many people of the day, and those of us who can look on the situation with historical perspective, were against the breakup of Standard. Standard had maintained low prices for their products, in favor of the consumer; paid relatively high wages, in favor of its employees; and provided a constant return on investment, in favor if [*sic*] its stockhold-

ers. The company paid fair prices to independent producers from which they bought crude, provided constant business for the railroads . . . If not a good corporate citizen, Standard had at least served as a stabilizing influence, indeed Rockefeller's Angel of Mercy, to the petroleum industry during its infancy.

The author offers three comments. The above propaganda would even make staunch conservatives, like William F. Buckley Jr. cringe (his father was a multimillionaire independent oilman); I bet the authors were paid well by a Standard Oil sibling to sell their integrity; and Amoco Supreme gasoline gets the best mileage in my car for the money.

Part III
Teapot Dome

"I am not worried about my enemies.... It is my goddamn friends who are giving me trouble."

—President Warren G. Harding (1923)

"Harding was not a bad man. He was just a slob."

—Alice Roosevelt Longworth, *Crowded Hours* (1934)

"I decline to answer on the grounds that it may tend to incriminate me."

—Albert B. Fall, former U.S. senator and secretary of the interior and the first cabinet member to be convicted and serve time in jail, pleading the Fifth Amendment during a Senate hearing. (1924)

CHAPTER SEVEN
A WHEELING & DEALING

THE JOB IS WORTH A HALF-A-MILLION DOLLARS

During the era of nominating presidents in smoke-filled rooms, the once powerful Republican "Ohio Gang" was leaderless. By 1920, their infamous political boss, Mark Hanna, was dead and his successor, Senator Joseph B. Foraker, had broken the Eleventh Commandment—Thou shall not get caught, especially taking bribes from Rockefeller's despised Standard Oil. The Ohio Gang had nominated six of the last ten presidents from Ohio, the Republicans had never won the presidency without carrying Ohio, and it appeared the Democrats would nominate Ohio Governor James M. Cox.

The Ohio Gang leadership vacuum opened the way for a sleazy, small-town lawyer, Harry M. Daugherty, to be handed control by default. Daugherty's political credentials were not impressive. He had been defeated as the Republican candidate for state attorney general and failed to win the Republican nominations for governor, U.S. Senate, and twice for Congress. He couldn't even get elected as delegate to the 1920 Republican National Convention.

Leading the delegate vote count were Gen. Leonard Wood, a Spanish-American War hero, and Governor Frank O. Lowden of Illinois. But a large dissatisfied bloc formed after Senate hearings exposed the buying of delegates and primaries with sacks of cash, a common practice by both parties. (Nothing has changed. Senator John McCain, Republican of Arizona, still believes big political contributions corrupt the political process.)

91

Daugherty's plan was to have Ohio nominate Senator Warren G. Harding as its favorite son and pray for a deadlock. Harding, the owner of a small newspaper, the *Marion Star*, had married a wealthy widow five years his senior and was enjoying the cordial life as a do-nothing senator. The risks made him queasy. He couldn't run for reelection and had lost a race for governor to Cox in 1912. Worse, his mistress had presented him with a daughter and a potential national scandal.

During the sweltering heat at the Chicago convention, aggravated by a waiters' strike and the hardship of getting ice for their bootleg booze, oilmen searched the hotels for a candidate to back. Wildcatter Jake Hamon from Oklahoma offered General Wood fifty-two votes from the Southwest and barrels of oil money for his campaign if he was named secretary of the interior. After being tossed out of Wood's headquarters, he was reported to have been shown the door by Governor Lowden before finding a welcome reception from Daugherty in Harding's empty campaign suite. No one knows what was said, but Hamon paid Harding's hotel bills, spread money around the convention to pick up Harding delegates, and bragged to his oilmen friends that the appointment as secretary of the interior was worth a half-a-million dollars.[27] Two other oilmen known to have contributed to Harding's campaign in Chicago were Col. James G. Darden, an independent oilman, and Harry F. Sinclair, president of Sinclair Consolidated Oil Corporation.

In a Blackstone Hotel suite, Will H. Hays, Republican national chairman, and seven senators met to break the deadlock on the fifth night of the convention. Senator Henry Cabot Lodge of Massachusetts, convention chairman, was concerned that he couldn't hold the delegates over the weekend. Senator Boies Penrose of Pennsylvania (a Standard Oil Senate mouthpiece) called General Wood and offered to swing the election to him if the senators could name three cabinet appointees. After Boies was turned down, the senators called Harry Daugherty into the smoke-filled room and ordained a fellow club member—Senator Warren Harding. Harding was nominated on the tenth ballot. Poker-playing Harding said of Daugherty's nomination plan, "We drew to a pair of deuces and filled."

The Senate cabal placed in nomination another of their own for vice president, Senator Irvine Lenroot of Wisconsin, not that he was

---

[27] Jake Hamon was shot a few months later. His married mistress was tried for the murder, but found not guilty. The murderer was never uncovered.

anxious to take the job. A senator is more powerful than the vice president. However, the convention woke up to the fact that two stodgy conservative senators on the ticket was one too many and nominated Calvin Coolidge, governor of Massachusetts, on the first ballot. In 1920 "Silent Cal" was known nationwide for his decisive action in 1919 when he called out the National Guard to quell the Boston police strike.

Daugherty and Hays kept Harding a secret from the voters during the campaign by keeping him on his porch in Marion, Ohio. Democrat James Cox and his running mate, Franklin D. Roosevelt, ran on President Woodrow Wilson's League of Nations platform as if it was the one-issue to save the world. But the voters didn't want any part of European entanglements or the League of Nations and preferred Harding's return to "normalcy" (whatever that means). Harding pulled 15,152,200 popular votes to Cox's 9,147,553 and 404 electoral votes to 137. Cox captured only the yellow-dog Democrat South. On Harding's coattails, the Republicans jumped from 48 to 59 in the 96-seat Senate and took the House of Representatives by the largest margin in history with 300 seats to the Democrat's 132.

As Daugherty promised the Senate power brokers, Andrew W. Mellon was named secretary of the treasury. The money man behind Gulf Oil would remain in the position for eleven years under Coolidge and Hoover. As customary, the winning party national chairman, Will Hays, was named postmaster general to hand out patronage plums. Edwin Denby, a mild-mannered wimp who had served three terms in the House, was appointed secretary of the navy because no one else wanted the job of dismantling the fleet after World War I. Harding's appointment of Harry Daugherty as attorney general rattled even the staunchest Republicans. Could they trust a shyster lawyer and political hack to prosecute the antitrust cases and war profiteers? William J. Burns, head of the detective agency that still bears the family name, was named chief of the Bureau of Investigation (predecessor of the Federal Bureau of Investigation).

Harding wanted to name his Senate pal, Albert B. Fall of New Mexico, secretary of state, but Daugherty had promised the prize to the Republican Senate clique's candidate, Charles Evans Hughes. Hughes had resigned from the Supreme Court to run against Wilson in 1916 and had represented Standard Oil. There were raised eyebrows over Harding's desire to name Fall, a short-tempered, steely-eyed Southwesterner with a Wyatt Earp handlebar mustache who toted a six-shooter on the Senate floor, to a position requiring diplomacy. Fall's dress of a string tie and Stetson and stories of how he shot a deputy sheriff and disarmed the notorious gunman, John Wesley Hardin, in an El Paso saloon didn't cast a diplomatic image, either. His reputation as the most rabid Democrat in the Southwest before turning Republican and accusations of bribery in connection with his election by the legislature as New Mexico's first senator earned Fall a long list of political and personal enemies.

It cannot be pinpointed who suggested Harding appoint Fall secretary of the interior, although the *New York Tribune* claimed Daugherty had promised the oilmen backing Harding that Fall would get the post.[28] Harding apologized to Fall for not naming him secretary of state and promised him a seat on the Supreme Court when a vacancy arose. One wonders if Harding knew that President Grover Cleveland had removed Fall from the Supreme Court of the territory of New Mexico after he climbed down from the bench to lead a posse tracking a bank robber.

Fall's Senate confirmation sailed through unanimously without a hearing to question his position on development of the public lands. This chagrined the conservationists led by Gifford Pinchot. Like today, there were heated conflicts over protecting Alaska's wilderness and drilling for oil on federal lands. Pinchot, former first chief forester of what is now the Department of Agriculture's Forest Service and currently revered as the "Father of Forestry," was opposed to Fall's development mind-set. Pinchot was also bitter. He believed he deserved a lifetime political appointment dating back to President Theodore Roosevelt, but had been fired by President Taft in 1909 for publicly criticizing the opening of public lands to development, including those in Alaska, by Interior Secretary Richard A. Ballinger. Taft, although conservation minded, didn't tolerate public squabbling. Fall was talking about oil drilling and transferring the Forest Service to the Interior Department. Some things will never change. Politicians and bureaucrats instinctively grab power and expand their turf. Pinchot had fought the creation of the National Park Service, saying it was "no more needed than two tails to a cat," and opposed creating national parks unless they were placed under the Forest Service.

---

[28] *New York Tribune* (February 6, 1924).

Pinchot rallied his former secretary, Harry A. Slattery, a lawyer, prolific letter writer, secretary of the National Conservation Association, and bachelor gadfly, to track Fall's movements and use his influence to create unfavorable press for the new interior secretary. Slattery rose from the positions as a clerk and personal secretary under two Democratic interior secretaries (Franklin K. Lane and Harold L. Ickes) to undersecretary of the interior under Ickes. Thus Fall was hounded by the Democrats and conservationists from the beginning of his tenure.

The Senate knew that Fall's passions were echoed by his fellow Westerners—Easterners should keep their noses out of Western development. Fall had vehemently opposed President Taft's 1912 executive order establishing Naval Petroleum Reserves in Buena Vista Hills and Elk Hills, California, and President Wilson's 1915 executive order creating a naval reserve at Teapot Dome, Wyoming. The executive orders removed the federal oil lands Taft had withdrawn in 1909 from the Interior Department's jurisdiction to prevent their loss to mining claims and placed them under the navy as an oil reserve in time of war. Oil companies had eyed the hundreds of millions of barrels of oil locked in the ground since, and Fall believed the reserves should be leased to earn the government royalties. Fall also knew an old oil prospector friend who was interested.

Fall first met fellow prospector Edward L. Doheny in 1896 during their quest for gold in New Mexico and had remained friends. Doheny had discovered rich oil fields in Mexico, Venezuela, and California, including downtown Los Angeles, and his Pan American Petroleum and Transport Company produced more crude oil than any Standard Oil sibling. At sixty-five, he had the energy of a man in his twenties, leprechaun blue eyes, and hundreds of millions of dollars. The staunch Democrat was the largest contributor to President Wilson's 1912 and 1916 campaigns, but had been turned down when he attempted to lease the Teapot Dome and Elk Hills reserves during the Wilson administration. In 1920 Doheny contributed to the Harding campaign, as well as to the Democrats.

THE $50-MILLION OIL DEAL

While the politicians were dividing the political spoils, Col. Albert E. Humphreys struck an oil bonanza in Texas's Mexia oil field. Standard

Oil of Indiana, left with little crude-oil reserves after the Supreme Court's 1911 dissolution, made an offer for 30 million barrels of oil at $1.50 a barrel through its chairman of the board, Col. Robert W. Stewart. (After the Spanish-American War, every gentleman and con man who had been in Cuba with Teddy Roosevelt claimed the title "Colonel.") Humphreys wanted Standard of Indiana stock instead of cash, but Stewart refused to sell $45 million in stock and give control of the company to the wildcatter. Stewart sent Henry M. Blackmer, president of Midwest Oil Company that Standard Oil of Indiana had recently acquired, and James E. O'Neil, president of Prairie Oil and Gas Company, another member of the busted trust, to talk to Humphreys. They were joined by Harry F. Sinclair of Sinclair Consolidated Oil Corp., whose subsidiary, Sinclair Crude Oil Purchasing Company, was partially owned by Standard Oil of Indiana as a result of a deal to feed its crude-oil-starved refineries.

The incestuous group persuaded Humphreys to sell Prairie Oil and Gas and Sinclair Crude Oil Purchasing the oil for cash. At the last minute, Humphreys wanted to make it a Texas-size deal by increasing the sale to 33,333,333⅓— barrels at $1.50 a barrel to round out the contract price at $50 million, the largest crude-oil purchase known at the time.

When Humphreys arrived to sign the contract, he was told a Canadian company, Continental Trading Company, was the buyer. Humphreys had never heard of Continental Trading and insisted Prairie Oil and Gas and Sinclair Crude Oil Purchasing guarantee payment. It is no wonder Humphreys had never heard of the company. Henry S. Osler, a Toronto, Canada, barrister, had not yet filed Continental Trading's charter in Canada. The paper company had no assets, and its officers and directors were law clerks who didn't have to divulge the corporation's real owners to the public or government.

After a drink to celebrate the deal, Humphreys left. Sinclair, Stewart, Blackmer, and O'Neil, signed another contract on behalf of their companies with Osler, president of Continental Trading. The second agreement provided that Prairie Oil and Gas and Sinclair Crude Oil Purchasing would buy the crude oil from Continental Trading at $1.75 a barrel, netting a potential profit of $8,333,333.33 for Continental Trading. In case of price fluctuations from the base price and to eliminate Continental Trading's need for cash, the purchasers were to pay Continental Trading the market price, allowing the paper company to pay Humphreys the contract price and keep a profit of 25¢ a barrel.

To avoid their corporate stockholders and directors learning about the deal and cash passing hands, Osler was instructed to buy United States 3½-percent Liberty Bonds with the profits and divide them among the four oilmen. Osler's legal fee was a 2-percent cut. If completed, it would earn him $166,666.67, a handsome fee in 1921, and equal to $1,683,333.67 in 2002. As general counsel for Imperial Oil (Canada), a subsidiary of Standard Oil of New Jersey, Osler knew how to handle secret deals.

WHAT DOES THE $50 MILLION DEAL HAVE TO DO WITH THE TEAPOT DOME?

Like a mystery, read on and spot the clues. It also proves what scoundrels they were. Flipping back to Chart 6:1 will help keep track of the incestuous companies, like Sinclair Consolidated Oil, which took over Prairie Oil and Gas.

A LITTLE BLACK BAG

By happenstance, the first strands of the web were spun during World War I when Doheny visited his son, Navy Lt. Edward L. Doheny Jr., aboard the *U.S.S. Huntington*. The commanding officer, Capt. John K. Robison, blustering and arrogant toward his subordinates, fawned before the elder Doheny's oil wealth and power of a man who had President Wilson's ear. Robison displayed his scant knowledge of oil by bragging that the Naval Petroleum Reserves were now protected by the navy. Doheny agreed, but warned that the reserves suffered from drainage. (There is that word "drainage" again from Chapter 2 under the Rule of Capture.)

President Wilson's secretary of the Navy, Josephus Daniels, had also been concerned about the potential drainage loss from the California naval reserves and asked Congress for authority to lease the edges of the reserves to protect the navy's oil. Congress passed the Naval Appropriations Act of June 4, 1920, that included an impressive-sounding amendment: "The Control and Protection of Naval Petroleum and Oil Shale Reserves." If you were looking for loopholes, the act was a sieve and a typical political compromise to placate Democrat Secretary of the Interior Franklin K. Lane and congressmen who believed the naval reserves should be leased. It granted the secretary of the navy the broad authority:

> ". . . to conserve, develop, use, and operate the same in his discretion, directly or by contract, lease or otherwise, and to use, store, exchange, or sell the oil and gas products thereof, and those from all royalty oil from lands in the naval reserves, for the benefit of the United States."

The amendment permitted the navy secretary to lease the lands under the recently enacted Mineral Leasing Act of February 25, 1920, which removed oil, gas, coal, and the so-called fertilizer minerals from the General Mining Law of 1872. The act also gave the interior secretary the discretion to lease the federal oil lands rather than grant mining claims that gave away the nation's oil resources for a pittance at $2.50 per acre to foreigners, like British/Dutch-owned Shell.

Fall's first step was to persuade Secretary of the Navy Edwin Denby and President Harding to transfer the Naval Petroleum Reserves back to the Department of the Interior. After a chat with Harding and Denby, Fall drafted an executive order effecting the transfer. Denby handed the order to Assistant Secretary of the Navy Theodore Roosevelt Jr. to work out the details. Young Teddy, son of former President Theodore Roosevelt, was the ideal man to handle the task. He had just left his position as an officer of the Sinclair Consolidated Oil Corporation and his brother, Archibald, was a vice president of several Sinclair subsidiaries. Harding signed the executive order on May 1, 1921, less than two months after he was inaugurated.

The interior secretary also had to appease the navy brass, worried about a civilian supervising their oil reserves. Was it coincidence or design that the newly appointed chief of the Navy's Bureau of Engineering that managed the Naval Petroleum Reserves was Adm. John K. Robison, who had learned about the danger of drainage from Doheny in 1917? Fall preyed on the navy's two biggest complaints. Royalties from drainage leases on the navy's California reserves were paid to the Treasury Department, and the admirals couldn't get their hands on the royalties for *their oil*. Worse, in 1913 Congress had revoked the secretary of the navy's statutory authority dating back to 1842 to construct storage depots without congressional approval, and the navy's requests to build fuel oil depots along the Atlantic and

Pacific coasts and Pearl Harbor, Hawaii, had been rejected.

Fall offered the navy the proverbial deal it couldn't refuse. Instead of leasing the naval reserves for royalties payable to the treasury, he would "convince" the oil companies to issue oil certificates redeemable for oil that wouldn't be charged against the navy's budget. Even better, the navy could use the oil certificates to pay for the construction of oil depots without budget authorization. Denby and the admirals put pencil to paper and figured they needed $200 million. They knew Congress would not appropriate the vast amount during peacetime, and the cost of the depots was far more than the navy would receive from leases to counter drainage. Admiral Robison agreed with Fall that the deal should be kept secret in case Congress got wind of it and interfered with a project crucial to national defense.

Doheny didn't need to be convinced. His Pan American Petroleum and Transport Company was familiar with the Elk Hills Naval Reserve from operating a small lease to offset drainage. He complained to Fall that the 55-percent royalty and low gas pressure made the lease unprofitable. Fall couldn't amend the terms of a government lease awarded by competitive bidding, but he had a plan. He arranged a contract between the navy and Pan American dated April 25, 1922, for Pan American to supply 1.5 million barrels of fuel oil to the navy base at Pearl Harbor, construct the necessary storage facilities, and for the navy to pay for the construction with oil certificates. The contract also provided that should the royalty oil be insufficient to deliver 500,000 barrels per year, the secretary of the interior would issue additional leases on the Elk Hills reserve to make up the shortfall. On June 5, 1922, an assistant secretary of interior issued an oil and gas lease endorsed by the secretary of the navy to Pan American for a quarter section in the Elk Hills reserve at royalties ranging from 12.5 to 35 percent.

Fall and Doheny knew that a quarter section (160 acres) was far too small to produce royalty oil at a rate of 500,000 barrels a year.

The admirals also knew it.

But only Fall and Doheny knew that on November 29, 1921, Fall had called his old prospecting pal and told him he needed the "loan" they had discussed. Doheny told his son to put $100,000 in cash in a little black bag and deliver it to Fall at his Washington apartment at the Wardman Park Hotel. Thus "a little black bag" became synonymous with political bribes.

99

DRAINAGE OR NATIONAL DEFENSE?

The Interior Department's Bureau of Mines and Geological Survey studied Teapot Dome's drainage potential and independently concluded leasing was not necessary. The navy's geologists agreed, but the reports were ignored.

Admiral Robison and most navy gold braid were shocked by the 1922 Washington Naval Conference, a disarmament agreement with Great Britain, France, Italy, Germany, and Japan to reduce the size of their navies. The United States made the largest concessions by agreeing to scrap thirty capital ships and not constructing replacements until 1936, leaving the navy with only eighteen capital ships.

The Pearl Harbor fuel depot was important—the Japanese might attack any day! The admirals were off by nineteen years. The 1941 Japanese sneak attack sank eight battleships, but the fuel tanks were untouched and supplied oil for the navy to regroup and defend the Pacific, so a little credit is due the navy's foresight.

An Expensive Teapot

Carrying Doheny's little black bag, Fall boarded a train to New Mexico in December 1921 to spend the Christmas holidays at home and buy a neighboring ranch. On New Year's Eve, Harry Sinclair arrived in his private railroad car, the "Sinco," with his lawyer, Col. J. W. Zevely.

The dapper Sinclair had come a long way from his modest youth in Wheeling, West Virginia, and early career as a druggist in Independence, Kansas.[29] He multiplied small oil leases in Kansas and Indian oil leases in Oklahoma when it was the Indian Territory until he controlled the largest independent oil company in the world and his net worth was $400 million. Sinclair had a penchant to outdo, outbuy, and outbluff when he wanted something. He was one of the first to have a corporate plane and, as the story goes, the first oilman to wear silk underwear in the Oklahoma oil patch. The avid sportsman also had the audacity to form a third major baseball league, the Federal League, in defiance of national baseball commissioner Judge Kenasaw Mountain Landis. In 1923 his horse, Zev, named after his lawyer, Colonel Zevely, won the Kentucky Derby.

---

[29] There is a tale that Sinclair acquired his initial oil investment money from an insurance claim for accidentally shooting off his big toe while hunting.

100

Fall and the navy agreed to lease Sinclair the *entire 9,481 acres* of the Teapot Dome Naval Petroleum Reserve in Wyoming if he constructed a pipeline from the reserve to Chicago at his cost, something Sinclair had to do to market the oil anyway. Sinclair agreed to build storage tanks on the Atlantic Coast and at Guantanamo Bay, Cuba, to be paid for with oil certificates. The deal not only awarded Sinclair a huge oil lease, the navy would be a perpetual customer for oil. The navy negotiators insisted on what they believed was a lucrative royalty rate to obtain the funds for the storage depots—12.5 percent on the first fifty barrels a day produced from each well and 50 percent on each additional barrel. Sinclair gladly agreed. He calculated the lease would net a minimum of $100 million and the average royalty would be less than what private landowners demanded for leases on proven oil reserves.[30]

Because of oil claims on Teapot Dome filed under the General Mining Law of 1872 before President Taft withdrew the oil lands from claims in 1909, Fall insisted Sinclair settle them before he issued the lease. The claims were dubious, but had been looked on favorably by previous Democrat Interior Department secretary, Franklin Lane. This opened cracks for cockroaches to crawl out of the woodwork.

Doheny had attempted to lease the Teapot Dome during the Wilson administration through Leo Stack, a small-time promoter, for 10 percent of the profits and payment of his expenses. When Stack's $5,000 bribe to a Wilson appointee failed, Doheny backed out of the deal and was reimbursed for his $15,000 investment by Stack, who obtained a loan to repay Doheny from L. L. Aitkin, president of Mountain States Oil, a Standard Oil of Indiana subsidiary. Stack then made a similar deal with the Pioneer Oil and Refining Company and Société Belgo-Amèricaine des Pétroles du Wyoming based on oil claims on Teapot Dome filed before Taft's withdrawal. Both were subsidiaries of Midwest Oil, a subsidiary of Standard Oil of Indiana. Sinclair met Henry M. Blackmer, president of Midwest Oil and his cohort in the Continental Trading scam, and bought the frivolous

---

[30] Royalties on private lands are computed in fractions except in California, where they have to be different and use percentages. The standard royalty is 1/8 (12.5 percent), but in cases of large reserves and during oil booms, the royalty is often 3/16 (18.75 percent) or 1/4 (25 percent). It is also a practice to pay a bonus when a lease is issued regardless of whether oil is found. Oilmen later testified the bonus on the Teapot Dome lease should have been at least $10 million. Sinclair paid nothing.

101

claims for $200,000 in cash and a promise to pay $800,000 from any oil produced.[31]

John C. Shaffer, a Fall political ally, oil promoter, and owner of a chain of newspapers, including the *Indianapolis Star, Denver Times, Rocky Mountain Post,* and *Chicago Evening Post,* approached Fall regarding his oil claim on Teapot Dome. Fall insisted Sinclair give Shaffer an interest in 420 acres of the lease. Satisfied Sinclair had taken care of the claims, Fall issued an oil-and-gas lease, locked it in his desk drawer, and sent his son-in-law to visit Sinclair. Sinclair gave Fall's son-in-law $198,000 in United States 3½-percent Liberty Bonds, all he had on board his private railroad car parked at Washington's Union Station at the moment. The following week, Sinclair handed him another $35,000 in bonds and $36,000 in cash. The odd total of $269,000 was never explained.

Sinclair assigned the lease to Mammoth Oil Company in which he owned all the stock. Through a dummy corporation he traded one-third of Mammoth Oil's stock for shares of Sinclair Consolidated Oil Corporation at a preferred rate and netted a $17-million profit. Sinclair Consolidated's shares shot up from 18¾ in January of 1922 to 33½ in April. He also formed a syndicate to market Mammoth Oil stock that raised $10.4 million for Mammoth Oil and earned the syndicate $20 million on profits from stock sales to the public. As Mammoth Oil's shares soared more than $55.50 and Sinclair controlled the syndicate, he was wallowing in more than enough cash to drill the Teapot Dome lease and build the pipeline.

Complaints of a secret Teapot Dome lease concerned Wyoming's two senators and lone congressman, F. W. Mondell, (the beautiful, but sparsely populated tenth largest state still only has one House member). The three received the runaround on their inquiries to Interior Assistant Secretary E. C. Finney. (Fall was out of town and couldn't be reached.) Navy Secretary Denby told them to call Secretary Fall.

Senator Robert "Fighting Bob" La Follette, liberal Republican maverick of Wisconsin, introduced a resolution to investigate the Teapot Dome leases that passed unanimously amid reports specula-

---

31 Midwest Oil's Teapot Dome claims were considered worthless. The Supremes had upheld President Taft's executive order withdrawing Teapot Dome from mining claims. *United States v. Midwest Oil Co.,* 236 U.S. 459 (1915).

tors had made more than $30 million on Sinclair Consolidated stock. La Follette and Senator Kenneth McKellar, Democrat of Tennessee, instituted an investigation into the high prices of crude oil and gasoline to determine if there was a conspiracy by the oil companies to raise prices. Nothing came out of the investigation other than La Follette reporting that Fall had been duped by the oil companies or had lied. Investigations into high oil prices have become standard fare (no pun intended in connection with Standard Oil). The venerable Senator Daniel Patrick Moynihan, Democrat of New York, joked in 1996, "It is in the oldest American political tradition that when anything happens [to oil prices] you investigate the oil companies."

The press notoriety drew Leo Stack from the slime. He urged Pioneer Oil and Refining and Société Belgo-Américaine des Pétrol du Wyoming to renew their claims, but was told they had been sold to Sinclair and offered $50,000 to forget about the deal. Stack smelled a rat and contacted two sleazebags, Frederick G. Bonfils and H. H. Tammen, owners of the *Denver Post,* then the yellowest tabloid in the West and a tool for blackmail. Bonfils and Tammen sent a reporter to New Mexico to check rumors Fall was making major improvements on his ranch. The snooping reporter uncovered two smoking guns. Fall, rumored to be broke, had paid ten years back taxes on his ranch and had received a thoroughbred horse, a breeding bull, and six prize heifers from Sinclair's ranch.

The newspapermen started a smear campaign against Sinclair's Teapot Dome lease in their paper and sent copies to President Harding and every member of Congress. Bonfils and Tammen were not the crusading newspapermen they pretended. They had made a deal for a fifty-fifty split of anything Slack received after paying his legal fees in his suit against Sinclair, Blackmer, Aitkin, Mammoth Oil, Standard Oil of Indiana, Pioneer Oil, and Midwest Oil for $5 million. Sinclair settled by paying $250,000 in cash and one-half the profits on 320 acres in Teapot Dome, with the right to buy them out for $1 million. The following week Bonfils and Tammen's newspaper published a Sunday feature article declaring Harry Sinclair to be a brilliant businessman and a great American.

CALL OUT THE MARINES

Col. James G. Darden, one of Harding's original backers at the convention and a longtime friend, had old oil claims on Teapot Dome. A weak Harding would do nothing to help Darden validate his claim. Fall told Darden that Sinclair would give him a piece of the action, but by this time Sinclair had the lease and was tired of paying for worthless claims. Darden formed a company to drill for oil on his Teapot Dome claim and enticed Attorney General Harry Daugherty to invest. The Spanish-American War veteran charged up Teapot Dome, not with a rifle, but with a drill.

When Fall heard that Darden was drilling on Teapot Dome, he called Assistant Secretary of the Navy Teddy Roosevelt, who recruited Maj. Gen. John A. Lejeune, the commandant of the Marine Corps, for the battle. Five armed Marines were dispatched to Wyoming to evict the trespassers. After completing their mission without firing a shot, Darden's representative took the Marines to lunch.

CHAPTER EIGHT
THE SENATE FOLLIES

FALL HAS AN ANSWER FOR EVERYTHING

F all prepared a lengthy report for President Harding to send to the Senate in response to its questions about Teapot Dome. Based on mythical geology and the threat of drainage, Fall assured the president it was in the nation's interest and there was no question the lease was within the law. He failed to mention that his Bureau of Mines subordinates had asked for legal opinions from the attorney general and two oil companies had challenged the legality of issuing oil certificates in lieu of paying royalties. Fall's blustering response was always the same. He was a lawyer, and he knew the law! He told Harding he had informally discussed it with Attorney General Harry Daugherty and was assured every step was legal.

Fall never discussed the leases with Daugherty. He didn't want to cut Daugherty and his poker-playing grafter pals in on the deal. The attorney general was under fire for not prosecuting antitrust and war-contract fraud cases and suspected of taking bribes for paroles. Daugherty also talked too much and had publicly complained he wasn't told about the Sinclair Consolidated stock play where the insiders made millions.

Before Harding sent Fall's reply to the Senate, Walter Teagle, president of Standard Oil of New Jersey, called Albert D. Lasker, a close friend of Harding and chairman of the Shipping Board (predecessor to the U.S. Maritime Commission). Teagle told Lasker that Standard Oil of New Jersey had no interest in Teapot Dome leases (Teagle would have drilled on the White House lawn if he thought he would find oil) and urged him to tell the president the lease "smells" and to stop it before it gave the oil industry a bad name. Lasker made an appointment to see the president that night and later recalled Harding's reply.

"This isn't the first time this rumor has come to me, but if Albert Fall isn't an honest man, I'm not fit to be president of the United States."

Everyone agrees that Warren G. Harding was not fit to be president of the United States. He probably wasn't fit to be president of your local Rotary Club. Harding submitted Fall's report to the Senate along with a letter stating that Fall and Denby had acted with his full approval. Harding never asked Attorney General Harry Daugherty for a legal opinion.

RETIREMENT OR AVOIDING THE HOT SEAT?

The secretary of the interior was not finished taking care of his old prospector friend. The Elk Hills Naval Petroleum Reserve drainage lease and construction of 1.5-million barrels of storage at Pearl Harbor had only set the scene for the big giveaway. On December 11, 1922, Navy Secretary Edwin Denby contracted with Pan American Petroleum and Transport Company to build a refinery and storage tanks at San Pedro, California, and connect it with a pipeline to the Elk Hills reserve. The next day, Fall issued Pan American a lease on the *entire* Elk Hills reserve (38,969 acres less 640 acres under drainage leases) at a royalty rate between 12.5 to 35 percent.

Fall resigned as interior secretary and retired to his New Mexico ranch in March 1923. The political climate in Washington was getting too hot for Harding's appointees. Republicans and Democrats alike were raining criticism on Attorney General Daugherty for his failure to prosecute fraudulent World War I contracts and antitrust cases. Members of Congress investigating Daugherty soon found they were being investigated by William J. Burns's Bureau of Investigation.

Col. (yes, another sleazy colonel) Charles R. Forbes, director of the Veterans Bureau, was under Senate investigation for taking kickbacks on veterans hospital contracts and selling surplus medical supplies that were not "surplus." Charles F. Cramer, the Veterans Bureau general counsel, committed suicide rather than face the disgrace and a jail term that Forbes eventually would serve.

Six weeks after Cramer's suicide, Jess Smith, Daugherty's unpaid gofer and bagman, was found with a bullet in his head in a suite they shared at the Wardman Park Hotel. President Harding couldn't believe it. He had a date that morning to play golf with his poker-playing pals, Jess, and Edward "Ned" B. McLean, publisher of the *Washington Post* and the *Cincinnati Enquirer.* William J. Burns, who lived at the hotel, took charge of the scene. The District of Columbia police were not amused that the head of the Bureau of Investigation didn't call them for a half hour, and Burns couldn't find the "suicide" weapon for ten minutes. Daugherty rushed to the scene after spending the night at the White House to "discover" that Jess Smith had burned Daugherty's personal papers in a metal waste can.

"Murder, She Wrote" fans and armchair TV sleuths would groan if Jessica Fletcher hadn't spotted the clues. The gun was found in the dead man's right hand and the bullet had entered his left temple and exited on the right, a feat impossible for a contortionist. How his head ended in the trash can with Daugherty's burned papers and why Daugherty's male secretary sleeping in a connecting room didn't hear the shot or smell the burning papers remains a mystery. The police records of the suicide were destroyed shortly afterward in a whirlwind of efficiency not seen since by the District of Columbia Police Department, which currently only solves one-third of the murders in the nation's capital.

In the meantime, Fall and Sinclair were in Moscow negotiating for Standard Oil of New Jersey's and Shell's oil concessions confiscated by the Communists. The smiling Kremlin leaders agreed to Sinclair's grandiose plan to develop the Baku and Grozny oil fields if he invested $115 million in the fields and arranged a $250-million loan for the Soviet government on the New York bond market. With a straight face, the Kremlin threw in an oil concession on Sakhalin Island on Russia's Siberian east coast as a bonus, notwithstanding it had been occupied by Japan since the Russo-Japanese War in 1905. When Sinclair's agents arrived on Sakhalin Island, the Japanese politely jailed them. The following morning the Japanese apologized, invited the oilmen to tea, and deported them.

The "oil deal of the century" had one catch—it was conditioned on United States diplomatic recognition of Soviet Russia. In preparation for lobbying the Harding administration and Congress on their

return, Sinclair's entourage of employees and former government officials required two decks on an ocean liner and an entire train from
Paris to Moscow. Richard O'Conner in *The Oil Barons* titled the chapter depicting the venture "The Sinclair Follies." Anti-Communism was
rampant in America, and Secretary of State Charles Evans Hughes had
recently demanded the Baku oil fields the Soviets had nationalized be
returned to Standard Oil of New Jersey, which had paid the Nobel
brothers $11.5 million for a half interest in their oil fields.[32]

Fall told the press on his return that conditions in Russia were
improving and the United States would soon recognize the Soviet
Union. He didn't mention that Sinclair gave him $25,000 in Liberty
Bonds and $10,000 in cash to cover his expenses on a trip paid for by
Sinclair.

President Warren Harding escaped from Washington's humidity
and political heat during the summer of 1923 by embarking on a jun-
ket to Alaska to see the Alaska Naval Petroleum Reserve No. 4 he had
ordered set aside after Fall's resignation. While visiting the territory,
then more than 90-percent owned by the federal government,
Harding learned more about Fall's shenanigans to deal away Alaska's
federally owned minerals.

WARREN G. HARDING
NOVEMBER 2, 1865 — AUGUST 2, 1923

President Warren G. Harding had a heart attack and died in San Francisco on his return from Alaska. It was first reported he died from tainted crab-meat. There were also rumors that he was poisoned. Those who knew him said he died at fifty-eight from the anguish of learning that his trusted friends had betrayed him and their country.

The vast majority of Americans trusted and liked their affable presi-dent. They were to learn that he was not competent to lead the country and probably never wanted the posi-tion that led him to an early grave and the ignominious label of being our worst president.

---

[32] Believers in an "Eastern Establishment" conspiracy must read Parts Four and Five.
Hughes had represented Standard Oil as an attorney, and President Hoover appointed him
Chief Justice of the Supreme Court in 1930.

THE SENATE HEARINGS

The first Senate hearing of the Committee on Public Lands and Surveys into the Teapot Dome lease was held on October 23, 1923, eighteen months after Senator La Follette's resolution passed to investigate the navy reserve leases. The Republicans had lost eight Senate seats in 1922, and committee Chairman Reed Smoot, Republican of Utah, was not inclined to air Republican dirty laundry.

On the other side of the aisle, Senator Thomas J. Walsh, Democrat of Montana and labeled a "Western Progressive," was hellbent to prosecute Fall and every Republican in sight. (Few things have changed in Washington.) Walsh and Fall were diametric opposites— self-righteous Walsh versus freewheeling Fall—the accuser short and slight, pale-faced, clipped-tongued, with a perpetual schoolmaster's stern gaze; and the defendant tall and rangy, bronzed by the sun, Southwestern drawl, with a gunfighter's steely eyes. Fall meet Walsh's penetrating questions with arrogance. He declared the leases were legal, in the nation's best interest, none of Congress' business, and he would do it again. He also lied when asked if Sinclair paid for his services in Russia.

Navy Secretary Edwin Denby's testimony proved his incompetence, naiveté, and lack of understanding of the lease terms. Harry Sinclair dazzled the Senate with bluster. When Walsh asked if Sinclair contributed to the Republican party, Sinclair admitted he did because he was a Republican, but he also contributed to Democrats. (Walsh was only following the congressional practice of pointing the blame to the other party, and Sinclair was showing Enron's Ken Lay how to spread the wealth.)

The next witnesses were geologists, lawyers, and oilmen testifying about drainage, government leases, and other dull issues that put a few senators to sleep and failed to earn headlines. Walsh's witnesses testifying on Fall's improvements to his ranch were regarded as petty political partisanship. It wasn't until December that Walsh, with trepidation, called Edward Doheny as a witness. Walsh and Doheny were both Democrats, originally from Wisconsin, and old friends. Doheny and his wife had nursed Walsh in their home after his wife died and Walsh was on the verge of a nervous breakdown. The two men had also discussed the problems of drainage from federal oil lands years earlier.

Walsh's systematic questioning was met by the Irish bantam's wit and counterpunches. He advised Walsh he possessed better data on drainage and oil matters than the Interior Department's Bureau of Mines bureaucrats, which was probably true. In 1919, they had announced America would run out of oil in precisely nine years and three months. When it came tit-for-tat time on political contributions, Republican Senator Smoot asked Doheny if he had contributed to the Democratic party. Democrat Doheny admitted giving the Democrats $75,000 towards their 1920 campaign debt and $25,000 to Harding's campaign to pay for photos of Harding in newspapers to rebut the insidious rumors that Harding was part Negro.

When the new committee chairman, Senator Irvine Lenroot, Republican of Wisconsin, asked if Fall profited in any way in connection with the granting of the Elk Hills lease, it should have raised eyebrows, Doheny answered, "Not yet," then said he would be glad to hire Fall if he desired to come out of retirement.

THE BIG LIE

Walsh insisted Fall appear before the committee again to explain how he could be spending money to upgrade his ranch when a drought and low cattle prices were driving cattlemen bankrupt. Fall sent word from New York that he was too ill to testify and went to Atlantic City. (If he was so ill, why did he go to chilly Atlantic City in December rather than to his ranch in sunny Three Rivers, New Mexico?) Fall's wife called Ned McLean and begged him to come to Atlantic City where a nervous Fall asked McLean to say that he loaned him $100,000. A neurotic McLean agreed, then boarded his private railroad car for balmy Palm Beach, Florida, where any rich playboy with a socialite wife like Evalyn Walsh McLean (owner of the Hope Diamond) should be instead of freezing his butt on the coast of New Jersey.

Fall wrote the committee that McLean loaned him $100,000 to fix up his ranch and he never received one cent from Sinclair or Doheny. Two days after Christmas, Senator Lenroot presented the letter to a skeptical committee that decided it required McLean's corroboration. (Any congressional committee meeting two days after Christmas must be damned serious or Grinches.) McLean's doctors and lawyer, A. Mitchell Palmer (attorney general under Woodrow Wilson), wrote the committee that McLean had "acute sinus" problems and travel would put his life in jeopardy. Walsh hopped on a train to Palm Beach to question McLean at the luxurious Breakers hotel. McLean waffled and admitted he didn't loan Fall $100,000. Fall, hiding in another room at the Breakers and realizing weak-kneed McLean might lose his nerve, was already on the telephone to Doheny.

Walsh gleefully spread the news that Fall had lied to his former brethren to guarantee that the press would pack the committee room to hear the official dirt. After Walsh gave his report, the Roosevelt clan appeared, not just brothers Theodore Junior and Archibald and their wives, but big sister Alice Roosevelt Longworth, who had more brains and gumption than her brothers combined. Accompanying Alice was her husband, Representative Nicholas Longworth, the Republican floor leader from Ohio and the next speaker of the House of Representatives, whose power and ability are memorialized by one of the House office buildings bearing his name. The previous evening the Roosevelt boys had told senators Lenroot and Walsh that Harry Sinclair told Archie to book him on the next ship to Europe and make sure his name was not on the passenger list. There was little naive Archie could tell the senators about what went on inside Sinclair's companies, except that he was resigning. He couldn't even recall all his positions with Sinclair's companies. Young Teddy, the assistant secretary of the navy, sat silent, aware he had been had. The Roosevelt boys marched out of the hearing with their integrity untarnished, but their smarts and common sense in serious doubt.

A few days later, Gustave Wahlberg, Sinclair's personal secretary testified. He had little to contribute, but let it slip that Sinclair had loaned Liberty Bonds to Postmaster General Will H. Hays when he was chairman of the Republican National Committee. Wahlberg wasn't sure, but suspected that Sinclair also gave Liberty Bonds to Secretary Fall. (The dry *Congressional Record* fails to disclose what went through the minds of the Democrats, but they probably had to restrain themselves from doing cartwheels in the Senate caucus room.)

Two days later, Doheny testified he had loaned Fall $100,000. That he gave Fall cash in a little black bag meant little to the oilman who shelled out millions in cash. Asked to prove it was a loan, Doheny presented Fall's promissory note a few days later. The fact that Fall's signature on the $100,000 promissory note had been torn off was difficult to explain. Even the Republicans didn't believe him.

But the biggest story began to unravel when Republican Senator Lenroot asked Doheny if Franklin K. Lane, the former interior secretary under Wilson, and other Democrats worked for Doheny. Doheny replied yes and, as if he was New York Yankees owner George Steinbrenner listing his high-priced free agents he had acquired, named one of Wilson's attorney generals, Thomas W. Gregory, and Wilson's secretary of war, Lindley M. Garrison. Then he hit the Democrats below the belt by giving the press tomorrow's headline. He also had employed William G. McAdoo, Wilson's secretary of war and son-in-law and the top contender for the Democrat nomination for president in 1924. It mattered little that McAdoo had only been retained as a lawyer to represent Doheny's interests in Mexico when his oil leases had been nationalized. The man on the street and scandal-hungry press saw a revolving door between government and oil companies that led to corruption and political payoffs.

The following day when it came time for Fall to appear, he entered the Senate caucus room leaning on a cane. No longer robust and arrogant, the broken man refused to testify under his Fifth Amendment right not to incriminate himself.

While the Senate was debating what action to take, the House appropriated $100,000 for President Calvin Coolidge to appoint two independent special counsels to prosecute the culprits and cancel the leases on the naval reserves.

Lawyers and T-Men

President Calvin Coolidge, accused of inaction in demanding Denby's and Daugherty's resignations by the Democrats and the press, stayed cool. Less than six months in office, he still had Harding's cabinet to deal with and, as the former governor of Massachusetts, he was a Washington outsider. The only thing said in Denby's defense came from Senator Walsh when he remarked that stupidity was not grounds for impeachment. After a bitter partisan debate, on February 11, 1924, the Senate passed a resolution demanding Coolidge force Denby's resignation. The votes were along party lines, with the Democrats only losing one vote from their ranks.[33]

---

[33] The box score on the resolution calling for Denby's resignation was 35 Democrats, two Farm-Labor, and ten Republicans for; and 35 Republicans and one Democrat against. (Did seven Democrats and six Republicans hide in the Senate cloakroom during the voting?) *Congressional Record*, 68th Cong., 1st Sess., 1924. 2055-68, 2245.

The Republicans who didn't follow the party line were labeled "progressives" by the Democrat press, as is still the case if "moderate" doesn't fit. Coolidge called them "damned cowards."

Coolidge stonefaced the Senate by mumbling the words of James Madison concerning the separation of the three branches of government and that he would seek the advice of the special counsel. When Denby submitted his resignation on February 18, Coolidge accepted it before the ink was dry.

Cal chuckled over the Democrats's choice for special counsel, Thomas W. Gregory. His name had to be withdrawn because he was employed by Doheny. Their second choice, former Democrat Senator Atlee Pomerane from Ohio, was a nonentity acceptable to the Senate clique. Feisty Republican Senator George Wharton Pepper of Pennsylvania pushed Owen J. Roberts of his home state for the Republican counsel. The biggest thorn was Senator Walsh, a professional hater who made a career of fighting corporations and Republicans. Walsh despised Pepper and mistrusted Roberts, who represented corporations as an attorney, but the Republicans controlled the Senate. Walsh refused to show up for the vote on Roberts. Like today, Pomerane and Roberts were acceptable compromises.

The conventional wisdom that Pomerane would be the leader was misguided. The cases would drag on for years and Roberts, younger by twelve years, was a tireless plodder. Roberts had the smarts to visit Senator Walsh to seek his advice. Walsh told him to trust no one. He and his staff had been spied upon, and his office had been broken into on two occasions. His most poignant warning was Attorney General Harry Daugherty's Department of Justice and William J. Burn's Bureau of Investigation couldn't be trusted.

Roberts reported his conversation with Walsh to President Coolidge. Why Coolidge did not force Daugherty's resignation cannot be explained, and Daugherty did not resign until one month later.[34] No-nonsense Coolidge proved his support of the special coun-

---

[34] There was a rumor that Coolidge couldn't persuade his Amherst classmate, Harlan Fiske Stone, to take the attorney general's position paying only $12,000 a year. Stone was making ten times that with a Wall Street law firm, but would take the pay cut if he was appointed to the Supreme Court, which Coolidge did eighteen months later. Stone cleaned up the Justice Department, starting with firing William Burns and naming the civil servant assistant director, J. Edgar Hoover, as the director of the Federal Bureau of Investigation, a job he would hold for forty-eight years. Hoover couldn't be connected with Dougherty's and Burns's corrupt cronies. Since 1919 he had been busy rounding up the "Red menace." (In January 1920, he arrested 10,000 radicals and forced the deportation of 556 "undesirables.")

113

sel by ordering the assignment of four Treasury Department Secret Service agents to handle their investigative work.

The incorruptible Secret Service T-men were ideal for the task. The serial numbers on the Liberty Bonds Sinclair gave the Republican National Committee allowed the tracking of transfers to possible pay-offs. Their first break was the discovery of large blocks purchased by the Continental Trading Company and Henry S. Osler. Continental Trading's records had been destroyed. Osler was less than cooperative and disappeared on an extended African safari. But the bond transfers led the T-men to Col. Robert W. Stewart of Standard of Indiana, Henry Blackmer of Midwest Oil, James E. O'Neil of Prairie Oil & Gas, and Harry Sinclair. Stewart suffered a memory loss, and Blackmer and O'Neil suddenly had business in Europe. In an age before computers and commercial plane travel, the T-men doggedly traced the Liberty Bonds received by Sinclair by rail and car to Fall's bank accounts in New Mexico and Texas.

The special counsel faced an uncooperative Interior Department in obtaining documents, and Doheny's attorney, Frank J. Hogan, had copies of Navy Department documents they were not given. Hogan also appeared to have copies of every document they had requested from the navy. Under pressure to take action from a press looking for dirt and Democrats seeking blood, the special counsel obtained indictments in the District of Columbia in June 1924 before they obtained sufficient evidence to proceed to trial. Fall and Doheny were indicted for conspiracy in connection with the Elk Hills leases, and Fall and Sinclair were indicted for conspiracy in connection with the Teapot Dome leases. Fall was charged with receiving a $100,000 bribe from Doheny and Doheny with bribing Fall. Why Sinclair wasn't indicted for bribery is a mystery unless you believe Roberts and Pomerane couldn't prove to a grand jury that Sinclair actually gave the bonds to Fall.

Sinclair's cockiness and possibly poor legal advice added to his troubles when the Senate subpoenaed him. He refused to plead the Fifth Amendment. Instead, he challenged the Senate's authority to question him after he had been indicted. The Senate cited him for contempt by a vote of seventy-two to one. Twenty-three Republican senators did not cast votes and complained that Walsh's questioning about the Liberty Bonds Sinclair had given Will Hays to pay off the

Republican National Committee's 1920 campaign debt was purely political. Senator Davis Elkins, Republican of West Virginia, cast the sole vote against the contempt resolution. He also cast the only vote against investigating Attorney General Harry Daugherty. As the vote was sixty-six to one, it appears twenty-nine senators had better things to do than vote. Elkins owned extensive oil, gas, and coal interests and had speculated in Sinclair Consolidated Oil stocks after the issuance of the Teapot Dome leases.

The Senate, prodded by Walsh and the Democrats anxious to expose corrupt Republicans during an election year, continued to hold hearings, notwithstanding their grandstanding politics might be detrimental to the special counsel's prosecution of the criminal cases. Thanks to Republican delays, the Senate Committee on Public Lands and Surveys failed to adopt a final report on the Teapot Dome investigation until January 20, 1925, well after the 1924 elections. The minority report presented by Senator Seldon P. Spenser, Republican of Missouri, defended Fall's leasing of the reserves and blamed the Democrat Wilson administration for the Naval Petroleum Reserves leasing policy and Senator Walsh, who had fathered the leasing legislation. The Republican minority report didn't pass the laugh test or the vote of the full Senate and was defeated forty-two to twenty-eight. Walsh's majority report only passed forty to thirty. No Democrat voted for the minority report, and every vote against the majority report was Republican. As the makeup of the Senate was fifty-one Republicans, forty-three Democrats, and two independents, it is clear that many Republicans had better things to do that afternoon than vote their conscience.[35]

Except for a few weeks of genuine fact finding, the fifteen months of hearings should have been called "The Senate Follies."

---

[35] *Congressional Record*, 68th Cong., 2nd Sess., 1925. 2133 *et seq.*

AL JENNINGS
WINNER OF THE MOST COLORFUL WITNESS AWARD

Al Jennings was one of four lawyer-sons of a judge. The brothers robbed trains to supplement their legal fees in the Oklahoma Territory. In 1897 the Jennings gang robbed a train of $300 and a watch. Al was caught and did five years of hard labor, but was readmitted to the Oklahoma bar. Finding the law practice not lucrative, he moved to Hollywood and expanded into real estate, movies, author of Wild West tales, politician, and part-time evangelist.

He testified that Jake Hamon told him he had spread a million dollars to Harry Daugherty, Will Hays, and Senator Boies Penrose in return for the appointment as interior secretary and leases on the naval reserves. That night he conducted an evangelical tent meeting. The collections for the ex-train robber who had found God were overflowing. Jennings lived to the age of ninety-seven still telling tall tales even after reporters exposed him as nothing but a petty crook. But there was probably a grain of truth in his testimony.

CHAPTER NINE
FALL'S FALL & OTHER OBITUARIES

TRIALS AND TRIBULATIONS

The Fall and Doheny conspiracy trial began in November 1926 and lasted three weeks. Washington's number-one criminal lawyer, Frank J. Hogan, representing Doheny, and the extremely able criminal attorneys handling Fall's defense outgunned corporate lawyer Owen Roberts. Atlee Pomerane, one reporter called "ornamental," didn't belong in a criminal courtroom. When the criminal defense lawyers finished their closing arguments, the jury was prepared to give Fall and Doheny medals for saving the U.S. Navy and protecting America from a Japanese invasion. Roberts and Pomerane sat at the prosecutors table as if they had wet their pants after hearing the jury's verdict—*Not Guilty!*

In October 1927, Fall and Sinclair went on trial for conspiracy, but a mistrial was declared when it was discovered Sinclair had ordered the jury shadowed by the Burns Detective Agency. In February 1928, the judge ruled Sinclair, William J. Burns, Sherman Burns (William's son), and others in contempt of court and sentenced William Burns to fifteen days in jail and Sinclair to six months and a $500 fine.

HARRY SINCLAIR'S FRIENDS HAVE FAITH

On December 6, 1927, Harry Sinclair was facing criminal contempt for jury shadowing, under sentence for contempt of the U.S. Senate, and had been indicted for bribery and conspiracy to defraud the government. The Supreme Court had ruled the Teapot Dome lease had been obtained by fraud and corruption. Harry swore he was innocent of all charges and was unanimously reelected to the board of directors of the American Petroleum Institute.

With Fall too ill to stand trial, Sinclair faced the conspiracy trial alone in April 1928. As the Supreme Court had held that the Teapot Dome lease had been obtained by "fraud and corruption," it should have been a proverbial open-and-shut case, but Frank Hogan was at his best. The jury took less than two hours to acquit Sinclair. As it takes two to tango and commit conspiracy, Fall could not be tried for the crime.

In April 1929, the Supremes affirmed Sinclair's Senate contempt conviction, and, in May, Harry of silk suits and undershorts began his three-month jail sentence. In June the Supremes affirmed his six-month sentence for jury shadowing, but reversed William Burns's conviction, Sinclair served six-and-one-half months with time off for good behavior and using his druggist skills in the prison dispensary.

Fall's bribery trial in October 1929 ended in a guilty verdict. Frank Hogan lost his first criminal case. It would have required Michelangelo to paint Fall as likeable to a jury. Nevertheless, the ill defendant looking far older than sixty-seven and sitting in a wheel-chair during the trial caused the jury to recommend leniency because of his age and health. The maximum sentence was three years. Fall only received a sentence of one year and a fine of $100,000.

Doheny faced the bribery charge in March 1930 at the age of seventy-three. After Hogan finished extolling his client's patriotism in helping the navy protect America's shores and his generosity by lending a few dollars to Fall, an old friend who had loaned him law books to study law while he was convalescing from two broken legs, the jury took less than one hour to acquit the loveable old man. Such inconsistencies make people hate lawyers and distrust the courts. Albert Fall was found guilty of taking a $100,000 bribe, but Edward Doheny was found not guilty of paying him the bribe. People said it was impossible to convict a millionaire. It also made many wonder about our jury system, unless you believe Doheny was a kind old man and didn't intend to bribe his crooked friend.

WHAT EVER HAPPENED TO WHAT'SHISNAME?

Albert B. Fall served nine and one-half months of his sentence. He was the first cabinet member convicted of a felony and to serve time in prison for a crime committed while in office. President Herbert Hoover refused to grant him a pardon. Because of poor health, he was allowed to serve the time in New Mexico, most of it in a prison hospital. He died a pauper in 1944 at the age of eighty-three and never paid the $100,000 fine. Many believed Fall was railroaded.

Edward Doheny died in 1935 at the age of seventy-eight. Bedridden during his last years, his Pan American Petroleum and Transport Company was merged with Standard Oil of Indiana in 1933. Pan American controlled the American Oil Company that gave Standard Oil of Indiana its name: Amoco.

Harry Sinclair passed away in 1956 at the age of eighty. His Sinclair companies were purchased by Standard Oil sibling Atlantic Refining (Arco). In 2000 Arco was swallowed up by BP Amoco. (See Chart 6:1.)

The other Continental Trading Company scoundrels disappeared into oblivion after assigning the balance of the contract to their companies for $400,000 when things got hot during the Senate hearings. None testified. James O'Neil of Prairie Oil and Gas lived the rest of his life in Europe and never returned to face charges. Henry Blackmer of Midwest Oil hid in Europe until 1949. At eighty-one, he returned and paid his fines and back taxes, but he was too old to be sent to prison. H. S. Osler remained in Canada, after all, he was only a lawyer and just accepted legal fees. After being acquitted of contempt of the Senate and perjury, Col. Robert Stewart was ousted as chairman of Standard Oil of Indiana in a nasty and costly proxy battle led by John D. Rockefeller Jr. The Rockefeller family still held 15 percent of the company's stock and thought Stewart gave Standard Oil a bad name.

Harry Daugherty returned to Ohio and retired on his ill-gotten gains.

Adm. John K. Robinson retired from the navy in 1926 at his permanent rank of captain. They say there is a bust of Robinson in the Engineering Building at the U.S. Naval Academy at Annapolis. Why he deserved the honor is uncertain, but Harry Sinclair contributed to its funding.

Ned McLean was committed to an insane asylum before the Doheny and Fall trials and died in a mental institution in 1941. His *Washington Post* was sold. Once a spokesman for conservative Republicans, it now espouses the liberal Democrat line.

William G. McAdoo remained tainted during the Democratic nomination campaign and saddled with the nickname "McAdieu." His battle for the nomination in 1924 with Alfred E. Smith went to John W. Davis on the 103rd ballot. McAdoo was supported by the South and West, "drys," and KKK; while Smith held the East, "wets," and Catholics. Davis was a compromise, a conservative Wall Street lawyer whose prime qualification was he didn't represent oil companies, although his clients included J. P. Morgan & Company. The Democrats campaigned with aluminum teapots, however, Coolidge, with the slogan "Keep cool with Coolidge," took 382 electoral votes and 54 percent of the popular vote. The Democrats only received 29 percent of the popular vote, the rest going to the Progressive Socialists led by former Republican Senator Robert M. La Follette. The Democrats only carried the solid South. It was the Roaring Twenties, a time of prosperity and bootleg booze. McAdoo was later elected to the Senate from California.

Will Hays, Harding campaign manager, chairman of the Republican National Committee, and postmaster general, left Washington in the middle of the Teapot Dome scandal for Hollywood to become moral supervisor of films as president of the Motion Picture Producers and Distributors of America. He remains best known for prohibiting movies containing long kisses, scenes of couples in bed without one foot on the floor, and sexual innuendos.

Senator Thomas Walsh's name came up for nomination as president during the 1928 Democratic convention, but the delegates ran from the acerbic senator like scalded dogs, and he hastily withdrew. In 1933 President-elect Franklin D. Roosevelt nominated Walsh for attorney general, but he died on the train on the way to the inaugural at age seventy-three.

Atlee Pomerene took time out in 1926 to run for the Senate in Ohio on his record as a dauntless prosecutor of fraud and corruption and was soundly defeated. President Hoover appointed Pomerane chairman of the Reconstruction Finance Corporation in 1932 to pick up conservative Democrat votes in an election year. It was no surprise when the job didn't last long.

Owen J. Roberts was appointed to the Supreme Court by Hoover in 1930. Legal historians credit him with blunting President Franklin D. Roosevelt's court-packing plan to add judges to the Supreme Court by switching from his conservative views to supporting Roosevelt's New Deal. It was claimed he played politics with a swing vote, and he was labeled the "Switch in time that saved the Nine."

Whatever successes Pomerene and Roberts are awarded in history, they were poor trial lawyers. How else could Fall, Doheny, and Sinclair beat the conspiracy charges based on the blatant facts and Doheny be acquitted of paying a bribe after Fall had been convicted of accepting the bribe?

Gifford Pinchot went on to become Republican governor of Pennsylvania and meddle in conservation and Prohibition matters. His minion, Harry Slattery, was canned as undersecretary of the interior by President Truman for talking too much. He wrote *The Story of the Teapot Dome Scandal* and his memoirs, *From Roosevelt to Roosevelt*, but was never able to get the tripe published by a reputable publisher.

Coolidge cooled the Teapot Dome issue by establishing the Federal Oil Conservation Board, consisting of the secretaries of war, navy, interior, and commerce, and revoking Harding's executive order transferring the naval reserves to the Interior Department and placing them back under the Navy Department. Every high school student should know, but doesn't because of our poor school systems, that Coolidge said, "I choose not to run" in 1928. But why did he say it? It was later discovered that he had suffered a mild heart attack and believed it was not prudent to run. He told one reporter he didn't run, "Because there's no chance for advancement." Coolidge got a bum rap as a sourpuss. He had a marvelous New England dry sense of humor. He was known for his deadpan expression, which prompted writer Dorothy Parker to remark after hearing that Coolidge had died, "How can they tell?"

Herbert Hoover, the only engineer elected president, defeated Al Smith, the first Catholic to run for president, drawing 58.7 percent of the vote. One week after settling in the White House, Hoover announced that no new federal oil leases would be granted and the secretary of the interior had been ordered to review the 20,000 existing federal oil leases to determine if they were legal and in compliance with the law.

In 1931 Secretary of the Interior Ray L. Wilber dutifully reported that 12,000 oil and gas leases had been canceled for noncompliance. Wilber's announcement was cheered by the conservationists and those who didn't know any better. Almost all the leases deemed in noncompliance were for the failure or refusal to drill for oil under the terms of the lease. There had been an oil glut since 1928 because of massive oil discoveries in Oklahoma, Texas, and Iraq, and the demand for oil was dropping. The nation was two years into the Great Depression. *By then oilmen and other scoundrels had already cooked up schemes that would dwarf the Teapot Dome scandal and create repercussions felt around the world.*

WHAT EVER HAPPENED AT TEAPOT DOME, ELK HILLS, AND PEARL HARBOR?

The Supremes ruled the Teapot Dome and Elk Hills Naval Petroleum Reserve leases were obtained by "fraud and corruption." It upheld their cancellation and ordered Pan American Petroleum and Mammoth Oil to pay the navy the value of the oil taken from the reserves. The contracts to accept oil certificates in lieu of payment of royalties and construct oil storage depots were likewise deemed obtained by fraud and corruption and canceled.[36] Pan American was denied payment for its drilling costs at Elk Hills of $1,013,428.75 and the costs of constructing the storage tanks at Pearl Harbor of $7,350,814.11. Mammoth's drilling costs were also forfeited. Mammoth's payment to the navy for the oil totaled $12,156,246.66 and Pan American's $34,981,449.62. The navy obtained the storage tanks at Pearl Harbor to help defeat the Japanese during World War II, as the admirals said they would.

---

[36] *Pan American Petroleum and Transportation Co. v. United States*, 273 U.S. 476 (1927); *Mammoth Oil Co. v. United States*, 276 U.S. 1 (1927).

PART IV
INTERNATIONAL SKULDUGGERY

"Oilmen are like cats; you can never tell from the sound of them whether they are fighting or making love."
> —Calouste Gulbenkian, "Mr. Five Percent"

Gulbenkian also said, "Oil friendships are greasy."

"An oilman is a barbarian with a suit."
> —Harry Doherty, president of Cities Service Company (Citgo)

CHAPTER TEN
THE FOREIGNERS

THE RUSSIANS

In the late 1860s, Tsar Alexander II opened oil exploration to private enterprise around Baku on the Caspian Sea, now the capital of Azerbaijan. In 1873 Robert Nobel, a chemist and the brother of Alfred (the inventer of dynamite), was sent to the Caucasus to buy walnut wood for rifle stocks by his brother, Ludwig, for their armament company. Instead, Robert became fascinated with oil and spent the money to buy a refinery. History doesn't record what Ludwig said when he learned of Robert's failure to follow orders, but within a few years, the Nobel Brothers Petroleum Company was Russia's largest oil company.

Baku's roads and transportation were impassable in the harsh winter, and there was a shortage of barrels in a land stripped of trees. The Nobels built the first oil tanker, the *Zoroaster*, named to commemorate the area the Zoroastrians called the "eternal pillars of fire" two thousands years earlier when flaming gas erupted and people prayed to things they didn't understand. As the Caspian Sea is land-locked, the tanker only supplied Russia. The only other nation bordering the Caspian at the time was backward Persia. Baku was in keeping with the oilmen's adage that oil is only found in godforsaken wildernesses[37] that defy man's attempt to drill and ship it to market.

---

[37] There are exceptions. Oil has been found in Beverly Hills and the front lawn of the governor's mansion in Oklahoma City. There is also oil in the Alaska National Wildlife Refuge (ANWR). Anyone who has been there will tell you that where the oil companies want to drill is *not* a wilderness, but admittedly godforsaken. In April 2002 Senator Ted Stevens, Republican of Alaska, said that anyone who says the ANWR drilling area is a wilderness is a liar and, if it was not against the Senate rules, he would challenge the liars to a duel.

The French Rothschilds banking house entered the oil business, but was rebuffed by the Nobels at the suggestion of a partnership. The Rothschilds bought the Batum Oil Refining and Trading Company (known by its Russian acronym, BNITO) and financed a railroad over the Caucasus from Baku to Batum on the Black Sea in 1883. The railroad opened the way to shipping through the Mediterranean, allowing BNITO to market one-third of the Russian production, second to the Nobels, who used four hundred tons of Alfred's dynamite to blast through the mountains and construct a pipeline to Batum.

The Russians, or to be more precise the Swedish brothers and French Jews encroached on Standard Oil's European domain. Through its Anglo-American Oil Company subsidiary, Standard Oil of New Jersey resorted to its standard (pun intended) practice of slashing prices and spreading reports that Russian kerosine was inferior and could explode and burn down your house, which was true. Standard Oil's offer to buy out the Nobels was rejected. They had more crude oil than they could refine, cheaper labor, and were closer to many European ports. By 1892, Russian oil had captured 29 percent of the European market.

THE BRITISH AND THE DUTCH

The Rothschilds retained London shipping broker, Fred "Shady" Lane, to find a distributor for their oil east of Suez. If Shady Lane was involved in a three-cornered deal, he would be representing at least two sides. Lane recommended fellow Londoner Marcus Samuel, a Jewish merchant, who jumped at the chance to get in bed with the Rothschilds and their money. Unfamiliar with the oil business, Marcus visited Baku and toured the Far East to survey the markets. Marcus Samuel must be referred to by his given name. His brother and partner was cursed with the name Samuel Samuel. Samuel was responsible for dealing with the Far East trading houses run mainly by shrewd Scotsmen blessed with the inherent ability to shave pennies off costs, which provided the brothers a vast and efficient distribution network.

Marcus showed his marketing savvy when he saw the *Zoroaster*. Bulk shipments would give him a jump on Standard Oil, still shipping kerosine in blue barrels and cans. When his kerosine reached its destination, Marcus filled bright red barrels and cans to distinguish them from Standard Oil's blue barrels. He formed Shell Transport and Trading Company, named to honor his father, a marketer of trinkets made from seashells. His first tanker, the *Murex*, was named after an ugly little snail shell. All of Marcus's tankers were named after seashells. He even named one the *Clam*. Today Shell's logo remains a scallop.

Marcus planned to ship the oil from Batum to the Far East through the Suez Canal, 3,500 miles shorter than Standard Oil's route from the U.S. Atlantic coast. The Suez Canal Company, controlled by Britain, had safety standards that required him to modify his tankers before they were permitted passage. He also had to overcome rumors in the halls of Parliament of "Hebrew influence" and danger of Russians using the canal initiated by Standard Oil's British representatives. In 1892, after the Rothschilds used their influence with Prime Minister Benjamin Disraeli, Lloyds of London rated the tankers safe ,and the *Murex* was permitted Suez Canal passage. No doubt the English Rothschilds' financing of Disraeli's purchase of control of the Suez Canal for Britain in 1875 helped persuade Disraeli.

The inevitable Standard Oil price wars against the Rothschilds and Nobels in Europe were already in full swing when the *Murex* sailed. Several attempts to split up the market failed. In 1895 the Rothschilds and Nobels agreed to divide the European market by allotting 75 percent to the Americans and 25 percent to the Russians, but Tsar Nicholas II nixed the deal.

Standard Oil turned to the Far East where it was being undersold by Shell with its cheaper transportation costs and entrenched trading system. A small company, Royal Dutch, had discovered oil on Sumatra in the Dutch East Indies, only a few days steam from the lucrative markets in Japan and Singapore. Shell attempted to buy Royal Dutch, which was open to a marketing arrangement, but refused to be bought. When Standard Oil proposed a buyout the Royal Dutch couldn't refuse, the Dutchmen refused and went to the Dutch government to assure that Standard Oil's application for a drilling concession in the Dutch East Indies was rejected. The "Royal" imprimatur in Royal Dutch signified King William III was behind the Dutch company and earning a few guilders from Royal Dutch.

Shell, not a threat like Standard Oil, obtained a concession in the wilds of Borneo amid malaria and headhunters that no one else wanted. It struck oil in 1897, but the heavy crude oil was high in sulfur and refined uneconomic yields of kerosine. Marcus Samuel attempted to sell the sour crude oil to the Royal Navy as bunker fuel for its ships it planned to convert from coal to oil for more than a decade, but failed.

Royal Dutch, in financial trouble and its managing director stricken with a heart attack, turned the reins over to Henri Deterding, a thirty-four-year-old aggressive whirlwind. Deterding believed Shell and Royal Dutch were a perfect match. Shell had a transportation and marketing network, and Royal Dutch possessed crude oil. What crude Royal Dutch didn't own was controlled by Deterding after he formed a combination of all Dutch East Indies crude-oil producers. But the two men were opposites. Deterding was all business, and the newly knighted Sir Marcus Samuel was a social climber looking forward to his election as lord mayor of London. Marcus proved his patriotism to England by turning down Standard Oil's unheard of buyout offer of $40 million and agreeing to a marketing joint venture with Royal Dutch in Asiatic Petroleum Company in 1902. The persistent Deterding finally won over Marcus Samuel in 1907 when they formed the Royal Dutch/Shell Group consisting of two separate entities, 60 percent Dutch and 40 percent British, that gave Deterding effective control. It continues today under its marketing name—Shell.

The Rothschilds traded their Russian crude-oil production and refinery for shares in Royal Dutch and Shell and became the largest shareholders in each in 1911. It was a smart move. Since 1901, Joseph Djugashvili, a former student for the priesthood, had been fomenting strikes and disrupting production at Batum refineries and Baku oil fields. Later, Djugashvili changed his name to Stalin. In the decade ending in 1914, Russia's oil exports dropped from 31 percent to 9 percent due to labor troubles and poor production practices.

WINSTON CHURCHILL BUYS AN OIL COMPANY

In 1901 William Knox D'Arcy, a mining millionaire, obtained an oil concession covering 500,000 square miles of Persia (five-sixths of what is now Iran) from Shah Muzzaffar al-Din for £20,000 and 16 percent of the annual net profits. D'Arcy never visited Persia. After several minor unprofitable discoveries and feeling the financial strain of the venture, he hired George Reynolds, a petroleum engineer. Reynolds drilled in the Maidan-i-Napti area, which every Persian knew meant "the Plain of Oil." The spot was Masjid-i-Suleiman, near an old fire temple that centuries earlier had spewed flaming gas. In 1908 Reynolds hit a gusher, and the following year, Anglo-Persian Oil Company was created as a public corporation. Anglo-Persian, known today as British Petroleum or BP, didn't have the finances or guts to compete against Standard Oil and elected to enter into a contract to sell crude oil, kerosine, and gasoline to Shell.

Winston Churchill became first lord of the admiralty in 1911 and immediately backed Adm. John A. Fisher's plans to convert the Royal Navy from coal to oil. Not only would oil push the speed four knots over a coal-burning battleship's twenty-one knots, it could save 80 percent in fuel and add 30 percent in cargo space. The fact that the navy planned to build fifty destroyers, seventy submarines, and five battleships that only burned oil was a hell of an incentive for a nation that had no oil to obtain a secure oil supply.

Churchill didn't trust Shell. Politically, Deterding was "too Dutch" and Marcus "too Jewish," as were the Rothschilds, who held tremendous influence over Shell. Many members of Parliament feared Shell would demand high prices and Anglo-Persian was financially weaker and a plum ripe for plucking. On June 17, 1914, Churchill proposed to the House of Commons that the government purchase 51 percent of Anglo-Persian for £2.2 million to guarantee the Royal Navy a supply of cheap fuel oil. Samuel Samuel, a member of the House of Commons, was no match for Churchill's eloquence and sarcasm during the debate. The bill passed 254 to 18. As a backup, wily Churchill personally negotiated with Deterding for fuel oil and a guarantee of Shell's tanker fleet in time of war.

On June 28, eleven days after Churchill proposed the Anglo-Persian purchase, Austrian Archduke Franz Ferdinand was assassinated in Sarajevo, igniting World War I. Britain declared war on Germany one month later, long before Anglo-Persian was prepared to supply the Royal Navy.

MR. FIVE PERCENT

Calouste Gulbenkian, an Armenian born in Turkey, was educated at King's College in London and received a degree in mining engineering in 1887 after completing his thesis in petroleum technology at the age of nineteen. His father, a wealthy oil merchant and banker, sent him to Baku to learn the petroleum business. Upon his return, he wrote articles and a book on Russian oil that turned him into a petroleum expert (at least on paper) at the age of twenty-one. Sultan Abdul Hamid retained him to investigate the Turkish Ottoman Empire's oil potential. Without setting foot in the Mideast, Gulbenkian wrote a report based on scant geology reports and interviews with visitors who had seen oil seeps. It must have been one hell of a report. The sultan offered him a concession covering the entire Ottoman Empire after transferring the potential oil lands to his personal account.

For several years, Gulbenkian dabbled in other deals, including oriental carpets that seems to be an Armenian monopoly, before taking over his aging father's oil and banking interests. This brought him into contact with Marcus Samuel and Henri Deterding. In 1907 he opened a Shell office in Constantinople and in 1912 organized the Turkish Petroleum Company (TPC) to develop the concession. The Turkish National Bank, of which Gulbenkian and British banks were major shareholders, held a 50-percent interest, and Shell and the Deutsche Bank each held 25 percent. Fearing foreign interference in the Mideast, the British bought the Turkish Bank's interests for Anglo-Persian. Gulbenkian's commission earned him the title "Mr. Five Percent."

British interests were protected by the British Foreign Office's insistence that the parties agree to a "self denying clause" prohibiting their direct or indirect involvement in petroleum throughout the Ottoman Empire except through the TPC. The day the Turkish grand vizier announced the formal transfer of Gulbenkian's dubious concession to the TPC, Archduke Ferdinand was assassinated.

THE SPOILS OF WAR

Two weeks after the November 1918 Armistice, Lord George Nathaniel Curzon, a member of Britain's War Cabinet and next foreign secretary, proclaimed, "The Allied cause had floated to victory upon a wave of oil." What teed off many Americans was that Lord Curzon failed to mention that more than three-quarters of the Allies' oil came from the United States. Mexico, through American and British companies, contributed twice as much oil as Anglo-Persian in Persia and Shell in the Dutch East Indies combined, one-third of which came from Edward Doheny's Mexican Petroleum Company. After Russia withdrew from the war, its contributions dried up.

Persian tribesmen, given gold and guns by German agents, blew up the pipeline to Anglo-Persian's refinery at Abadan and put a leak in Britain's secure source of supply. American oil was the Allies' savior during the war.

CHART 10:1 WORLD CRUDE-OIL PRODUCTION 1916-1918
(Millions of Barrels)

Nation	1916	1917	1918
United States	300.8	335.3	355.9
Russia	65.8	63.1	27.2
Mexico	40.5	55.3	63.8
Dutch East Indies	12.5	13.2	12.8
Persia	4.5	7.1	8.6
Other	33.4	28.9	35.2
World Total	457.5	502.9	503.6

Mineral Resources of the United States. Bureau of Mines. (1922), pgs. 388-389.

The United States didn't attend the 1920 League of Nations San Remo Conference to slice up Turkey's Ottoman Empire between Britain and France. The United States wasn't a member of the league, and President Wilson said Americans did not believe in colonial powers carving up land occupied by poor dark-skinned people. (Wilson failed to mention Puerto Rico, the Virgin Islands, Hawaii, and American Samoa.) With our State Department representatives not in attendance except at cocktail parties, it was a Standard Oil of New Jersey official who uncovered TPC documents showing that Britain was trying to hog all the Mideast oil.

Winston Churchill, the British colonial secretary after World War I, was busy drawing the boundaries of Iraq, Syria, Lebanon, Palestine, and, as an afterthought, Jordan.[38] It wasn't easy. Sir Mark Sykes, the muddling British negotiator, had divided the war spoils with France in 1915 in the Sykes-Picot Agreement. Similar to slicing a pie before baking it, Sykes forgot about the oil potential in Mesopotamia's Mosul region and gave it to France as part of its mandate over Syria. Foreign Minister Arthur J. Balfour added to Churchill's bargaining power by

---

[38] Legend is Jordan's southern boundary was drawn by Churchill with a squiggle for no apparent reason other than Churchill had partaken of a few brandies. The zigzag became known as "Winston's Hiccough."

maintaining 50,000 British troops in the Mideast.[39] As usual, the French whined and wouldn't fight, allowing Britain to grab the Mosul and add it to its new mandate called Iraq.

Dividing the spoils of war included the TPC, renamed the Iraq Petroleum Company (IPC). For reneging on the Sykes-Picot Agreement, Britain gave the German-owned Deutsche Bank's 25-percent interest to a newly created French oil company, Compagnie Française des Pétroles (CFP), in which the French government owned 25 percent. Britain's oil supremacy in the Mideast was secure. Anglo-Persian held 100 percent of the Persian concession and 50 percent of IPC covering the former Turkish Empire. Gulbenkian kept his 5-percent commission. Britain's puppet Iraqi king, Faisel, extended IPC's term to 2000 and decreed that IPC's chairman must be British.

BRITISH PETROLEUM—BP

At the outbreak of World War I, the British government acquired the German Deutsche Bank's petroleum-marketing facilities in Britain for Anglo-Persian that was curiously called *British Petroleum*. Anglo-Persian changed its name to Anglo-Iranian in 1935 after Shah Reza Pahlavi renamed the nation Iran, banned the use of the name Persia, and ordered all mail addressed to Persia be returned. After Anglo-Iranian was nationalized by Iran in 1951, its name was changed to British Petroleum, then shortened to *BP* so it could sell its gasoline to unsuspecting American motorists.

AMERICA'S OPEN DOOR POLICY

In 1919 Washington was alarmed by the Department of the Interior's prediction that America's oil production was reaching a peak and would soon decline. On the Senate floor, Senator James Phelan of California referred to England as the "great oil cormorant of the world."[40] He wanted to know why Britain hadn't paid its $4-billion wartime debt to the United States instead of investing its capital and

---

[39] Balfour is better known for the Balfour Declaration, his letter dated November 2, 1917, to Lord Edmond Rothschild that declared Britain's support for a Zionist home in Palestine. The Arabs claimed they were double-crossed. The British had promised the Arabs their own country if they rebelled and fought against the Turks.

[40] *Congressional Record*, 66th Cong., 1st Sess., 1919. 4163. Senator Phelan was a pal of Standard Oil of California and in favor of drilling in the Naval Petroleum Reserves in California.

maintaining troops in the Mideast to keep American oil companies out. The last straw was the "British octopus," Shell, was drilling for oil in Senator Phelan's home state of California. But what riled the entire Senate was Phelan's reading of a speech by Sir E. Mackay Edgar, an Anglo-Persian investor, on the Senate floor.

> " . . . America is reaching the end of some of her most valuable raw materials . . . Her magnates are . . . scouring the world for reserves . . . but wherever they turn they will find that British enterprise has been before them . . . Even if they do not lie within the British Empire, they are controlled by British capital. America one of these days—and not very distant days, either—will have to come to us for the oil. . . ." [41]

The following year, Congress passed the Mineral Leasing Act of 1920 to curtail the giveaway of oil, coal, and the so-called fertilizer minerals. The act included a provision denying federal mineral leases to foreign corporations whose countries denied Americans the reciprocal right to mine for minerals. Many felt the law did not go far enough. Bills were introduced to embargo British and Dutch oil, but cooler heads prevailed to avoid trade wars. In 1921 Interior Secretary Albert Fall reported to the Senate that Britain controlled all the Mideast oil fields and was preventing American exploration around the world—a good reason to drill in Teapot Dome and Alaska. A few months later, Harry Sinclair and two Standard Oil siblings were denied leases in the Dutch East Indies. When Secretary of State Charles Evans Hughes complained and the Netherlands in effect told him to "stuff it," Fall's Interior Department refused to issue Dutch-controlled Shell federal oil leases under the Mineral Leasing Act of 1920 until the Netherlands granted Americans leases. The Senate debates led to President Harding's demand for an "open door" policy to allow American oil companies access to British- and Dutch-controlled oil.

Britain, sensing a strong anti-British sentiment in Congress and America's behind the scenes inducing of several South American nations to ban granting oil concessions to Anglo-Persian and Shell, condescended to open the door, but only a crack. In 1922 the IPC invited American oil companies to join the party, if they would agree

[41] Ibid. 4785.

to the "self-denying" clause prohibiting development anywhere in the IPC concession area except through IPC. Secretary of State Hughes gave his okay, justifying it as a method of the Americans getting their foot in the door.

THE RED LINE AGREEMENT OR THE DOOR CLOSES AGAIN

Seven companies, Standard of New Jersey, Standard of Indiana, Standard of New York, Atlantic, Gulf, Texaco, and Sinclair, entered into negotiations that were to drag on for six years. Sinclair and Texaco quit after discovering they not only had to negotiate with the British and Dutch, but the snotty French and a stubborn Armenian. After a few years, the interests of Gulf, Atlantic, and Standard of Indiana waned and were assigned to Standard of New Jersey and Standard of New York.

The American lead fell to Walter C. Teagle, president of Standard of New Jersey, which was forced to buy five-sixths of its crude oil to keep its refineries operating. Standard of New York was also crude short. Teagle realized he wasn't going to walk away with anything but a token amount after October 15, 1927. IPC's first well north of Kirkuk in the Kurdish region blew in at 95,000 barrels of oil a day.[42] After six years of wrangling, Teagle settled for 23.75 percent for the Americans (11.875 percent each for Standard of New Jersey and Standard of New York), which left Shell, Anglo-Persian, and CFP each with 23.75 percent and Gulbenkian, who had refused to budge, with his 5 percent intact. The Armenian still complained. He didn't have the ability to refine and market the cheap oil and had to sell it to CFP.

There are several tales how the self-denying clause was explained to the Americans, but all agree that Gulbenkian took a thick red pencil and drew a line around the entire Middle East except for Persia and Kuwait. Anglo-Persian and Shell claimed it conformed to British Foreign Office maps of the Ottoman Empire in 1914. They lied. Bahrain had been a British protectorate since 1820, as were the Trucial States (now the United Arab Emirates) since 1873, and Ibn

---

[42] The *Bible* told Gulbenkian and the geologists where there was oil. It is where Nebuchadnezzar threw Shadrach, Meshach, and Abednego into the fiery furnace (escaping burning natural gas). Oil in the Kurdish region explains why the Kurds never received an independent nation promised under the Treaty of Sèvres in 1920. The British wanted the Mosul to be part of Iraq.

Saud had controlled the center of the Arabian Peninsula called Nejd since 1906. But the fib might keep American oil companies from poaching on their private Mideast bonanza of dubious legality. Gulbenkian's concession had been issued by a tyrannical and thieving Sultan Abdul Hamid, who had been deposed, and the Turkish Ottoman Empire no longer existed. To the victor belongs the spoils, and, as the United States never declared war on Turkey, it was not entitled to a slice of Turkey.

The Red Line Agreement was signed on July 31, 1928, closing the door to the Mideast again.

CALOUSTE GULBENKIAN

Mr. Five Percent made untold millions from Mideast oil. After the Red Line Agreement was signed, he took a Mediterranean cruise. One day he asked what a ship with its superstructure and smokestack in the rear was. He had never seen an oil tanker. He never visited the Mideast either.

Gulbenkian bought the famous Ritz Hotel in Paris where he lived for many years. He died at the age of eighty-five, attributing his longevity and sexual prowess to trading in his mistresses before they reached eighteen.

MAP 10:1
THE RED LINE AGREEMENT—1928

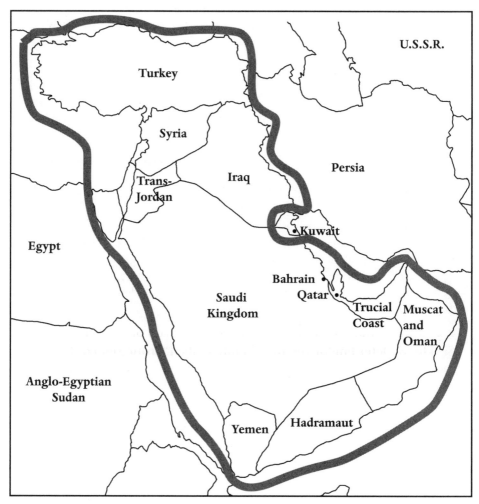

CHAPTER ELEVEN
Too Much Oil!

THE ACHNACARRY AGREEMENT

S cotland in the fall is breathtaking. Grouse hunting and fishing are at their height. Achnacarry Castle, the seventeenth-century home of the Camerons of Lochiel and chief of Clan Cameron, was an ideal place for sports-loving oilmen to enjoy the outdoors and chat about the Red Line Agreement they had created a few weeks earlier, if you are wondering what Scotland has to do with oil and scoundrels. Sir Henri Deterding of the Royal Dutch/Shell Group rented the castle and hosted the two-week stay. His principal guests were Sir John Cadman of Anglo-Persian and Walter ("the Boss") Teagle of Standard of New Jersey.

William L. Mellon, president of Gulf Oil, also dropped by. He didn't have a title, but his family had more money and political power than the other guests. His uncle and the big bucks behind Gulf, Andrew Mellon, was secretary of the treasury under presidents Harding, Coolidge, and Hoover. Uncle Andy had so much money, he had to build the National Gallery of Art to hold his art collection. Uncle also came in handy when he was American ambassador to Great Britain and Anglo-Persian and the British government tried to keep Gulf out of British-controlled Kuwait. (Anglo-Persian and Gulf split Kuwait fifty-fifty.)

During the afternoons they weren't fishing and hunting, they discussed oil and decided there was *too much*. Prices were dropping due to production in Venezuela, Mexico, Romania, Russia, and the United States. They followed Rockefeller's belief that a combination to maintain prices was more profitable than price wars. Shell and Standard of New York were engaged in a fierce price war Deterding started after Standard of New York bought cheap oil from Russia that Deterding claimed belonged to Shell. Also on the agenda was putting up a united front against Russia to regain the oil fields Shell and Standard of New Jersey had purchased from the Rothschilds and Nobels that the Communists had confiscated.

Iraq crude-oil production was a minor problem. They merely had to purchase a nominal amount to keep the ignorant Iraqis happy. By cooperating, they could keep crude-oil prices low and maintain their profits from refining and marketing. To hell with their partner, CFP, that had no other source of crude oil, and Gulbenkian, whose income was from crude-oil production.

The Europeans thought the United States antitrust laws were a nuisance and were pleased the Webb-Pomerane Act of 1918 exempted combinations exporting from the United States from antitrust law restrictions. Anglo-Persian wasn't concerned about the British laws prohibiting conspiracies and combinations in restraint of trade. Its majority shareholder was the government and Winston Churchill, currently chancellor of the exchequer (the British elegant title equivalent to the American secretary of the treasury), had approved a fifty-fifty split of the African market between Shell and Anglo-Persian. As the government now owned 56 percent of Anglo-Persian, Churchill was in favor of greater profits for the exchequer and recommended that Cadman and Deterding have a chat with Standard Oil about similar alliances.[43]

Deterding, Cadman, and Teagle are credited (blamed) for drawing up and having the sense not to sign the seventeen-page "Pool Association" dated September 17, 1928, that would become known as the "Achnacarry" or "As Is" Agreement. "As is" meant eliminating price competition by setting quotas for the members' respective worldwide market shares as they were in 1928. The market share would remain "as is." Members producing in excess of their quotas were required to offer the surplus to another member. They also

---

[43] The author proffers that Winston Churchill was not a scoundrel. Americans would have elected him president if his father rather than mother, Jennie Jerome, had been an American. (I'm biased, as evidenced by naming my last two dogs Winston and Maggie (as in Thatcher), both great names for English bulldogs.)

agreed to assist one another by allowing the use of each other's facilities on a favorable basis and to draw and exchange crude oil or refined products from the nearest source to its destination, regardless who owned it, and split the savings on the transportation costs.

As market quotas and price fixing violated United States antitrust laws, they would be avoided by a slick maneuver. World crude-oil prices would be based on the price of oil on the Texas Gulf Coast plus transportation costs to the markets regardless of where the oil was produced. The *Gulf plus* price system added substantial margins. United States crude-oil production costs were the highest in the world. To add to the profits, the tanker distance between the Texas Gulf Coast and Europe was greater than the distance from the Mideast or Russia to Europe. Coupled with their agreement to exchange crude oil and petroleum products for delivery to the nearest market, the Gulf-plus price added to their hidden profits they would secretly split. In oil industry jargon, the difference in tanker costs was termed a "transportation differential." Behind closed doors it was called "phantom freight."

As the Achnacarry meeting's purpose was secret, the only comment about the two weeks in the Scottish Highlands reported to the press came from Walter Teagle, "The hunting was lousy."

Henri Wilhelm August Deterding

In 1936 Deterding was forced to retire from Shell because of his outspoken Nazi sympathies. He divorced his second wife (a Russian), married his German secretary, and moved to Germany where he became a bosom buddy of Hitler. He died in Germany in 1939.

For the Achnacarry Agreement to be successful, the hunters and fishermen had to persuade other major producers to join the club. Seventeen American companies joined the conspiracy that included not selling crude oil or refined products to outsiders. Russia joined the cartel in 1929. The Communists understood planned economies and dealing from a position of strength. They kept the Western oil companies out of Russia and negotiated a guaranteed share of the European market, including in Britain. As 25-percent owner of CFP, the French government went along with the agreement. France set import quotas to allow its fledgling CFP to compete in the French market and kept the "Anglos" out of its oil-producing colonies.

The biggest problem facing the Achnacarry plotters was cheating and the growing number of American independent oil companies. They fell short of ever controlling 50 percent of the American exports. There were also difficulties in interpreting the general terms of their seventeen-page agreement. No one could agree on the division of the markets, which required another meeting in January 1930 to devise a Memorandum for European Markets. In December 1932, the "Big Boys" met again to formulate a second amendment with the unwieldy title "Heads Agreement for Distribution" that included how to handle virgin markets, cheaters, and new entrants. Cheaters and expansion were partially solved by permitting the members to purchase other companies after "frank discussions" with affected members and the preparation of a list of refiners to whom they would sell crude oil. (A retired John D. Rockefeller Sr., then ninety-three, would have chuckled at their plan.)

Another insidious document was the "Draft Memorandum of Principles" of January 1, 1934. To eliminate cutthroat competition and increase their gasoline margins, the scoundrels agreed to cut advertising costs and claims of product superiority. Today that would mean that Exxon couldn't claim it was putting a tiger in your tank. For those who lived during the era, the plan was un-American. They not only agreed to curtail newspaper ads, billboards and signs, but stop giving away free dishes, cigarette lighters, and other handouts. (The author's father never went on a trip without a free ESSO [now Exxon] road map; and his mother collected Shell glasses my father got free with a fill-up.)

When the Federal Trade Commission subpoenaed oil company documents in 1948, Standard of New Jersey claimed that it had *verbally* terminated the marketing agreements and that they "never amounted to anything"; and "Any activities that may have survived came to an end in September 1939, as a result of the outbreak of the war. They were never resumed." They lied. In 1944, a war year when Britain was fighting to exist, Britain's auditor-general protested phantom freight charges from the Mideast. The Gulf-plus pricing system, market quotas, exchanges, and phantom freight existed for decades, and vestiges are still practiced outside the United States.[44] What had been a formal structure became institutionalized and an accepted way of doing business, and in some cases condoned by governments.

AMERICA'S ROARING AND CONFUSING 1920S

At the beginning of the decade, Americans were told that the United States was running out of oil. The farsighted president of Cities Service Company (now Citgo[45]), Harry L. Doherty, was an oxymoron—a conservationist-oilman. In glasses that looked like the bottoms of Coca-Cola bottles and a neatly trimmed Vandyke beard, he appeared more like a stereotypic college professor than one of Big Oil's hard-nosed business moguls. He entered the oil business when one of his Midwestern gas and electric utilities drilled for natural gas and hit an oil field.

Doherty believed oil fields should be unitized and the production controlled in order to conserve the gas and water pressure that raised the oil to the surface. He originally called his concept "rationalization." Wasn't it rational that the nation not waste the precious resource and leave three-quarters of the oil in the ground under the archaic Rule of Capture? Unitization simply required the oil companies to cooperate in the development and production of a common pool of oil in order to obtain the maximum efficient rate of production through the elimination of unnecessary drilling and uncontrolled production.

His insistence that the federal government enforce a unitization law, if not done voluntarily, drew the ire of every red-blooded oilman, large and small. Doherty's pleas were ridiculed by Big Oil's lobbying arm, the American Petroleum Institute (API), and William Farish, president of Humble Oil Company, a Standard of New Jersey subsidiary and the largest crude-oil producer in Texas. Although an API

---

[44] In the 1990s, I negotiated oil supply agreements on behalf of a client in the Pacific. After a long day of haggling on one of the beautiful islands, we adjourned to the pool bar for a well-deserved libation. When the representatives of X and Y oil companies (mentioned earlier in the chapter) began to discuss quotas and fixing prices in several island nations, I gulped my vodka and tonic and left after mentioning American oil company lawyers shouldn't be within earshot.

[45] Although a visionary, Doherty never could have imagined his company, Citgo, would be owned by Petroleos de Venezuela SA, the Venezuelan national oil company, controlled by Venezuelan President Hugo Chavez, a left-wing, anti-American nut.

141

director, Doherty was refused permission to address its annual meetings in 1924, and he had to hire a hall across the street to give his rationalization sermon.

Doherty took his case to President Calvin Coolidge in August 1924. Coolidge was leery about anything connected with oil. The Republicans were reeling from the Teapot Dome scandal, and 1924 was an election year. But Silent Cal, never one to waste anything, moved quickly after the election. In December, he created the Federal Oil Conservation Board (FOCB), composed of the secretaries of war, navy, interior, and commerce, to investigate ways for the nation to conserve oil.

With unitization under attack, the politically attuned FOCB recommended oil company cooperation to conserve oil, but fell short of proposing compulsory unitization. In 1926 Charles Evans Hughes, former secretary of state and Supreme Court justice and later appointed chief justice by President Herbert Hoover, vigorously attacked unitization as counsel for the API. Hughes contended that mineral extraction did not involve commerce between the states, thus was outside the jurisdiction of the federal government under the Constitution's commerce clause, and agreements to curtail oil production were exempted under the antitrust laws. (Years later, the Supremes ruled differently.)

CHART 11:1 SHOULD ANYONE BELIEVE THE INTERIOR DEPARTMENT'S DIRE PREDICTIONS?

Year	U.S. Production Million bbl/day	Prediction
1885	0.01>	Little or no chance of oil in California.
1891	0.01	Little or no chance of oil in Kansas and Texas.
1909	0.50	U.S. oil will be exhausted by 1935.
1914	0.72	U.S. oil will be exhausted by 1936.
1920	1.21	Peak production reached. U.S. needs foreign oil.
1922	1.53	U.S. oil will be exhausted by 1942.
1939	3.47	U.S. oil will be exhausted by 1952.
1949	5.07	U.S. must now import oil.
1951	6.16	U.S. oil will be exhausted by 1964.

In retrospect, Interior's predictions are comical. Bureaucrats thrive on apocalyptic forecasts that make their jobs more important, and politicians slant the statistics to serve their political bias. The United States became a net importer of crude oil in 1948 and reached its peak production of 11.3 million barrels a day in 1970. Crude-oil production has steadily declined since, and the politicians have cried wolf too often. In 2002 United States production was 5.85 million barrels a day, and it currently must import 58 percent of its petroleum needs. (*See Endnotes for sources.*)

In 1926 Hughes also argued on behalf of the API before the FOCB that the petroleum industry, guided by the API, is best equipped to police its own problems without governmental interference. Today we still hear the same fallacious argument that industries should police themselves—even after the Enron debacle and fraud. It is the equivalent of letting the inmates run the jail.

Oil shortages were forgotten by 1928 with the elephant oil discoveries in Oklahoma and Texas. Oklahoma's Greater Seminole field alone was producing more than 500,000 barrels a day. Sir John Cadman of Anglo-Persian addressed the 1928 API meeting on "economic cooperation," and in 1929 Sir Henri Deterding endorsed the "Export Petroleum Corporation" to limit American exports. The API proposed a "Marketing Ethics Code" and formed a committee to survey worldwide production and consumption that recommended the United States limit its production to its 1928 output, *not coincidentally identical* to the quotas in the "As Is" Agreement.

The FOCB approved the API proposal like an obedient puppy, but was reined in by Attorney General William D. Mitchell's ruling that the FOCB did not have the power and it was contrary to the antitrust laws. In 1929 FOCB chairman, Secretary of the Interior Ray Lyman Wilber, proposed an interstate compact for the states to allocate production and govern conservation. By this time the public and Congress were aware of the worldwide oil surplus. The nation was also sliding into the Great Depression. The politicians and public forgot about the issue, similar to today's forgetfulness after a so-called "energy crisis" passes—when gasoline prices drop at the pump and the gas-guzzling SUV drivers stop complaining.

CHAPTER TWELVE
THE SEVEN SISTERS

ABU AL-NAFT
I'm the Sheik of Araby
Your Love belongs to me
At night when you're asleep
Into your tent I'll creep

Abu al-Naft—the "Father of Oil"—was Frank Holmes, a rough-hewn mining engineer from New Zealand. In 1923, after hearing tales of oil seeps in the tiny archipelago of Bahrain off the coast of Saudi Arabia, he visited Sheik al-Khalifha, whose family had run the 240-mile square sheikdom since 1783. The sheik wasn't interested in oil, it messed up his carpets. If Holmes wanted to do something worthwhile, he should drill for water. In order to get on the good side of the sheik, Holmes drilled and found water. The sheik was so pleased, he gave Holmes an oil concession. Before they finished celebrating, the British reminded the sheik that Bahrain had been a British protectorate since 1820, and, if he read the fine print, he wasn't supposed to make deals with foreigners unless they were British.

Holmes asked Anglo-Persian if they were interested, but they scoffed at the idea there was oil in Bahrain. He tried to sell the concession to Walter Teagle of Standard Oil of New Jersey for $50,000. Teagle, turned down the bargain. Bahrain was within the Red Line Agreement he was negotiating to gain a share of Mideast oil. Teagle later called his failure to grab the deal a "billion dollar error." Gulf Oil purchased the concession for the trifling amount to supplement the expensive crude it was purchasing from the IPC, but turned chicken after reading the Achnacarry Agreement it had signed that banned it from operating inside the Red Line. Gulf sold the concession to Standard Oil of California ("Socal" before it became Chevron), up to then too far away from the Mideast to be a factor in the European market and not a member of the Achnacarry conspiracy.

The British Foreign Office advised Socal that it wasn't British, which Socal knew because it was from California. Then the Foreign Office pulled out the British treaty with Bahrain and pointed to the clause requiring all companies operating in the protectorate to be British. However, as the Americans were screaming for an open-door policy and Bahrain was only 240 square miles, they tossed Socal a small bone. To save face, the Foreign Office insisted Socal must conduct its Bahrain business under a British subsidiary. Socal selected Canada, still British enough to have a picture of King George V on its money. By the way, the Foreign Office added, as the ignorant sheik requires British protection, all contracts and correspondence must be funneled through the British representative in Bahrain.

Socal struck oil in Bahrain in May 1932 after breaking through the British red tape and Gulbenkian's Red Line Agreement that actually wasn't applicable. Bahrain had been a British protectorate since 1820, long before Gulbenkian's concession was granted in 1904 and approved in 1914. Bahrain is too small to become a major oil producer or even join OPEC. But as any Bedouin will tell you: *Never let the nose of a camel to slip under the tent flap—his big ass is sure to follow.*

Holmes had also sold Gulf Oil the Kuwait concession outside of the Red Line Agreement. Anglo-Persian pulled the old British-nationality-in-the protectorate-treaty routine to keep the American oil company out. They also claimed there was no oil in Kuwait and had several dry holes to prove it. But Sheik Ahmad al-Sabah, of the Sabahs who have ruled Kuwait since 1756 and still do thanks to American smart bombs dropped on Iraq in 1991, was adamant someone drill for oil. Japanese cultured pearls had ruined Kuwait's natural pearl industry, and his neighbors in Bahrain were being paid oil royalties. After the ambassador to Britain and a Gulf major shareholder, Andrew Mellon, stepped in, Anglo-Persian saw the writing in the sand. Although Kuwait was tiny (about the size of Hawaii's land mass), this time Anglo-Persian wouldn't permit the Americans to run off with a single gem from the crown jewels. Anglo-Persian and Gulf split the concession fifty-fifty.

In May 1938, Gulf and Anglo-Persian struck the first of dozens of gushers that would make conservative Gulf Oil think it was one of the big international oil companies. Frank Holmes earned the title Abu al-Naft and was awarded a piece of the action for his services as Sheik al-Sabah's representative for the rest of his life.

Abu al-Naft also had an ambiguous entree into what would be the jewel of all oil concessions—Saudi Arabia. There his success is either credited or blamed on Harry St. John Philby. Philby was an adviser to Abdul Aziz bin Abdul Rahman bin Faisal al Saud (Ibn Saud), the ruler of a kingdom in the middle of the desert that would soon be called Saudi Arabia. The curmudgeon had been the British resident commissioner in Transjordan during the carve up of the Mideast and was labeled an "Arabist," a British Foreign Office term that translates: "The bugger not only bothered to learn fluent Arabic, he claims we are screwing the Arabs." Philby's resignation from the British Indian Civil Service was a good career move. He became a trader in Jidda and renewed his friendship with Ibn Saud. As Ibn Saud's friend and adviser, he received exclusive concessions that might be worth a fortune, including the Ford dealership, if the country ever built roads, and the wireless franchise, if the conservative Wahhabis could be convinced that the radio wasn't the handiwork of the devil.

After Philby's conversion to Islam, he took the name given him by Ibn Saud, Abdullah, "Slave of Allah." Most Saudis thought his name should be Abdulqirsh, "Slave of Sixpence," which explains why Philby asked the IPC to compete against Frank Holmes's recommendation that Socal be issued an oil concession. Philby became a secret well-paid adviser to Socal during the negotiations while remaining a sometimes paid adviser to Ibn Saud. Anglo-Persian, representing IPC, never had a chance. They came to the bargaining table with £10,000 in British sterling ($50,000 in 1933 and $600,000 in 2002). Philby told Socal that Ibn Saud was hard up for cash, preferred gold, and thought India's paper rupees with a picture of English King George V was insulting. Socal offered gold, £35,000 up front, another £20,000 in eighteen months, and £100,000, if it found oil. The offer actually consisted of loans and advances on royalties, but Philby didn't mention to Socal that there wasn't a snowball's chance in the desert of getting any money back if they didn't find oil.

Ibn Saud didn't trust the British. During the British drawing of Mideast boundaries, Ibn Saud had lost land to Jordan, Iraq, and Kuwait. Ibn Saud believed boundaries were made by conquests, not Englishmen in short pants with a red pencil. He didn't know what a mile was and had asked the British, "How long does it take a camel to walk a mile?" Not only that, the British had sent a woman, Gertrude Bell, to the boundary negotiations. Ibn Saud was also slighted when the Arabs couldn't agree on boundaries in the empty deserts and the British pulled out their red pencil and drew "Neutral Zones" between his land and Iraq and Kuwait.

In March 1938, Socal discovered oil that would develop into a concession containing more than one-fourth of the world's oil reserves. Socal's gushers were put on hold in October 1940 until the end of World War II. The Italian Air Force, flying from Ethiopia to bomb the British protectorate of Bahrain's oil field, mistakenly bombed the Dhahran oil field in neutral Saudi Arabia. Unable to defend the entire Persian Gulf, the British plugged the oil wells in Kuwait. And unable to rely on Italian aerial navigation, the Americans shut in most of the Saudi crude-oil production before the United States entered the war except for shipments to Bahrain to aid Britain's war effort and pay Ibn Saud a small allowance.

HARRY ST. JOHN PHILBY

Philby died wealthy after surviving a late-in-life primitive circumcision when he converted to Islam. It did not stop him from having a child at the age of sixty-five by a slave girl Ibn Saud gave him. In 1940 Ibn Saud tipped the British off that Philby was going on an anti-British tour of America. The British tossed Philby in jail. Ibn Saud did not like the British, but he believed that advisers shouldn't shoot their mouths off in public.

After Ibn Saud died, his son, King Saud, publicly spit on Philby and expelled him from Saudi Arabia for accusing his regime of corruption.

Philby's enmity toward his native England was passed on to his infamous son, Kim, a high-level British intelligence officer who defected to Russia. Kim's treachery makes the CIA's and FBI's recent moles look like amateurs. As MI6 liaison to the United States, he also spied on America. Kim Philby was known to be pro-communist while a student at Cambridge.

Dividing the Mideast

The IPC, led by Anglo-Persian, gobbled up the rest of the Mideast, including tiny Qatar, smaller than Connecticut, and the Trucial States, a federation of seven emirates about the size of Maine now named the United Arab Emirates (UAE) that ranks third in world oil reserves. Americans know little about the UAE. They don't burn American flags, and nothing important happens there. Another possible explanation is American teachers can't pronounce the names of the seven emirates and are afraid former Abu Dhabi Sheik Shakhbut's name will upset classroom decorum.

Socal expanded its concession to include the entire nation of Saudi Arabia (more than three times the size of Texas) to keep out the British and Germans. With more crude oil than it knew what to do with and having no international markets, it invited Texaco, another Red Line Agreement outsider, to share its Saudi Arabian and Bahrain concessions. They combined their production and markets east of Suez behind their "Blue Line" to form Caltex and compete against the other major companies.

By 1947, Socal and Texaco were under pressure by Ibn Saud to produce more oil, but neither had sufficient access to the European markets. They decided to build a pipeline to the Mediterranean and ship Saudi oil to Europe that cost less than 10¢ a barrel to produce and invited Standard of New Jersey and Standard of New York to share in the bonanza. Both jumped at the offer, but the bugaboo of the Red Line Agreement reared its ugly head. Shell and Anglo-Iranian agreed to work out a deal, but Gulbenkian and the French pip-squeak, CFP, cried foul and went to court when the Americans claimed the Red Line Agreement was illegal. Ibn Saud brought them back to the bargaining table by refusing to permit any oil companies in Saudi Arabia unless they were American. Standards of New Jersey and New York agreed to purchase 40 percent of the concession for $347 million ($2.6 billion in 2002), then the largest financial deal in history, but puny by today's megabuck mergers. At the last minute, Standard of New York wilted and only purchased 10 percent, leaving Standard of New Jersey, Socal, and Texaco each with 30 percent of the world's biggest crude-oil conglomerate—the Arabian-American Oil Company (ARAMCO).

ARAMCO ended British oil dominance in the Mideast. It was now time for cooperation. In 1948 the Federal Trade Commission issued a report entitled "The International Petroleum Cartel" that read like an indictment of the oil companies for fixing prices. Its release was delayed until 1952 because the State Department, Defense Department, and Central Intelligence Agency claimed their oil was needed for national security. President Harry Truman had it "sanitized" before its release and ordered the Department of Justice to drop the criminal charges and file an antitrust civil action one week before President Dwight D. Eisenhower's inaugural.

The Achnacarry Agreement members no longer needed the independent oil companies. The eight oil companies holding Mideast oil concessions controlled more than 90 percent of the world's oil exports, and the United States was a net importer of oil. Their agreement to set quotas for each Mideastern oil-producing nation was effective control over the balance of the world's oil supply at the prices they set.

Enrico Mattei, director of Italy's state-owned oil company, Azienda Generali Italiana Petroli, frustrated with dealing with the Mideast oil cartel and their high prices, contemptuously called them "Sette Sorrelle," the Seven Sisters. Mattei didn't mention CFP, the weak French stepsister that greedily sopped up her sisters' crumbs. He was drumming up support against the Anglo-American cartel's control over European oil prices. The name "the Seven Sisters" stuck. Today we know them by their trade names:

> Standard of New Jersey (**Exxon**) and Standard of New York (**Mobil**) are combined as Exxon-Mobil; Standard of California (**Chevron**) took over **Gulf** after Kuwait nationalized its principle crude source and later merged with **Texaco**; Anglo-Iranian is now **British Petroleum** or BP (BP-Amoco); and **Shell**.

THE SEEDS OF IRAN'S DISTRUST OF WESTERNERS?

The power of the Seven Sisters is best illustrated after Iran nationalized Anglo-Iranian's concession in 1950 for what the Iranian nationalists believed were serious breaches of the concession agreement. (Anglo-Iranian was shortchanging Iran on royalties.) And, as an Iranian told the author, "their snotty England-knows-best attitude." The nationalists, led by Prime Minister Muhammad Mossadegh, had taken over the reins of power and left Shah Muhammad Pahlavi an impotent figurehead. The British filed a complaint with the International Court of Justice at the Hague (World Court), claiming it was contrary to international law. It was a stall, every law student knew Iran was within its rights as long as it paid due compensation. The claim took a lot of chutzpah. Prime Minister Clement Attlee and the British Labor Party were busy nationalizing British industries.

Anglo-Iranian, with the backing of the British government, which owned 56 percent of its stock, threatened nations and companies alike that they would be cut off if they purchased *their* Iranian oil. The American Sisters persuaded President Truman that nationalization would spread through the Mideast if America didn't support Britain. Without oil exports, Iran's production plunged from 665,000 barrels a day in 1950 to 28,000 in 1952, and Iran's economy collapsed. But there was never an oil shortage, although oil prices rose. The Seven Sisters, with a surplus within their cartel, merely opened the oil spigots in Saudi Arabia, Kuwait, Iraq, and Venezuela.

In a coup engineered by Britain's MI6 and America's CIA that reminded President Eisenhower of "something out of a dime novel," Mossadegh was ousted, and the shah was restored to power. But that didn't mean Anglo-Iranian had won. The shah could not lose face. Assistant Secretary of State George McGhee, a former independent oilman, was aware Anglo-Iranian had been unreasonable in its dealings with Iran. Even the American Sisters admitted Iran was unfairly treated. After protracted negotiations, Anglo-Iranian's interest was reduced to 40 percent. Anglo-Iranian was so piqued, it changed its name to British Petroleum. The rest of the concession was split among the Seven Sisters: Shell 14 percent and Exxon, Chevron, Texaco, Gulf, and Mobil 8 percent each, leaving their ugly stepsister, CFP, with 6 percent.

When the Department of Justice heard that the Seven Sisters—the companies it accused in their antitrust suit based on the FTC's "The International Petroleum Cartel" report—were dividing the spoils, it recommended 36 percent be given to American independents. The State Department, at the request of the oil companies, asked the accounting firm of Price Waterhouse to "certify" reliable applicants because Price Waterhouse did the accounting for most of the American Sisters. The Justice Department's objection to an accounting firm that was in bed with the oil companies was ignored. (Shades of Anderson-Enron debacle?)

The American Sisters' generosity was underwhelming. Each surrendered 1 percent and held onto 7 percent, leaving the eighteen Price Waterhouse "qualified" independents labeled "Iricon" to divide 5 percent.[46] Throughout the negotiations the American Sisters bluffed that they would pull out. They already had more oil than they could market. They argued, if they gave away 36 percent, they couldn't control the high-flying independents. Hell, look what the independents did in the Saudi-Kuwaiti Neutral Zone in 1948 that led to the Iranian nationalization. During Senate hearings on multinational oil companies, a Standard Oil of New Jersey vice president admitted including the independents was "window dressing."

CHART 12:1 SEVEN SISTERS MIDEAST OIL CONCESSIONS — 1950

Country	Concession	Ownership	Percent
Iran	BP	British Gov't	56
		Burma Oil	22
		Private shares	22
Iraq	IPC	BP	23¾
		Shell	23¾
		CFP	23¾
		Exxon	11⅞
		Mobil	11⅞
		Gulbenkian	5
Saudi Arabia	Aramco	Chevron	30
		Texaco	30
		Exxon	30
		Mobil	10
Kuwait	KOC	BP	50
		Gulf	50
Bahrain	BPC	Chevron	50
		Texaco	50
U.A.E		Same as Iraq	
Qatar		Same as Iraq	

Iran Concession in 1953

		BP	40
		Shell	14
		Exxon	7
		Mobil	7
		Chevron	7
		Gulf	7
		Texaco	7
		CFP	6
		Iricon	5

---

[46] The division to the American independents was: Richfield 25 percent, Atlantic, Signal, Hancock, San Jacinto, Getty, Tidewater (controlled by Getty), and Standard of Ohio 8.33 percent each, and *ten individual independents* 16.67 percent. To save you time looking for your calculator or figuring out where the decimal point goes, each of the ten unmentioned independents was entitled to a 0.0833-percent share of the Iranian oil.

The Justice Department didn't fare well in the civil case against the Seven Sisters and stepsister, either. BP, Shell, and CFP said, "We're outside United States jurisdiction." Exxon, Chevron, Mobil, Texaco, and Gulf signed consent decrees neither admitting nor denying the charges and promising never to do whatever they were accused of again.

THE NEUTRAL ZONE & THE INDEPENDENTS

In 1948 Saudi Arabia and Kuwait decided to grant oil concessions in the Neutral Zone carved out of the barren desert by the British in 1922 when they could not agree on the borders. The concession was unique. Each nation would accept bids for its one-half interest, but the oil companies were required to develop the concession as a single entity. The State Department, fearing it might be criticized for favoring the American Sisters, recommended only American independent oil companies be permitted to bid and rationalized that the area was only 2,000 square miles.

The Alice in Wonderland State Department didn't know that American independent oilmen were like Mad Hatters craving to drill anywhere, anytime, at any cost. Kuwait awarded its half-interest to a consortium of Phillips, Sinclair, and Ashland called Aminoil, short for American Independent Oil Company, for a $7.5-million bonus, 15 percent of the profits, a royalty of 35¢ a barrel with a minimum guarantee of $625,000 per year, and a million-dollar yacht for Emir Ahmad al-Sabah.

But that was nothing. J. Paul Getty's Getty Oil paid Saudi Arabia $9.5 million up front, a 55¢-a-barrel royalty with a minimum guarantee of $1 million a year plus a commitment to furnish the Saudi Army with gasoline.

The Seven Sisters went bonkers. The crazy independents paid too much and screwed up their royalty payments. Aramco's royalty to Saudi Arabia amounted to only 33¢ a barrel, IPC and Anglo-Persian (BP) were paying roughly 16½¢ to Iraq and Iran, and Gulf and Anglo-Persian were paying a mere 15¢ to Kuwait. When the gushers came in, it made J. Paul Getty America's richest man. If the Neutral Zone, the size of Delaware, was a nation, it would rank nineteenth in world oil reserves.

AMERICA'S FIRST BILLIONAIRE

Contrary to conventional wisdom, John D. Rockefeller was probably not America's first billionaire. Rockefeller's fortune reached only around $900 million, as he had given away a good part of his wealth before he died. J. Paul Getty was named America's first billionaire by *Fortune* and *Forbes* in 1957. He also held the distinction of being the stingiest billionaire in the world after he installed a pay phone in his English manor house for his guests. Getty's parsimony was legendary.

Getty was a spoiled brat born of a hard-working oilman father. In his early years, he did little except flit around Europe chasing women and obtaining a dubious Oxford diploma. World War I forced his return to America to search for oil in Oklahoma for his father's company with the promise of 30 percent of any profits. It was a good deal. Daddy was putting up the money, and, if he kept a low profile, he wouldn't be drafted during the war. In his autobiography, Getty claimed he volunteered, but the military never called the splendid physical specimen.

He took over his father's oil company at the age of thirty-eight after the old man's death. Daddy left an estate valued at $10 million to his wife in trust and only $500,000 to his son, from which he deducted $250,000 for one-third in the company J. Paul had not paid under their agreement. This left his mother with the controlling two-thirds of the company she would literally hold after her death and her son's death through the Sara Getty Trust. Mother and father made it clear they didn't approve of their son's lifestyle.

Getty's first three marriages at the ages of thirty-one, thirty-four, and thirty-six were to *teenage* girls, and he didn't wait until the divorce decrees were final before taking his next marital vows. He had sons by the first and the third wife, but none by the second, possibly because he preferred diddling her sister before, during, and long after a marriage that lasted less than two years. He married his fourth wife when he was thirty-eight and she was twenty-two, although he had dated her when he was thirty and she was fourteen. Wife number four had to wait until the divorce from number three was final. By that time, she had given birth to J. Paul Getty Jr. She also presented him with his fourth son.

Getty was forty-seven when he had his first of many face-lifts and married twenty-four-year-old wife number five. The playboy wasn't one to come home every night to be with his wife and children in the modest homes he provided. He was too busy bedding other women in his private apartments (plural) or yacht or in hotels as he traveled around the world. After his divorce from wife number five, Getty stuck to women enamored with his money.

Like many wealthy snobs, Getty was drawn to power, titles, and people who fawned over him. During the 1930s, he became too friendly with Hitler's friends, which resulted in his being unable to pass FBI security investigations and a period when the State Department revoked his U.S. passport. Getty fell in with the wealthy artsy crowd impressed with his art collection. Several critics said that Getty was into collecting more for the thrill of picking up a bargain and flaunting his purchases than art. One of his most infamous bargains was furniture from the Austrian Rothschilds' palace that had been looted by the Nazis in 1938.

Getty's sexual peccadilloes and craving for social status did not deter him from being an astute and highly successful oilman. He wrested control of the Tidewater Oil Company from Standard Oil of New Jersey and was proud that a share of Getty Oil stock was worth more barrels of oil-per-share value than Exxon's stock, which he called the true measure of an oil company. After his early days working for his father, he preferred to buy companies for their oil in the ground rather than risk drilling for it. He ran Getty Oil during his last twenty-five years without setting foot in its corporate headquarters while he lived in England to avoid U.S. income taxes. He purchased Sutton Place, a fourteen-bedroom manor outside of London, as a Getty Oil Company subsidiary, thereby avoiding exorbitant British Inland Revenue income taxes. Until his death at the age of eighty-four, Getty Oil officials had to fly to England or rely on the phone to discuss business with their CEO.

England was also a good place to avoid his four living sons, three of whom worked for Getty Oil for a brief time in their youth. His eldest son, George, worked for Getty until he committed suicide at the age of forty-nine, many say because he felt unable to meet his demanding father's expectations. His other sons lived on their Sara Getty Trust inheritance in their worlds of money, celebrities, booze, and drugs. No one can imagine what staid and proper Getty said when his son, J. Paul Getty Jr., told him that his grandson's name was Tara Gabriel Galaxy Gramophone Getty or when the boy's mother died of an overdose of heroin.

Getty changed his will twenty-one times during his last eighteen years, rewarding his few so-called friends, mainly obsequious women, and cutting out his children. Most of his estate was bequeathed to the J. Paul Getty Museum in Malibu, California, the richest art museum in the world, which Getty never saw.

J. PAUL GETTY QUOTES

"I just fleeced my mother."

"If you can count your money, you don't have a billion dollars."

"My wives married me; I didn't marry them."

"When I'm thinking about oil, I'm not thinking about girls."

"Heard Hitler's speech and thought it worthy of consideration." (Diary notation.)

"The Arabs have been gulled, bilked—in a word. suckered. Arabs know that the Western powers arbitrarily established unrealistically low prices for Arab oil and kept them there for decades."

PART V
THE BLACK GIANT

"Every woman has a special place on her neck and, when I kiss it, they start writing me a check. I may be the only man on earth who knows how to locate the spot."

> —Columbus Marion "Dad" Joiner (He admitted the checks weren't always good.)

"The trouble with this country is that you can't win an election without the oil sector, and can't govern with it."

> —Franklin Delano Roosevelt (1934)

CHAPTER THIRTEEN
An Ocean of Oil

Hard Times

The summer of 1927 cursed East Texans with a fourth year of drought that weathered their crops of corn, sweet potatoes, and cotton. The descendants of Scotch-Irish and Germans had no choice but to scratch the soil with their mules in the broiling sun. They knew what poor dirt and dirt poor meant. The Great Depression came early to Rusk County's inhabitants to test their God-fearing fundamentalism. Their only faint glimmer of hope was sixty-seven-year-old Columbus Marion Joiner finding his promised "ocean of oil," but no one had seen him in months.

Columbus was in Dallas raising money to drill a wildcat well. Unlike Hollywood's stereotype Texas oilmen in Stetsons and boots, he wore a white shirt, tie, wingtip shoes, and often sported a straw bowler. Born on a farm in Alabama in 1860, he never knew his Confederate soldier father killed in 1864. He left school at eight after his mother died, and it was left to his sister to teach him to read from the only book found in backwoods homes—the *Bible*. He ventured to Tennessee as a young man, where he read the law and was elected to the state legislature. Unable to make a go of it as a lawyer and defeated for reelection, he moved to oil-rich Oklahoma to buy and sell oil leases. Some say he made and lost a fortune, others that he barely eked out a living before being drawn to Dallas.

The old man's stature had been whittled down by rheumatic fever as a child that left him bent over from the waist, but the malady never affected his vigor. Head down, he scurried with his hands flailing behind him as if he was swishing flies off his backside. His boyish charm and baby-smooth complexion, the latter he attributed to daily doses of carrots, seldom failed to pique the ladies' interest.

Nineteen-year-old Dea England went to work for Columbus in 1927, her first job out of secretarial school. One of her tasks was to prepare lists of potential investors in his ocean of oil. She purchased yesterday's newspapers at the Adolphus Hotel for a penny. What better sources of investors were there than the obituaries of doctors, bankers, and wealthy merchants? Their widows were ripe for plucking. Spinster daughters, the *femme sole,* were not forgotten. They loved the letter-writing lothario's eloquent flattery. The *Bible* and poetry-quoting con man held the record for the most books borrowed at the Dallas Public Library and was often seen bent over and hustling towards his next mark with a *Bible* or book tucked under his arm.

The lobby of the Adolphus Hotel was one of his haunts where he connived with his 325-pound cohort, Doc Lloyd. Doc often remarked that Columbus was the only interesting man he knew who didn't smoke, drink, or use profanity, all of which Doc did with exuberance. More than seventy, Doc still radiated infinite energy. He called himself Dr. A. D. Lloyd, but his real name was Joseph Idelbert Durham. Some say he changed his name because of bad checks, others because of a string of wives he left without divorcing. It is reported that the spellbinding con man had practiced medicine, was a druggist in Cincinnati, and worked as a chemist for the Bureau of Mines. Doc admitted running a medicine show as Dr. Alonzo Durham, peddling elixirs that cured whatever ailed the gullible. A teller of tall tales, he played the role of an adventurer in knee-high boots, jodhpurs, and a sombrero.

Columbus was a promoter and lease hound, a breed looked down on by real oilmen. He bought and sold oil leases under the theory of *blash—buy low and sell high.* In 1925 he had obtained a lease on the 975-acre farm of Daisy Miller Bradford. Daisy was a widow and no fool. Unlike most women he flimflammed, when irritated by the old diddler, her tongue had a sharp bite; and she was angry. He was late paying his 50¢-an-acre delay rental payment that would excuse drilling for another year. Daisy was crucial to his scheme. Her farm lay in the center of 5,000 acres he had leased, and she had reduced the standard one-eighth royalty to three thirty-seconds if he drilled the first well on her farm.

The promoter was busy preparing engraved $25 Rusk County Oil Syndicate certificates that looked like miniature stock certificates. Each certificate represented a 25/75,000 interest in a well on eighty acres in Daisy's lease based on a value of $75,000 he picked out of the air. If you recall, your elementary school teacher made you compute fractions to the lowest common denominator, so each certificate owner held a 1/3,000 interest. As a bonus, he included another 500 acres of "prime oil lands he would personally select" entitling the owner to a 1/500 undivided interest in the 500 acres. IF (a big IF) he sold all 500 shares at face value, he would gross $12,500 to cover the drilling costs and retain a 62,500/75,000 interest, broken down to its lowest common denominator: 5/6, one hell of a deal IF he struck oil, another big IF. BUT (a very big BUT) what if he can't sell 500 shares? And, as Arthur Anderson wasn't around to do the auditing, what IF he sold more than 500 certificates?

Columbus's promotion gimmick had an impressive title: GEO-LOGICAL, TOPOGRAPHICAL & PETROLIFEROUS SURVEY, PORTION OF RUSK COUNTY, TEXAS, Made for C.M. Joiner by A.D. Lloyd, Geologist and Petroleum Engineer. The first person Doc's report impressed was young Dea England. She had to fold and stuff hundreds of copies into envelopes, including a map outlining the Joiner and Lloyd anticlines (a geologist's term for underground domes) affixed with a *genuine* United States copyright mark, so it had to be true.

Doc lied when claimed he based his report on wells and thousands of seismic registrations in the area. There were no wells or seismic records. The only explanations for naming the fictitious Joiner and Lloyd anticlines are that he wanted to name something after himself and his pal, Columbus, or it was a scam. Doc's cover letter included in the mailing asked Columbus to *continue* sending him core samples and cuttings from the well, although Columbus hadn't started drilling.

Times were hard. Receipts from the mailings barely covered costs and his living and widow-wooing expenses, forcing Columbus to journey to Rusk County to con money from the locals. In the tiny town of Overton, he met two true believers in his promise of an ocean of oil, Walter and Leota Tucker, general store owners. After a moment of dismay at finding the Tuckers bankrupt and their store closed,

161

Columbus gave Walter Tucker a one-quarter interest in Daisy's well for his past faith and future services and told him to sell one-eighth and give him the cash as payment. Walter, honest and highly respected in Overton, had little trouble selling the one-eighth for $900 to local businessmen and believers in the ocean of oil.

With little cash and a satchel full of $25 Rusk County Oil Syndicate certificates, they set out for Houston County to buy secondhand drilling equipment. Columbus told Walter about the rudiments of poor-boying a well. They were not Standard Oil and didn't have Rockefeller's millions, so they had to drill with spit, sweat, and prayers—poor-boying with secondhand equipment. This meant dealing with a character in the oil patch that makes used-car salesmen look like Billy Graham, a used oil-equipment dealer. Columbus barely bought enough used equipment to start drilling. As he couldn't afford a boiler with sufficient steam to power the drill rig, he settled for two used mismatched small boilers the drilling crew named "Big Joe and Little Joe." Big Joe had powered a cotton gin for twenty years. The drill pipe was rusty and bent, described by one driller as "a heavy streak of rust."

Tom Jones was hired as the driller. As chief of the drilling crew, he was responsible for the drilling and maintenance. Drilling crews consist of skilled roughnecks, who work on the rig floor and wrestle the drill pipe, and roustabouts, oil patch slang for common laborers. Tom swallowed when he saw his crew made up of Walter Tucker (a general store owner), farmers, and fifteen-year-old John Tucker, whose father drafted him as an unpaid roustabout. John's duties were stoking the boilers and catching catfish for the crew's supper. In oil field slang, the crew would be called *weevils,* a derogatory term for inexperienced men named after a pesky beetle. Tom's wages were $4 a day and an added $2 *if he struck oil.* It wasn't top pay, no doubt because jobs were hard to come by and Tom's principal occupation had been a hard rock miner, but at least he had worked on a drill rig.

IF AT FIRST YOU DON'T SUCCEED . . .

Tom groaned at the sight of the dilapidated drill rig. Doc Lloyd estimated the Woodbine sand formation containing oil was at a depth of 3,550 feet, and the drilling rig was only designed to drill 2,500 feet. It may have been Leota Tucker's cooking or because there was no other work that convinced Tom to stay. The Tuckers planned to live in a tent at the site until Tom "brought them a gusher." Living next to the well would keep out thieves and oil scouts oil companies hired to spy on each other's drilling operations.

There are numerous tales of how the location of the Daisy Bradford No. 1 well was selected. An often-told anecdote is that Daisy insisted it be moved several hundred feet so it wouldn't dirty her washing on the clothesline. Most agree it was at least a half-mile from the spot Doc selected.

Progress was slow, but not sure. Tom spent days teaching the weevils and repairing the antiquated drilling rig. The boilers, Big Joe and Little Joe, barely powered the rig, and Columbus's failure to pay the crew or send money for supplies meant no work. Oil scouts reported checking the well a dozen times and not witnessing drilling. Six months after spudding, the rusty used pipe twisted and jammed. In oil patch jargon, they were "stuck in the hole" at only 1,098 feet.

USED OIL-EQUIPMENT DEALERS (A PERSONAL EXPERIENCE)

In 1980 I took my eighteen-year-old son with me to buy a secondhand pump jack from Uncle Billy, a used oil-equipment dealer in Oklahoma. As we sipped a Coca-Cola laced with bourbon, a ritual Uncle Billy enjoyed during negotiating, a poor-boy operator arrived I will call "Clyde" because my mother told me never to make fun of idiots and drunks. I told Uncle Billy to deal with Clyde. I was in no hurry, and it was part of my son's education.

Clyde needed a large compressor that Uncle Billy swore was a steal at $18,000. Two hours of negotiation, including a double shot of Jack Daniel's in Clyde's Coca-Cola, resulted in Clyde paying $8,000, a 1/16 interest in his gas well, and his Chevy pickup for the compressor and a sixteen-foot boat Uncle Billy had taken in a previous trade.

After Clyde left, my son asked Uncle Billy if he was aware that there was an eight-inch hole on the other side of the boat hidden under a canvas.

Uncle Billy nodded and spit a wad of tobacco. "An' I reckon Clyde will larn about it, too, when the damn fool puts it in the lake."

Lawyers call that *caveat emptor*—let the buyer beware.

Daisy, like many landowners, was shocked to learn that oil lessees had the right to use the water and timber on the lease for drilling. Poor-boy operators fired the boilers with wood instead of oil to save money. Although disheartened by her farm being denuded of trees, she handed Columbus a check for $100 and demanded, "Go raise the rest, and get me an oil well."

As usual, Columbus was physically bent and financially broke. He mailed out Doc's report and a new batch of $25 Rusk County Oil Syndicate certificates and wooed a few more widows. This time he was forced to discount them for up to 50 percent of the face value to scrape up enough cash to start drilling again.

Another myth folks enjoy repeating is how they determined where to drill the Daisy Bradford No. 2. The new driller, Bill Osborne, asked Columbus where he wanted the rickety 112-foot wooden derrick rolled on logs to spud the new well. The crew, no longer inexperienced weevils, yelled in unison, "Downhill, any direction as long as it's downhill."

Money was harder to find than the crew's five-gallon-a-day still in the pathless woods. Columbus paid for the crew's wages and repairs on the antiquated drill rig with cash raised from the $25 certificates, sometimes discounted to $10, which circulated throughout East Texas like money. News that the Texas Company (Texaco) drilled a dry hole southeast of Daisy's lease dried up the chance of selling the $25 certificates at any price. A year of sporadic drilling when Columbus raised money ended when the corroded drill pipe twisted and broke in the hole at 2,518 feet. Columbus's ocean of oil seemed the pathetic dream of an old man when a Texaco oil scout uttered the worse damning slur you can say to an oilman, "I'll drink every barrel of oil you can get out of that hole," and reported that Texaco had drilled its well to 3,500 feet in less than six weeks.

Two weeks of attempting to fish the broken pipe from the hole were futile. Bill Osborne quit. He hadn't been paid in months. The crew returned to their farms to eke out a living and feed their families. Walter Tucker packed up his family and moved back to Overton.

THE DAISY BRADFORD NO. 3

Walter found a job as a bank clerk. By the end of the first week on the job, the true believer convinced R. A. Motley, the bank president, to lend Columbus $100 to rent a wall hook and hire an experienced driller to fish out the broken pipe. The nearest wall hook was owned by Ed Laster in Shreveport, but Ed told him that the meandering drill hole wasn't worth saving. Columbus had no choice but to raise enough money to hire Ed to drill the Daisy Bradford No. 3 at $6 a day and the promise of $4 a day in oil leases, *if he struck oil*. Ed wanted to construct a new derrick and relocate the hole 500 feet to a level area. Columbus insisted he couldn't afford it and pleaded with Ed to move the old wooden rig. Before the tractor pulled the derrick 200 feet, the rig floor hit a rock and snapped the timbers like a pencil. After swaying, the tottering landmark became the East Texas version of the Leaning Tower of Pisa and couldn't be moved. But it could be leveled, and, if there was an ocean of oil down there, a couple of hundred feet shouldn't matter.

A *Henderson Times* headline read 1200 FEET IN TWO DAYS. The crew was amazed what Ed Laster's skill and "almost new" drill pipe could do. But Columbus's funds soon ran out, and it was back to using rusty pipe. When there wasn't enough money to buy wood from adjacent farms, the crew burned used automobile tires salvaged from junkyards that cast black plumes in the sky neighbors could see for a mile until Big Joe exploded and badly scalded Ed and one of the crew.

Columbus organized another syndicate. This time he went big time with $100 certificates. Each new $100 Rusk County Oil Syndicate certificate promised a 1/300 interest in 80 acres surrounding the well and entitled the owner to an additional undivided four-acre interest in 320 acres on Daisy's lease. Dea England recalled her math from secretarial school and figured it required 1,200 acres, but she had faith in Columbus, even when he sold one lease several times.

Ed drilled the Daisy Bradford No. 3 to 2,600 feet, deeper than they had ever drilled, but still far short of 3,550 feet where Doc claimed the oil-bearing Woodbine sand would be found. Not that it mattered. Columbus had only spent a few hundred dollars raised from the new syndicate. Ed was about to quit when Daisy told him Columbus had called to ask if Ed would take a core sample when he brought prospective investors from Dallas. The veteran driller knew it was a scam, but he persuaded R. A. Motley to advance the money to rent a core barrel to sample the formation being drilled. The prospects were not disappointed when the crew pulled the core sample from the well and laid it on the drill rig floor like seasoned roughnecks. Columbus smelled the rock cylinder and rubbed his hand along its course grains, then hesitated as if in deep thought before pronouncing they where close to the Woodbine. The crew celebrated that night. Their charade garnered enough money to pay their back wages and start drilling again.

Encouraged by the ruse, Columbus persuaded Ed to send telegrams reporting he was taking more core samples and nearing the Woodbine. The news piqued the interest of oil scout Don Reese of the Sinclair Oil and Refining Company. Don's admiration for Ed soared when he learned that the well was at 3,400 feet—900 feet more than the rig was designed. The oil scout was surprised when he asked Ed for cuttings from the well and Ed agreed if Don gave him the Sinclair geologist's report. Drillers never give cuttings to oil scouts. To make sure the cuttings weren't salted, Don sneaked back that night and snitched more cuttings. Don wasn't aware that Ed wanted a geologist's report. Doc Lloyd had never visited the well. Ed was devastated when he read the geologist's report: the Woodbine was at least another 1,500 feet deeper and probably would not contain oil, but saltwater.

Another friendly oil scout (all good oil scouts must be friendly), Hank Conway from the Amerada Oil Company, offered to lend Ed a core barrel, aware Ed was not taking cores and Columbus was pulling a scam by flashing core sample reports around Dallas. Ed couldn't refuse. The well was bottomed at 3,456 feet—only 94 feet from where Doc claimed he would hit the Woodbine. When Hank returned with the Amerada geologist's analysis, it was almost identical to the Sinclair report.[47]

OIL SCOUTS OR SPIES?

Oil scouts of the era obtained inside information on the drilling progress of other companies, such as the depth of the well, the formations penetrated, whether oil or gas was found, and any data that might help their company cut drilling costs, reduce risks, or tip them off to possible oil strikes. They often frequented card games, saloons, and whorehouses to pick up the valuable information oil companies wouldn't disclose. Oil scouts were not above sneaking around a well at night to steal drill cuttings and peek at records.

Spies was a good name for the scoundrels.

---

[47] That the geologists' reports were similar was surprising. Many oilmen believe, if you ask two geologists a question, you will receive at least four opinions. *No nasty letters from geologists accepted.*

166

Although Doc Lloyd's report had been discredited and Ed had no faith in the scoundrel, he was determined to drill to 3,550 feet before Columbus's lease terminated in two weeks. Two days later, he noticed the drill hack-sawing, an indication it was cutting into hard sand. When he examined the cuttings, he saw sand streaked with a rainbow of color. He ordered the crew to take a core sample and go home. It was a sign of oil, but he didn't want the crew raising their hopes and blabbing about a possible oil strike. He put the core sample in the trunk of his car and drove home. When he opened the trunk, he gazed on the most beautiful sight he had ever seen—nine inches of Woodbine sand dripping oil.

Do Unto Others Before They Do It Unto You

Ed's elation turned to panic when he recalled leaving the bucket of cuttings on the rig floor. If an oil scout found the Woodbine cuttings, the news would break, and oil lease prices would skyrocket, making it impossible for Columbus to buy the leases he owed Ed under his contract. His panic turned to dread after he raced back to the rig, blowing a head gasket in his old jalopy on the way. Someone had stolen the bucket of cuttings.

The dejected driller sat on the rig staring into the black night that began as a dream of riches and twisted into a nightmare. With his car disabled, he couldn't get back to town to telephone Columbus. Last week he had sold a small lease a mile from the well for a pittance to put food on the table for his family. When news of the strike broke, it would be worth thousands. Car headlights approached, and Don Reese, the Sinclair scout, climbed from his car and grinning told Ed who did it. Don told him he had found the bucket of Woodbine cuttings and thought Ed had placed it as a scam, so he hid the bucket. The scout said that because they were friends he wouldn't tell anyone. Ed smiled, unable to admit or deny Don's accusation, but told him to pick up leases in the area.

As they say in Texas, Ed Laster was as happy as a pig in slop when he telephoned Columbus to tell him he hit the Woodbine sand oil. The old promoter casually told him to put a sample on a bus and not tell anyone. Then came the crushing blow. Columbus said that Doc Lloyd would take over as driller.

Ed realized he was about to be double-crossed. He called a friend

167

at the Mid-Kansas Oil & Gas Company. For a sample of the core and drilling log data, he made a deal for a one-quarter interest in a 1,000-acre lease near Daisy's farm that Mid-Kansas Oil & Gas could obtain for a $1 an acre. It would be worth hundreds of dollars an acre . . . maybe thousands.

It was hate at first sight. Doc told Ed he was demoted to assistant driller and that he knew of a new system to cement the hole without reaming it. An angry Ed said he would ruin the hole.

The following day, Don Reese arrived at the drill site and was surprised to see Columbus, Daisy, Motley, and the Tuckers watching Ed, Doc, and the crew recovering a core sample. Don told Columbus, if he didn't obtain a piece of the core, he would be fired. Columbus winked and gave him a thumb-size piece of the core and thanked him for his help. After Don showed the sample to his supervisor, everyone at the Sinclair office laughed. He should have known that the old con man had salted the well and was fleecing more money out of widows.

Daisy telephoned Ed and asked him to met her at her brother's motel in Henderson. She didn't trust Doc and was angry. Columbus's lease ran out the next day, and Daisy wouldn't renew it unless Ed was in charge, Columbus furnished new equipment to complete the well, and he assigned 100 acres in the lease to her brother. The old con man had no choice but to sign.

When Ed returned to the well, the crew told him that Doc had drilled another seventy-five feet deeper and through the Woodbine. Every oilman, from experienced petroleum engineers to green weevils, knew that Doc's drilling risked hitting saltwater generally found beneath oil. Saltwater could have flooded and destroyed the well. Ed raced to Henderson to punch the eminent geologist, petroleum engineer, and medicine show huckster in the nose, but the scoundrel had skipped town.

DID THEY OR DIDN'T THEY?

There has always been a question whether Columbus and Doc attempted to sabotage the well. As the years pass, Columbus "Dad" Joiner's legend grows, and he becomes more revered. Today it is rarely mentioned. Make up your own mind as you read the next chapter.

CHAPTER FOURTEEN
BOOM & BUST

THE GAMBLER

Columbus wheedled a free drill-stem test from the Miller brothers of El Dorado, Arkansas, who had developed a new method of testing the bottom pressure and fluids. Amused the con man couldn't pay for the test, they invited Pete Lake, an El Dorado haberdasher and oil deal backer, and Haroldson Lafayette Hunt Jr., a gambler turned oil-man after winning an oil well in a game of five-card stud. The two came to gamble if the well showed promise and the old promoter needed cash.

H. L. Hunt would become a legendary billionaire oilman, but in September 1930, he was forty-one years old and short of cash. The "spiffy dresser" (one biographer's description) didn't have an office, but could easily be spotted in a bar or hotel lobby wearing a jauntily askew fedora and chomping a giant panatella and wheeling and deal-ing. In El Dorado, he lived with his wife, Lydia Bunker Hunt, and five children. When in Shreveport, Louisiana, the traveling man had a second wife, Frania Tyc (really Tiburski) Hunt. Hunt and Frania had two children and one in the oven. Shreveport, an oil town only 100 miles from Eldorado, was good reason for Hunt to call himself Maj. Franklin Hunt when with young Frania.[48]

Hunt's nights were often reserved for high-stakes poker under the alias "Arizona Slim." Although a gambler, wildcatting wasn't Hunt's

---

[48] Numerous accounts have been written about H. L. Hunt's three wives and fifteen chil-dren, although Hunt barely mentioned Frania in his several autobiographies. Many lawyers became wealthy as a result of his fourteen living children squabbling over a couple of bil-lion dollars inheritance.

style. To Hunt, the odds of hitting a wildcat well were worse than hitting an inside straight. He preferred to move in with oil scouts and buy leases and let the wildcatter take the risk. Another way was to take over a poor boy's well with Pete Lake's backing. Hunt was disappointed when Columbus told him that D. H. "Dry Hole" Byrd was financing the well completion. He would have to be satisfied with moving fast if the old con man's drill-stem test proved positive. He didn't have long to wait. Before the crew could complete the drill-stem test, an odor of gas filled the air, and the rig shook like leaves in a windstorm. A deep rumble from below turned into a roar that could be heard for a half of a mile. Mud, gas, and oil shot through the top of the derrick, and one of its legs snapped like a twig. Nature's furious blast of hydrocarbons trapped beneath the surface for millions of years had erupted in a gigantic belch.

A swarm of well-wishers (no pun intended) clustered around Columbus, but the old con man shooed them off, saying, "It's not an oil well yet."

Ed Laster said it "would make a pretty good well, *if* we can bring it in."

Hunt didn't say a word. He was too busy planning where to obtain oil leases.

R. A. Motley lined up Columbus, Doc, Ed, and the crew for a picture. At the last moment, Columbus motioned to Hunt and called, "This picture's going down in history, boy, you'd better get in it." Columbus was right, it would be one of the most-reproduced photograph in petroleum history. Hunt shouldn't have been in the picture. He had nothing to do with the discovery that would make him a billionaire. Doc shouldn't have posed shaking Columbus's hand, either. When the picture was plastered on the front pages of the newspapers, two of Doc's wives arrived looking for the scoundrel.

JOINER FINDS OIL ON MILLER FARM read the bold headline in the *Henderson Times*. It was the best news heard in East Texas since Sam Houston kicked Santa Anna's butt at San Jacinto in 1836. Within days, thousands of men desperate for work in the early days of the Depression roared into East Texas along with oil patch trash—con men, gamblers, whores, and thieves. Overnight a town christened "Joinerville" rose along the highway where a one-lane dirt road turned off to the Daisy Bradford No. 3. The shantytown of shacks and tents held more than two thousand within weeks and might have held thousands more if it had water and plumbing. (Don't look for it on a map, it burned down during the boom, and all that remains is a road sign.)

Wildcatters flooded East Texas. It meant little that the drill-stem test only showed a trace of oil. They would have rushed in if there was a rumor of the black gold. Most major oil companies, more cautious, sent oil scouts and geologists. Their bloated corporate bureaucracies didn't believe there was oil in East Texas. The exceptions were the always aggressive Shell, an embarrassed Sinclair, and Humble Oil and Refining Company, a rapacious Standard Oil of New Jersey subsidiary.

Rusk County farmers were the first to reap the bonanza. The price of oil leases jumped to $400 an acre overnight—ten times what the barren land would have sold for the month before. Within two weeks, more than 2,000 oil leases were filed in the county court-house. Shrewd farmers held back leasing all their land. If they could get $400 now, what would the land be worth *if Columbus Joiner actually struck oil?*

Hunt managed to acquire 400 acres to the east and south of the Daisy Bradford No. 3 dirt cheap with the little cash he had in his pocket, earned playing poker and $2,500 won betting the Philadelphia Athletics would beat the St. Louis Cardinals in the World Series. Humble Oil gobbled up 13,000 acres, most at less than $20 an acre, and Shell and Sinclair each leased 5,000 acres.

THE DAY OF RECKONING

Always one of the first to arrive after an oil strike were oil field map-makers. Unlike county land plats, oilmen need diagrams of boundaries showing the mineral-interest owners and the location of wells that hit oil or gas or were dusters. During booms, county clerks were unable to update land plats fast enough and didn't record where wells were drilled. It was only a short distance to Henderson from Ft. Worth for mapmaker W. W. Zingery. His first night in town, while two wildcatter friends plied a Humble Oil landman with corn liquor, he traced a Humble Oil map in the next room to get a head start on the other mapmakers. Zingery was at the county clerk's office when it opened the next morning and slipped the clerk a few dollars to let him stay after closing.

The following day Zingery was raking in thousands of dollars selling maps and dealing for leases. It was inevitable the mapmaker would be offered a $100 Rusk County Oil Syndicate certificate used like money by the locals. Zingery spotted that Columbus had only set aside 320 acres for bonuses that required 1,200 acres. As he was double-checking the records in the clerk's office, he met another notorious scoundrel found in the oil patch that is sneakier than an oil scout, slyer than a used oil-equipment dealer, and with the morals of the hookers parading the streets in boom towns, who had uncovered the same insufficiency—*a lawyer.*[49]

The lawyer told Zingery he was from Dallas and planned to file suit against Columbus in the federal court in Dallas on behalf of a widow who had bought Columbus's certificates. Zingery knew that big-city lawyers made a federal case out of everything so they could flimflam the country folks. He retained a local lawyer, anxious to keep the legal fees in East Texas and a hometown advantage, who called Judge R. T. Brown at home. That Saturday afternoon the involuntary receivership was filed in the case of *W. W. Zingery v. C. M. Joiner.*

East Texans were shocked when the county land records revealed Columbus had oversold the Rusk County Oil Syndicates by 350 percent and had sold one lease eleven times. But the savior of Rusk County was revered as "the Daddy of the East Texas oil field." He was no longer Mr. Joiner, but "Dad Joiner," a title he carries today.[50] Doc Lloyd started a rumor that "Big Oil," led by Humble Oil, was attempting to steal the oil field from the small independent oilmen. Every local newspaper supported Dad Joiner. The Tyler Texas *Courier-Times* called him the "Second Moses" being tied up in court by "big boys" and "oil trusts." Walter Tucker and R. A. Motley organized the "Joiner Jubilee" to support Dad. The parade and barbecue in Overton, a town of fewer than 400, drew 5,000 cheering partisans.

In the meantime, Ed Laster and the crew labored to make the well produce oil. They knew the Daisy Bradford No. 3 had not given up a

---

[49] No nasty letters from lawyers accepted. The author regrets having to admit he was a lawyer. In those days it was unethical for attorneys to advertise in the Yellow Pages between astrologers and auctioneers. The scoundrels could only hand out cards, unlike their immoral counterparts, the prostitutes, who wore bright beach pajamas when walking the streets to attract clients.

[50] As everyone started calling him "Dad," from this point on, so will the author.

172

single barrel of oil and were finally ready to bring in the well on October 2, 1930. True to his word, Dry Hole Byrd supplied new equipment and tanks to store Dad's ocean of oil. A carnival atmosphere swept over Daisy's farm, clogging the roads with cars and buggies for miles. Soda pop and moonshine flowed freely as thousands gathered to celebrate and watch the dull tasks of cementing the casing and swabbing the well.

For three days, the throng waited. By October 5, 1930, the crowd had swelled to 10,000. Byrd kept their spirits high by recounting how he earned the nickname "Dry Hole." After drilling more than fifty dry holes, the wildcatter hit two gushers on the same day. When Ed announced he had to shut down because they had run out of firewood, Walter Tucker and R. A. Motley persuaded onlookers to remove the spare tires from their cars for use as boiler fuel. Not even the black fetor of burning rubber hovering over the crowd daunted the faithful.

In the late afternoon, Ed jumped from the rig and shouted to shut down the boilers and for everyone to douse their cigarettes. Daisy Bradford recalled the ground shaking and her knees buckling. A distant rumble turned into hell's thunder, and the rickety rig shook. With the roar of a locomotive, a black pillar erupted over the derrick and rained Dad Joiner's promised ocean of oil on the crowd.

Ed turned the valve and shunted the gusher into the tanks as Dry Hole Byrd read the gauge. Dry Hole whispered the reading to Dad. It was Dad's ocean of oil, and he should tell the crowd that the well flowed at 6,800 barrels a day.

"I dreamed it would happen, but I never really believed it," Dad whispered to Doc as they faced the cheering crowd.

"The Lord blessed us with oil, then blessed us with rain," folks said. Seven years of drought ended with a deluge. Creeks swelled, and roads turned into an ocean of mud. Cars and trucks mired over their axles in the Texas red slime. But few cared about the mud. The Daisy Bradford No. 3 had became erratic and had dropped to 250 barrels a day. In oilmen lingo, it flowed in heads, belching a few barrels, then coughing and dying for hours.

Hunt figured the well was on the upper edge of a pool and being fed irregularly. As two recently drilled wells to the east were dusters, the field had to be to the west. Unfortunately, three of his four leases were

173

to the east, so he drilled on his only lease to the southwest. He hit a well that produced 100 barrels a day. He glumly reported he "only had a show of oil," not wanting to disclose his small bonanza. With every dollar he could borrow, he made a deal with Sinclair Oil and Refining Company to sell his oil delivered to a depot on the nearby Missouri-Pacific Railroad and built a pipeline from the field to the railroad. Hunt would earn 15¢ a barrel for transporting independent oilmen's oil, and he wouldn't be dependent on Standard of New Jersey's subsidiary, Humble Oil, that controlled oil pipelines and prices in Texas.

On Dad Joiner's day of reckoning before Judge R. T. Brown, everyone showed up in court but Dad. Col. Bob Jones, Dad's attorney, said Dad was too ill and presented Dad's defense. Judge Brown, who would earn the sobriquet "the Sage of East Texas," banged his gavel and issued one of the most famous rulings in the history of the Texas judiciary:

> I believe that when it takes a man three-and-one-half years to find a baby, he ought to be able to rock it for a while. This hearing is postponed indefinitely.

Zingery withdrew his suit after his first taste of East Texas justice and laid low. Attacking Dad Joiner was an invitation for a gunfight. For weeks the Dallas lawyer couldn't find Dad to serve him in the federal court case until a $100 bill slipped to a bellhop uncovered Dad hiding in a room in the Adolphus Hotel. Here, too, justice was swift. Colonel Jones, pleading he was only a "country lawyer" (translated: watch out city shysters), claimed Dad could not protect his investors and develop the oil leases with devious lawyers and the threat of Big Oil nipping at his backside. He requested Dad be granted a voluntary receivership so he could control the destiny of his ocean of oil for the folks in Rusk County. The judge agreed.

THE BEST OIL DEAL IN AMERICAN HISTORY

Hunt offered to buy out Dad as they walked out of the courthouse. Dad replied he would only be "buying a pig in a poke." Undaunted and with only $109 in his pocket, Hunt borrowed $30,000 from Pete Lake. He promised H. L. Wilford, a promoter pal of Dad's, $25,000 if he steered Dad to the bargaining table. News that two wells drilled to the northeast and southeast of Daisy's well were dry holes told him it was time to deal. Then he promised Frank Foster, the driller on the Deep

Rock well being drilled one mile west of Dad's leases, $20,000 to tell him if the well was a producer before the news was made public.

On the morning of November 25, 1930, Hunt and Dad embarked on what was to be thirty-six hours of almost nonstop negotiations in suite 1553 of the Baker Hotel in Dallas. There are numerous conflicting tales of what went on in the suite, but no one really knows. Rumors that Hunt enticed him with booze and ladies of the evening are untrue. Dad never touched the devil's brew, and Dea England was now more than a secretary. The twenty-two-year-old was also more than the seventy-three-year-old man could handle. What is known is that three hours before they signed the contract, Hunt secretly received word from Frank Foster that the Deep Rock well had cored ten feet of the Woodbine sand dripping oil.

As the two celebrated the deal over a plate of cheese and crackers, Dad said, "Boy, I hope you make fifty million dollars."

Dad sold his interest to Hunt for $1,335,000—$30,000 in cash, $45,000 in promissory notes, and $1,260,000 in oil payments. Oil payments are a promise to pay a sum *if and when oil is produced*. If the leases did not produce the amount due based on a 7/32 interest on the first half or the 7/64 interest due of the second half, Hunt's obligation ended. What did Hunt receive in return? More than 300 lawsuits, according to Hunt's attorney. Dad did not have clear title to two acres out of 5,000 acres in his bloc of leases. Hunt's plan was simple—settle the claims for a small amount or drag the case through the courts for years. In the meantime, Hunt would drill and produce oil.

Broke again, Hunt went to R. A. Motley to borrow $5,000, but the small bank was overextended because of the oil boom. Luckily, Leona Tucker was in the bank and loaned Hunt the money at 8-percent interest (more than twice the going rate). The Tuckers had leased their farm ten miles from Daisy's farm for $30,000. Land they couldn't sell for $30 an acre last month was leased for oil at $100 an acre.

Two weeks later, the Deep Rock well gushed in at a rate of 3,000 barrels a day, and Hunt's first well was producing 100 barrels a day. On the strength of his leases and pipeline, he borrowed $50,000 from a Dallas bank. The Hunt Oil Company was now a booming oil business.

THE BOOM

Fourteen miles north of the Daisy Bradford No. 3, Ed Bateman, a poor boy wildcatter, drilled on the farm of Mrs. Lou Della Crim.

Malcolm Crim, her son, was dubious when the first crew laughed at the dilapidated rig and left. Weeks later, Bateman was about to throw up his hands in defeat. He had drilled to 3,600 feet, as deep as the Daisy Bradford No. 3, and the old-fashioned, fish-tail bit could only cut one or two inches of the hard rock an hour. Bateman's savior was a Hunt Oil Company oil scout. He loaned Bateman a new roller bit on the condition that he advise him if he struck oil before telling anyone so Hunt could pick up cheap leases in the area. A week later, the Lou Della Crim No. 1 blew in at 22,000 barrels a day.

Within days, oil leases between Daisy's and the Crim's farms cost up to $5,000 an acre. By then Hunt had signed up hundreds of acres at less than $100 an acre. And the boom didn't stop there. Twelve miles north of the Crim farm, a third well gushed 20,000 barrels a day. The Black Giant, as the East Texas oil field became known, would prove to be forty-five miles long and range between five and fifteen miles wide, extending from Rusk and Gregg counties to Upshur County in the north and Smith and Cherokee counties on the west and south. Within nine months of Dad's discovery, there were 625 wells producing more than one million barrels a day of flush production. The Black Giant was the biggest oil strike in U.S. history. Oil leases bonuses soared to $15,000 an acre.

Kilgore, in the center of the oil field, exploded from a sleepy town of 700 to 10,000 boomers within two weeks of Bateman's well. Malcolm Crim and other store owners on Kilgore's main street tore down the rear of their stores and drilled for oil until forty-four wells sprouted on the richest block in America. A well was drilled through the marble floor of a bank, a church was torn down to set up a rig, and derrick legs overlapped on small lots until every landowner had his own oil well under the Rule of Capture.

Back in Dallas, Dad celebrated with Dea, collected oil payments from Hunt for a wildcat well play in West Texas, then celebrated with Dea again. Dad had more money than he had ever seen and had escaped going to jail for fraud, although few believe you could have found twelve jurors in East Texas who would have convicted the old con man and hero. Dad's money disappeared faster than Dea could say "Neiman Marcus." Hunt wasn't surprised when Dad showed up on occasion to ask for an advance on his oil payments. He reminded the old promoter that oilmen did not invest their own money on wildcats, but gamble on speculator's money. Hunt also ominously warned that the price of oil was dropping.

HUMBLE OIL AIN'T HUMBLE

Humble Oil & Refining Company didn't take its name because it was modest and unpretentious. It was organized in 1917 by independent oilmen and named after Humble, Texas, a small town north of Houston, to compete with Gulf and Texaco. Two years later, it secretly crawled into bed with despised Standard Oil of New Jersey when it sold 50 percent of its stock to the predator. It became a wholly owned subsidiary in 1925, the first crack in Texas antitrust laws barring out-of-state corporations from doing business in Texas.

By 1925, Humble was the largest crude-oil producer in Texas and in 1928 became the largest oil pipeline company in the United States. Its domination over prices was evidenced by purchasing three times more crude oil than required for its refineries and exporting the surplus. (Remember the Achnacarry Gulf-plus price fixing scheme in bonnie Scotland?)

Humble's president between 1922 and 1933, William Farish, was so ruthless, he was elected president of Standard Oil of New Jersey to replace Walter Teagle. There are those who claimed, not without reason, that Teagle and Farish cooked up the secret 1919 merger so Standard Oil could sneak back into Texas. Teagle and Farish had been pals since they worked together on the National Petroleum War Service Committee during World War I.[51]

THE SQUEEZE

Humble Oil, the largest purchaser of crude oil in East Texas, cut the price from $1.30 to $1.15 a barrel in January 1931. As the Texas Gulf prices were the basis of world prices under the Achnacarry Agreement, the ripple was felt around the world. During March and May, Humble led the other major oil companies (derogatorily called "Big Oil" and pronounced "Big Awl" in Texas) in price cuts on purchases from independent producers to 67¢ a barrel, then 35¢, then 15¢. Desperate small oilmen sold at any price in order to keep producing and emptying their storage tanks until the price fell to 10¢ a

---

[51] For Humble Oil's side of the story, there is the *History of Humble Oil & Refining Company: A Study in Industrial Growth*. In its self-serving "autobiography," Humble claimed it would have discovered the East Texas oil field six months before Dad Joiner and avoided the nation's worst crude-oil-price crisis, but didn't get around to drilling the well as planned.

barrel under the same scheme used by Rockefeller in the 1870s. Big Oil, which purchased 90 percent of America's crude oil, kept its high profit levels through inflated export prices and maintaining their regular refining, pipeline, and marketing margins. Drivers pulling their cars up to the pump in New York, Chicago, and Peoria saw little drop in gasoline prices during the Great Depression.

Independent oilmen in Texas and Oklahoma felt the brunt as they opened their wells to the limit at 10¢ a barrel, particularly in the Black Giant that gushed more than one-third of America's total oil needs. Humble Oil blamed the oil glut on the independents, but it drilled more wells than any other operator and built a pipeline to the oil field. The Texas legislature, upon hearing that Humble's Texas pipelines earned $12 million in 1931, passed the Common Purchaser Act requiring pipelines to carry oil at reasonable prices without discrimination. Humble answered by refusing to purchase oil in several fields to tighten the noose and admitting that its pipelines had actually made $22 million in 1931.

Texas, one of the first states to enact petroleum conservation laws, had passed a statute in 1919 charging the Texas Railroad Commission (TRC) with protecting correlative rights and prevention of the physical waste of oil. The TRC's original infamous Rule 37 provided that wells must be a minimum of 150 feet from the lease lines and 330 feet from the nearest well producing from the same formation. At first blush, the spacing rules appear to ban drilling on each tiny lot in downtown Kilgore, however, Rule 37 contained an exception for small lots under the populist Texan's belief that every Texan should have the opportunity to have his own oil well. As a result, of the 24,000 wells drilled in the Black Giant during the 1930s, 16,000—two-thirds—were exception wells.

In January 1930, Ross Sterling, a founder and former president of Humble Oil, was sworn in as governor of Texas. Sterling refused to fund the Common Purchaser Act requiring Humble to carry the independents' crude oil and listened to the advice of Humble's president, William S. Farish. Farish insisted Texas's conservation law permitted the TRC to not only regulate *physical* waste, but *economic* waste—producing oil in excess of market demand—which sounded identical to the deal his boss, Walter Teagle, and his chums cooked up at Achnacarry Castle in 1928. This took chutzpah. In 1929 the Texas

178

legislature had amended the laws to provide that "waste shall not be construed to mean economic waste." In August 1930, the TRC issued an order limiting Texas's total oil production to 750,000 barrels a day.

East Texas independents thumbed their noses at the TRC's order—they were producing more than one million barrels a day from the Black Giant. When the case reached the federal court, the judge came down hard on the TRC.

> "[U]nder the thinly veiled pretense of going about to prevent physical waste the Commission has, in co-operation with persons interested in raising and maintaining prices of oil . . . set on foot a plan which is seated in a desire to bring supply within the compass of demand."[52]

Oklahoma was also feeling the price squeeze caused by the crude-oil deluge. Governor William "Alfalfa Bill" Murray ordered the Oklahoma National Guard to close down the Greater Seminole and Oklahoma oil fields and personally shut off the four oil wells on the lawn of the governor's mansion until the return of "dollar oil."

Texas Governor Ross Sterling vacillated several times before ordering the Texas National Guard to close down the East Texas field.

THE TEXAS RAILROAD COMMISSION

The TRC was the brainchild of Governor Jim Hogg in 1891. Originally its antitrust duties were to break the stranglehold of the damnyankee (one word) railroads over agricultural and commercial freight rates. Its jurisdiction was expanded to administer corporate charters and ban monopolies and out-of-state corporations from preying on Texas citizens. As monopolies were under its jurisdiction, it seemed natural that oil would be taken under its wing. The TRC was so powerful, Hogg persuaded Senator John H. Reagan, one of the sponsors of the Interstate Commerce Act, to return to Texas and become its first chairman.

In 1988, in an unofficial expansion of the TRC's duties, TRC Commissioner Kent Nance began attending Organization of Petroleum Exporting Countries (OPEC) meetings to chat with the Arabs about how to raise oil prices.

---

[52] *MacMillan v. Texas Railroad Coms.*, 51 F.2d 400, 405 (W.D.Tex. 1931), *rev'd per curium and dismissed*, 287 U.S. 576 (1932) (moot after law amended).

CHAPTER FIFTEEN
DOLLAR OIL

HOT OIL

Kilgore looked like a scene from a farcical 1930s movie when 1,200 Texas National Guard troops disembarked from a train to enforce martial law, complete with mounted cavalry and a band. They were joined by a half-dozen Texas Rangers in case people started shooting. The next day, two old World War I fighter planes landed in the grass at the foot of Proration Hill, named after a Humble Oil lease, where the troops were to be bivouacked.

Politically and morally, Governor Sterling could not have selected a worse choice as commanding officer. National Guard Brig. Gen. Jacob F. Wolters was a pompous ass who loved to play soldier and parade around in his campaign hat and billowing riding pants. When he wasn't playing weekend warrior, he was the general counsel of Texaco. His second in command, stiff-necked Col. Walter Pyron, spent his normal workday day as a Gulf Oil official. Wolters's reading the declaration of martial law to quell "the state of insurrection and open rebellion" was greeted with laughter. He banned more than twenty-five citizens meeting and prostitutes selling their wares in bright-colored beach pajamas, commenting that the nearest beach was more than 100 miles away. Wolters couldn't ban prostitution. The ladies were fined $20 every week to pay for Kilgore's police force that had expanded from one lone cop to more than twenty.[53]

---

[53] Part Five, *The Black Giant,* was originally written as a film script. It was rejected by Universal Studios, in part, because it was too corny to be true and the characters were unbelievable.

Martial law helped Big Oil squeeze the independent oilmen. In a letter to Walter Teagle, William Farish wrote, "only the shock and pain of low prices" would bring the independents in line under "the law of the tooth and claw." With the troops in place, the TRC issued an order limiting the Black Giant to 400,000 barrels a day and each well to 225 barrels a day. At that rate and with crude oil at 10¢ a barrel, wells capable of producing 20,000 barrels a day would only gross $22.50 a day.

ADAM SMITH'S LAW OF SUPPLY AND DEMAND

During the boom when crude oil was priced at 10¢ a barrel, a normally 5¢ Coca-Cola sold for 10¢ and hamburgers that once cost 10¢ sold for 25¢.

A U.S. District Court ruled the TRC order unconstitutional. However, the joy in the oil patch was short lived. Governor Sterling and General Wolters brazenly refused to obey the court's order even when cited for contempt. The governor personally took over issuing the prorationing orders and cut the per well allowable to 165 barrels a day, then 150 . . . 125 . . . 100, until February 25, 1932, when he dropped the allowable to 75 barrels a day. An independent oilman grossing $7.50 a day couldn't afford to pay his workers. Landowners also felt the pain when their royalties of one-eighth the value of the oil was cut below 95¢ a day. Many independent oilmen went bankrupt and were forced to sell out to Big Oil. The second squeeze was the TRC order only prohibited the production of wells, not the drilling. Big Oil could afford to continue to drill wells and buy more leases.

Governor Sterling pointed to a recent Supreme Court decision upholding Oklahoma's prorationing statute as constitutional exercise of the state's police powers. Oklahoma had used more finesse in crafting its statute and orders to solely protect correlative rights of the landowner. The Supremes believed the fairy tale and ruled that "None of the commission's orders has been made for the purpose of fixing prices of crude oil or has had that effect,"[54] notwithstanding Oklahoma Governor Alfalfa Bill Murray declaring its purpose was to return to "dollar oil."

---

[54] *Champlin Refining Co. v. Oklahoma Corp. Coms.*, 286 U.S. 210, 232 (1932).

Martial law and Humble's tooth-and-claw plan worked. The price of crude oil crept up to 85¢ a barrel before falling again. In November 1932, the Texas legislature passed the Market Demand Prorationing Act after a heated debate that it was price fixing. But it didn't stop the production of bootleg or "hot oil." The tale is told that hot oil got its name one winter night when a National Guardsman complained to a hot oiler that he was cold. He was told to lean against a tank truck recently filled with illegally produced crude that was still hot after coming from deep in the ground.

Soldiers drawing $2 a day and railroad workers paid $4 for a ten-hour shift were easily bribed to let a tank truck through a roadblock or attach cars to a train leaving East Texas. Hot oil flowed from wells hidden in the deep pine woods, like a moonshiner's stills, or wells inside of what looked like a house, and was transported out of the area by pipelines built in the dead of night. When the National Guard began detecting the pipelines with metal detectors, fire hoses were laid underground to carry the hot oil. The U.S. Bureau of Mines estimated 25 million barrels of hot oil were produced in East Texas in 1932 and 35 million barrels in 1933.

H. L. Hunt and many independents fought Big Oil by building refineries to sell petroleum products rather than give their crude oil away to Humble at 10¢ a barrel. A simple distillation "teakettle" refinery that ran 2,000 barrels of crude oil a day could be built for between $10,000 to $25,000. The Black Giant's sweet light crude could produce 18 gallons of gasoline per barrel plus roughly 16 gallons of kerosine and fuel oil. The gasoline could be sold for 5¢ a gallon. After the costs of refining and storage, a teakettle could generate profits on gasoline alone of 70¢ a barrel and pay for the construction of the refinery in less than one month. The teakettles' "Eastex" gasoline was sold by independent stations throughout the Southwest and Midwest for 10¢ or 11¢ a gallon, undercutting the major oil companies. Eastex gasoline carried no octane guarantees, but 60 octane ran a tin lizzie Ford and was a welcome bargain to motorists during the Depression. It was also a thorn in the backsides of major oil companies attempting to maintain high gasoline prices.

FDR's New (Bad?) Deal

The 1932 elections were welcome in Texas. President Franklin D. Roosevelt had the good sense to have Texan John Nance Garner as vice president, although "Cactus Jack" said, "The vice presidency ain't worth a pitcher of warm piss." Governor Ross Sterling was defeated for reelection by Miriam "Ma" Ferguson—a woman! Before Sterling left office, in a unanimous opinion written by Chief Justice Charles Evans Hughes, the Supremes slapped him down by ruling his martial law proclamation declaring a "state of insurrection, tumult, riot, and a breach of the peace" was a "subterfuge and unconstitutional."[55]

But even Roosevelt's New Deal couldn't solve the biggest problem in East Texas. The Black Giant was acting like no other oil field. It didn't contain a sufficient gas drive to raise the crude oil to the surface in several areas, and the pressure was dropping. If the pressure continued to drop, most of the ocean of oil would remain imprisoned underground forever. Geologists, who have at least two answers or opinions on everything, were dumbfounded, although many offered opinions anyway.[56] While waiting for the geologists and petroleum engineers (a fairly new profession at the time) to arrive at a solution, the befuddled TRC shut down the entire field, which doubled hot-oil production.

The petroleum engineers determined the oil field was not driven by gas, but water from the west and the underground aquifers feeding the Black Giant were not flowing sufficiently to replace the oil being produced. When the TRC opened the field, it set allowable production at twenty-eight barrels a day to test whether the aquifer flow and crude-oil extraction were in balance, but the rate was far below the break-even point for the small producers. The courts invalidated the TRC's order limiting the allowable on a per-well basis rather than the area drained on a lease, as they did *all nineteen* of its prorationing orders in 1932, absolving the hot oilers of any crime.

Roosevelt's most colorful cabinet appointment was Interior Secretary Harold L. Ickes. The power-hungry, renegade Republican curmudgeon coveted his title during the Democratic administration and in his memoirs, *Autobiography of a Curmudgeon*. The tyrant ran the Interior Department with wiretaps and spies and occasionally locked the department's doors at 8:00 A.M. to personally chastise and fine bureaucrats who were late. Ickes remained interior secretary throughout Roosevelt's administration (thirteen years) and one year

---

[55] *Sterling v. Constantin*, 287 U.S. 378 (1932).

[56] See footnote 47.

into Harry Truman's administration, when Harry realized that one curmudgeon in Washington was more than enough and forced Ickes to resign.

The interior secretary grabbed more power with his appointment as oil administrator under the National Recovery Administration (NRA). The NRA was part of Roosevelt's National Industrial Recovery Act (NIRA) under Gen. Hugh Johnson. Ickes refused to report to Johnson, who Ickes said was afflicted with "mental saddle sores" and "halitosis of intellect."

Ickes was concerned that the American oil industry was wasting oil and teetering on the brink of collapse. Crude oil at 10¢ a barrel was below its cost to produce. The federal government also had a selfish interest. It owned one-third of the nation's lands, including more than one-half of the oil lands in the Western states. The Department of the Interior was and still is the largest collector of oil and gas royalties in the country, and the federal government badly needed income during the Depression. Like the Texas farmers, Ickes had no problem in figuring that a royalty of one-eighth of $1 was ten times more than one-eighth of 10¢.

As in any crisis, government officials are flooded with advice from those they regulate. Ickes had the good sense not to listen to Walter Teagle of Standard of New Jersey and Harry Sinclair of Teapot Dome infamy when they urged him to set federal price and production controls. What intrigued Ickes was Teagle's suggestion that the East Texas oil field be shut in and purchased as a Naval Petroleum Reserve. The purchase of the East Texas field would garner a big profit for Standard of New Jersey's subsidiary, Humble Oil, which owned 13 percent of the field at the time. It would also eliminate the pesky independent oilmen who were producing too much oil. Ickes put aside the idea when told the federal coffers couldn't afford the purchase and he failed to persuade President Roosevelt to transfer the Naval Petroleum Reserves back under the Department of the Interior.

Ickes realized that the East Texas field was the heart of the hot oil. In May 1933, he reported to President Roosevelt that crude-oil prices had collapsed to 4¢ a barrel and 500,000 barrels a day of hot oil was escaping out of East Texas. It convinced Roosevelt to issue an executive order authorizing Ickes to send fifty federal agents to East Texas to stop the running of hot oil. Ickes had grossly exaggerated the figures. The price was 10¢ to 15¢ a barrel, and the best estimates were that hot oil was running at 125,000 barrels a day. But Ickes got what he wanted—control. He wired the governors of all the oil-producing states to dictate each state's production quota based on Bureau of Mines estimates of the nation's oil demand.

ICKES LIED OR DIDN'T READ THE NEWSPAPERS

On May 13, 1933, the week Ickes reported the crisis to Roosevelt, the *Petroleum Times* wrote: "Disturbing news from East Texas where the increase in production alone in the past few days is many times greater than the total output in Rumania . . . this formidable increase in production has been met by the international group posting crude prices down to ten cents *in order to kill the efforts of the independents.*" (Emphasis added.)

At the urging of the API, the Bureau of Mines number-crunchers had gathered oil statistics since 1930. In most cases, they were spoon-fed the statistics on production, storage, and consumption by major oil companies and the API. Even the Washington bureaucrats were aware there was no way to determine the amount the hot oilers were producing. There were seventy-five teakettle refineries, not including a refinery the oil G-men raided that distilled 500 gallons of moonshine a day.

The oil G-men combed the fields alone. The Texas National Guard had withdrawn after the Supremes ruled that Governor Sterling's declaration of martial law was unconstitutional. The principal federal bureaucratic enforcement method was, as expected, *paper.* The NRA's Federal Tender Board required all oil to be accompanied by a certificate proving the black goo was produced under the board's allowable production. As the reader learned in Chapter 2, crude oil is fugacious and fungible. It migrates and can be freely exchanged. The oil G-men couldn't tell the difference between federally certified oil and hot oil migrating across the country. The going rate for a bogus Federal Tender Board certificate and seal off a Houston printing press was $5, including the "official signatures" of such notables as Jeff Davis, R. E. Lee, Hal Ickes, Frank Roosevelt, and Ed Hoover.

The stream of hot oil increased by 40 percent in 1933 due, in part, to corruption and incompetence. Texans found it easier to bribe a federal agent than a Texas National Guardsman. Many oil G-men were poorly paid political hacks with little or no experience in the oil field.

OIL AND BUREAUCRATS DON'T MIX
(A PERSONAL EXPERIENCE)

During the oil crises of the early 1970s (there were two or three, depending on whom you ask), I was the director of the Office of Hearings and Appeals in the Department of the Interior. I was required to transfer five members from my office to the recently established Federal Energy Administration, four lawyers and one clerk. When I complained to my deputy for administration, Gilbert Lockwood, a friend and consummate bureaucrat (he got things done without making waves), he smiled and advised me to transfer the most incompetent and/or lazy nerds in the office. We never found out what happened to the secretary who couldn't type, but two of the four lawyers we got rid of were promoted and absorbed into the Department of Energy in 1978.

A big boost to push up crude-oil prices came in 1934 when Congress levied a 21¢-a-barrel tariff on imported crude oil and $1.05 on refined products, forcing Big Oil to raise their prices paid the independents. East Texas hot oil dropped an estimated 23 percent in 1934, partly due to the demand for oil falling 8 percent during the Depression year, according to the Bureau of Mines.

Big Oil had a few more tricks up their sleeves to keep their prices and profits up. Although the national average price of gasoline dropped from 20¢ a gallon in 1930 at the start of the Depression, it averaged between 17¢ and 18.9¢ a gallon between 1931 and 1935. At the time, Eastex gasoline sold for 10¢ or 11¢ a gallon. Big Oil was also engaged in price wars among themselves in parts of the nation and enticing motorists with free maps, glasses, trading stamps, cigarette lighters, and ashtrays. The country boys selling Eastex gasoline from hot oil and even some legitimately produced oil under the Federal Tender Board responded with practical items—a dozen eggs, five pounds of tomatoes, or chicken dinners with a fill-up.

The Achnacarry Agreement cohorts pushed their January 1, 1934, "Draft Memorandum of Principles," and its provisions began to creep into the NIRA Oil Code to "eliminate cutthroat competition." Claims

187

of gasoline superiority were banned. Newspaper ads and billboards were restricted, the size of signs at dealer stations were limited, and the amount of free "giveaways"—glasses, maps, etc.—were curtailed. Ickes claimed he was unaware that the Big Oil scoundrels were planning to deprive Americans of their cherished "freebies" at the gasoline stations when he welcomed Big Oil's lawyers and executives to Washington to help draft the NIRA Oil Code. The foxes in the chicken coop also lowered their costs by prohibiting an oil company from paying for the repair and painting of the stations, except the pumps the oil companies owned. Dealers were required to post the prices and forbidden to change them for a minimum of twenty-four hours or sell below the posted price. Of course, everyone cheated, and the regulations were impossible to enforce. The giveaways didn't end until World War II, but it shows what scoundrels they were.

When competition at the pump became unbearable, the major oil companies decided to take refiner "dancing partners" in East Texas and the Midcontinent.[57] To stem the flow of cheap gasoline, they agreed to purchase gasoline from independent refiner dancing partners that had been selling cut-rate gasoline to independent distributors and stations. Their plan allowed the dancing partner-refiner a greater profit and raised the price of gasoline. Many majors "married" their dancing partners by buying them out, as Rockefeller did around the turn of the century. In the end, out of the seventy-five teakettles once refining Eastex gas, there were less than thirty left.

In 1939 the Supremes ruled that the majors who took dancing partners violated the Sherman Antitrust Act by conspiring to fix gasoline prices.[58] The defense of the sixteen companies charged was they were acting under the NIRA Oil Code and that the oil administrator, Harold Ickes, condoned their plan. Tricky Ickes refused to testify and claimed he never signed anything. Then the seventy-year-old curmudgeon went on his honeymoon with a bride forty years his junior.

---

[57] The oil industry considers the Midcontinent between the Mississippi River and the Rocky Mountains except for Texas, which is in a class by itself. Most dancing partners were in Texas, Oklahoma, and Kansas.

[58] *United States v. Socony Vacuum Co.*, 310 U.S. 150 (1939). Law students in antitrust law class must pour over the dry (117 page) case holding that any combination to fix prices is a per-se violation of the Sherman Antitrust Act. But few know that Chief Justice Charles Evans Hughes had to recuse himself from the case because he had represented the scoundrels as a lawyer.

The final blow to the NIRA Oil Code came in December 1934 when the Department of Justice faced Fletcher "Big Fish" Fischer, a country lawyer. He had "read the law" and during the early days of the oil boom maintained his law office above a gasoline station in Tyler, Texas. Full of country metaphors and with grammar that would have made his English teacher cringe (if he had an English teacher), Big Fish devoured the Justice Department lawyers before the Supreme Court like a shark. Two months later, in a decision written by Chief Justice Charles Evans Hughes, the Supremes ruled the provisions of the NIRA Oil Code unconstitutional.[59]

Congress filled the void with the Interstate Oil Compact Act of 1935, permitting the oil-producing states to coordinate and adjust the Bureau of Mines demand forecasts, and the Connally Hot Oil Act of 1935. The latter bill was sponsored by Senator Tom Connally, Democrat of Texas and a strong backer of "dollar oil." The act prohibited the interstate transportation of oil produced in violation of state conservation laws and carried stiff fines and jail terms. Connally gave credit to J. Howard Marshall for drafting the law. Marshall, a Texas lawyer and oilman working in the Interior Department, had drafted the Federal Tender Board regulations and oversaw the writing of the NIRA Oil Code.

WHAT HAPPENED TO J. HOWARD MARSHALL?

Marshall died in 1995, leaving an oil fortune of more than $1 billion. You probably never would have heard of him except for his marriage to a twenty-something voluptuous stripper, Anna Nicole Smith, when he was eighty-nine and kicking the bucket at ninety. The court awarded the widow $88 million in March 2002 after battling Marshall's sons over the estate for seven years. As for Nicole's true age, she told Larry King on CNN she was twenty-seven and had a son when she was seventeen who is now sixteen. Newspapers claimed she was twenty-six when she married Marshall. She also told King she plans to have another child via a one-night stand. No doubt Marshall married Nicole for her mind, and she married him out of love. (At least that is what Nicole claimed on her "reality" TV show in 2002.)

---

[59] *Panama Refining Co. v. Ryan*, 293 U.S. 388 (1935).

Before the era of hot oil came to an end, more than 100 million barrels of hot oil poured from the Black Giant (4.2 billion gallons if you are an environmentalist). But that's not to say prorationing violations didn't occur. Humble Oil was convicted of violating the Connally Hot Oil Act almost two decades later.[60]

By the end of 1935, the major oil companies controlled 60 percent of the East Texas field. Humble's 1,500 wells constituted 16 percent of the field, making it the largest producer. Hunt Oil owned 250 wells and was the largest independent oil company in the field. Prorationing was working. Most oilmen, including Hunt, believed it was tied to the meaningful conservation of the Black Giant and was finally being relatively fairly enforced. Hot oil dropped to 12.8 million barrels in 1935 and 2.8 million barrels in 1936. But most important to the peace in the East Texas oil field, crude oil was selling at $1 a barrel.

LEGENDS

The tales of Dad Joiner and H. L. Hunt are an amalgam of fact and legend that will never die. The acts of Governor Ross Sterling, Interior Secretary Harold Ickes, and the federal government are recorded history. There were too many characters to emerge from the East Texas field to enumerate in this brief irreverent history nor can the number of scoundrels and Texas oil millionaires be counted.

H. L. Hunt and Dad Joiner remained friends for the rest of their lives, although Dad sued Hunt when he learned of Hunt's inside information from Frank Foster on the Deep Rock well during their negotiations. To show Hunt that he bore no hard feelings, Dad sent him a crate of pink grapefruit for Christmas during the litigation. The two wheeler-dealers settled the case behind closed doors. No one knows what the final settlement was, and Dad never complained.

H. L. Hunt died at eighty-five, a renowned right-wing billionaire, health food fanatic, and cheapskate, although he was known to bet $10,000 on a college football game. The author's one invitation to have lunch with him in his Dallas office consisted of a cheese sandwich on whole wheat bread, carrot sticks, and a Coca-Cola. He told me it was *real* American cheese, "not processed cheese food with chemicals and preservatives Kraft foists on the unwary public." We discussed oil and politics in the afternoon before he went home to his

---

[60] *Humble Oil & Refining Co. v. United States*, 198 F.2d 753 (10th Cir. 1952).

190

Dallas mansion, a replica of George Washington's Mount Vernon, only bigger.

Throughout his life, Hunt was haunted by rumors and accusations that he swindled Dad Joiner. Hunt called it his "greatest business coup." Friends and family claimed he merely conned a con man. But no one can deny that H. L. Hunt was one of America's greatest independent oilmen . . . he battled Big Oil and won.

Dad Joiner and his secretary, Dea England, went to Juarez, Mexico, where Dad got a quickie divorce from his wife of more than fifty years and married Dea. He was seventy-one, and she was twenty-three. Dad wandered across Texas for the rest of his life looking for another ocean of oil, but never hit another gusher. He died in Dallas at the age of eighty-seven, broke. But the lovable scoundrel will always be remembered as the Daddy of the East Texas oil field.

Dad's East Texas oil field and its impact on petroleum conservation laws was not his only contribution to the law. A decade later, the Supreme Court applied the Securities Act of 1934 to sales of oil and gas lease fractional interests to Dad's mailing of promotional literature to hundreds of people on one of his wildcat oil ventures. The Supremes noted that oil and gas leases "were notorious subjects of speculation and fraud."[61]

Dad's ocean of oil, the Black Giant, still spouts oil. It can no longer gush the 500 million barrels of oil it contributed during World War II towards the defeat of Nazi Germany. However, it is still a mighty force in producing jobs in East Texas and reducing America's dependence on foreign oil.

Market-demand prorationing based on economic waste brought about by Dad Joiner finding too much oil is no longer required, but is followed in natural-gas-producing states. It ended in 1973 during the Arab embargo when America woke up and discovered it was dependent on foreign oil for 36 percent of its needs. Actually, economic waste should have ended a quarter of a century earlier, but Big Oil was still running things and Americans paid too much for oil, as you will see in Part Six.

---

[61] *Securities & Exchange Coms. v. C.M. Joiner Leasing Corp.*, 320 U.S. 344, 352 (1943). After the Supremes ruled that he couldn't send prospectuses without registering them with the SEC and obtaining its approval, Dad retired.

VISIT EAST TEXAS

Venture to Kilgore and spend a few hours at the East Texas Oil Museum depicting America's biggest oil boom. It's extremely well done and includes accurate depictions of Kilgore's muddy streets, businesses, and the oil fields of the 1930s. You shouldn't miss its actual size replica of a wooden drill rig of the era. For visitors at Christmas time, Kilgore's dozens of old steel oil derricks adorned with bright colored lights is a Texas Christmas delight.

If you are in the mood for a short drive into East Texas's pine forests, ask one of the museum guides to direct you to the Daisy Bradford No. 3. When the author last visited in 1997, it was still coughing up a few barrels a day for the Hunt Oil Company

PART VI
MODERN SCOUNDRELS

"Oil is the excrement of the devil."
> —Juan Pablo Pérez Alfonzo, former Venezuelan minister of mines and hydrocarbons

"The meek may inherit the earth, but not the oil rights."
> —J. Paul Getty, billionaire oilman

"We proclaim loudly that the United States needs to be given a big hard blow in the Arab area on its cold insolent face."
> —Muammar al-Qaddafi, Libyan head of state

CHAPTER SIXTEEN
OPEC

THE BIRTH OF **OPEC**—ALMOST AN ABORTION

The Organization of Petroleum Exporting Countries (OPEC) is not a bunch of Arabs with a whole lot of oil. Yes, OPEC has almost 80 percent of the world's oil reserves, but they are not *all* Arabs. Of OPEC's eleven members, Venezuela, Nigeria, Indonesia, and Iran are not Arabs, but seven member nations are Muslim Arabs. Chart 17:1— Estimated Principal World Oil Reserves & Production—2002 shows the top thirty nations with more than 96 percent of the world's oil reserves and a few demographics that might concern arabphobes and conspiracy worrywarts.

A common misconception is that OPEC embargoed the United States because of its support of Israel during the 1973 Yom Kippur War. It was the Organization of Arab Petroleum Producing Countries. Earlier after the 1967 Six-Day War, Saudi Arabia, Kuwait, and Algeria embargoed the U.S. and Britain, and Libya and Iraq stopped shipping oil to everyone until all five realized there was a crude-oil surplus, and they needed the oil money to run their governments.

The OPEC cartel was the brainchild of a left-wing Venezuelan, Juan Pablo Pérez Alfonzo. After the overthrow of corrupt dictator Marco Pérez Jiménez in 1958, Pérez Alfonzo returned home from exile for the third time and was appointed minister of mines and hydrocarbons by the new president, Romulo Betancourt. During his banishment, he lived in Washington, D.C., and studied the American petroleum industry. Pérez Alfonzo was fascinated by the Texas

Railroad Commission and market-demand prorationing, especially the TRC's driving force behind higher crude-oil prices that forced Americans to pay more than the world market price.

No sooner had Pérez Alfonzo arrived home than President Dwight Eisenhower implemented the 1959 Mandatory Oil Import Program (MOIP), which drastically cut 40 percent of Venezuela's oil exports and its major source of government income. (Oil exports are still one-half of the Venezuelan government's income.) Pérez Alfonzo flew to Washington to plead for a special quota for Venezuela, but was given the finger. Americans didn't want anything to do with the pinko Venezuelans and were angry at the Venezuelan government's failure to protect Vice President Nixon from anti-American mobs during his 1958 goodwill visit. The United States position was firm, but on the shaky grounds that the MOIP was for "national security" reasons. Only oil imports from Canada and Mexico shipped by land instead of tankers to avoid attacks by submarines were favored. (No joke.) Of course, oil had to be shipped in and out of Hawaii, the Virgin Islands, Alaska, and Puerto Rico.

Pérez Alfonzo understood the farce. The United States was protecting its oil industry from cheap imported crude oil from the Mideast, Africa, and Venezuela by passing the "national security" costs to American consumers used to paying 50 percent more for domestic crude oil. He had the impossible task of protecting Venezuela's petroleum industry from cheap Mideast crude oil.

MOIP MEXICAN MERRY-GO-ROUND

There were no pipelines from Mexico, and it was too expensive to truck the crude oil from the oil fields to Texas. Mexican crude oil was shipped by tanker to Brownsville, Texas, loaded in bonded trucks, and driven across the border to Matamoros, Mexico, where it drove around a circle and back to Brownsville. Thus it legally entered the United States by land under the MOIP.

Pérez Alfonzo journeyed to the First Arab Oil Congress in Cairo, Egypt, to chat with Venezuela's competitors. Mideastern crude oil had two big advantages. Most Venezuelan crude oil was heavy gunk and sour, making it less valuable for refining into gasoline. Second, Venezuela's 80¢-a-barrel production costs far exceeded the 20¢ average cost in the Mideast, a sizable difference when the world price of crude was around $1.80. His aim was to introduce market-demand prorationing à la the Texas Railroad Commission to raise the per-barrel price and obtain a guaranteed share of the export market for Venezuela.

At first, the Cairo confab looked like it might be a bust. Of the 400-odd delegates, three-quarters were from Egypt and Syria, neither of which were major oil exporters and were in Cairo to "show the masses the importance of oil" and "coordinate the efforts of the Arab governments." Socialist-leaning Egypt and Syria, joined as the United Arab Republic, wanted a share of the oil largess and didn't invite the Mideastern non-Arab Iran, a major crude exporter. Not wanting to be blind-sided by the Arabs, the shah sent an observer to see what the Arabs were up to. Iraq, another large exporter, refused to get involved with Egypt's socialist president, Gamal Nasser, and did not send an official delegation.

Pérez Alfonzo might have gone home empty handed if Wanda Jablonski, a correspondent for *Petroleum Week*, hadn't introduced him to Abdullah Tariki of Saudi Arabia. Tariki, the son of a camel caravan operator, had studied geology and petroleum chemistry at the University of Texas and worked as a geologist trainee for Texaco. Some say he became anti-American after Texans tossed him out of bars believing he was a Mexican. As Saudi Arabia's only trained geologist and petroleum chemist, he became its director of Oil and Mining Affairs in 1955 by default. If King Saud knew his nickname was the "Red Sheikh," Tariki would have been boiled in oil.

Tariki and Pérez Alfonzo gathered a few attendees from Kuwait, Iraq, and Iran at the Maadi yacht club outside of Cairo, far from the Arab Oil Congress and hubbub of delegates who knew little about oil other than it made a lot of money they would love to get their hands on. They signed the unofficial nonbinding Maadi Pact that was to be kept confidential, except for a few leaks to the press, including the Czech brunette bombshell, Wanda of *Petroleum Week*. The Maadi Pact declared that the producing nations should receive 60 percent of the profits, be consulted on price changes, establish national oil companies to manage conservation and production, and expand into refining.

Noteworthy, the Maadi Pact was signed by Kuwait, the largest Mideast oil producer, which insisted on no notoriety because it was still a British protectorate and was not supposed to muddle in international matters, especially oil; Saudi Arabia and Venezuela by two left-leaning connivers; and two guys from Iran and Iraq who weren't supposed to be there. Tariki and Pérez Alfonzo, elated with their progress, hopped on a plane for Texas to attend the annual meeting of the Texas Independent Producers and Royalty Owners. The Texans were bitching about America importing 9 percent of its needs in cheap foreign crude oil under the MOIP and were glad to hear there was a movement to limit imported crude-oil production and raise prices. A happy Pérez Alfonzo took Tariki to Venezuela where pinko President Betancourt pinned a medal on the Red Sheikh.

After demands on the producers by the five Maadi Pact nations to *consult* with them before changing prices, on August 9, 1960, Exxon Chairman Monroe "Jack" Rathbone reduced the posted price in the Mideast by 5¢ to 14¢ a barrel without warning. Saudi Arabian light crude dropped from $1.90 to $1.76, a cut of 7 percent. Exxon's reason for cutting the posted price was valid, but its brashness in not discussing it with the countries was lamebrained. Russia was flooding Europe with bargain basement-priced crude far below the Seven Sisters' prices.

Tariki and Pérez Alfonzo screamed nasty oaths in public and rubbed their hands in glee behind closed doors. It was time to unite. Scheduling a meeting was chaotic. Iraq refused to go to Cairo, and Egypt had broken diplomatic relations with Iran. The meeting was held in Baghdad, and the Egyptians were told not to come. All the Maadi Pact signers' oil representatives showed up. Pérez Alfonzo arrived late because of an attempted coup in Caracas and a detour to Moscow to brief his Kremlin pals. Tiny Qatar showed up uninvited, but it wasn't allowed to join because it was too small and might make the group look too Arab. On September 14, 1960, OPEC was born of five nations that exported 80 percent of the world's crude oil.

OPEC's resolutions followed the Maadi Pact concepts, except they *demanded negotiations* over price changes, which was both reasonable and necessary. Crude oil represented between 90 percent to almost 100 percent of most member nation's exports and like percentages of their national budgets. However, their insistence that prices return to the pre-August 9 level was naive because of the market glut. They backed their demands by agreeing, if as a result of a unanimous OPEC decision the oil companies attempted to employ sanctions, the members would not break ranks and accept the benefits to the detriment of the others. This point was offered by Iran, still smarting from the Seven Sisters' boycott after its 1951 nationalization of Anglo-Persian. (Later, Iran was the first to break the commitment. To save face at the next meeting, OPEC voted unanimously to allow everyone to break the rule.)

The Western press gave OPEC's creation scant attention. Moscow's *Ekonomicheskaya Gazeta* reported, "The establishment of such an organization is a new feature in the struggle of the peoples of economically underdeveloped countries against the domination of monopoly capital." The *New York Times* picked up a Reuters wire story fifteen days later and buried it in the inside pages with a brief announcement and misspelled Qatar "Aqtar." The Seven Sisters refused to acknowledge OPEC's existence and chuckled at its provision requiring unanimous decisions. How could three backward Arab nations, an egotistical shah, and a coffee republic ever agree on anything?

The Second OPEC Conference was held in Caracas in January 1961 to organize its bureaucracy into four departments: administrative, technical, enforcement, and public relations. OPEC didn't get around to establishing an economics department until 1964 after someone mentioned the law of supply and demand. They selected Geneva, Switzerland, as its headquarters because of the Arabs' practice of boycotting meetings held in countries they were squabbling with at the moment. But they had to move to Vienna, Austria. Switzerland didn't believe OPEC was important enough to be accredited as an international organization and was wary about a bunch of riffraff troublemakers wandering around Geneva with diplomatic status. By then Qatar, Libya, and Indonesia had joined OPEC.

Fuad Rouhani of Iran was selected as OPEC's first secretary general. The shah instructed him not to let the group do anything stupid. But that was the least of Rouhani's problems, OPEC couldn't agree on anything important in the early 1960s.

Venezuela wanted to reduce production in order to increase prices and prorate the market among the members. It was losing markets and needed cash.

Iran, under the shah, also needed cash. He was hell-bent to regain Iran's status as the Mideast's number-one oil producer and build up his army and air force. He also said prorationing was a pipe dream . . . the Arabs would cheat. (He was right.)

Kuwait sat waiting for its independence from Britain in June before saying anything. Also, as the smallest member and the largest Mideast oil producer, it didn't want to cut its production.

Iraq was also waiting for Kuwait's independence so it could invade it. It did, giving Saddam Hussein the idea thirty years later. Iraq was defeated by British, Saudi, Jordanian, and U.A.E. troops. (The U.A.E. was a British protectorate, and Britain was financing Jordan's army.) Iraq boycotted OPEC meetings until 1963.

Saudi Arabia was concerned that Iran, Iraq, and Egypt were becoming too powerful, and King Saud wasn't about to screw up the money rolling in from Aramco (Exxon, Mobil, Texaco, and Chevron).

The only major OPEC victory during the 1960s was an accounting issue that added 11¢ to OPEC's take during a period of a crude-oil surplus. Crude oil hovered around $1.80 a barrel until 1970. OPEC added three members: Abu Dhabi (1969), which included the other United Arab Emirates in 1974, Algeria (1969), and Nigeria (1971), bringing its membership to eleven.

THE PINKO FOUNDERS LEAVE OPEC

The "Father of OPEC," Pérez Alfonzo, came to the conclusion that OPEC was run by greedy sheikhs and a shah and Venezuela was led by corrupt politicians. He resigned as minister of Mines and Hydrocarbons in 1963 after writing off OPEC as the savior of the masses and labeling oil "the excrement of the devil."

Abdullah Tariki, the "Red Sheikh," had the audacity to accuse the king's brother-in-law of taking *baksheesh* on a Japanese oil concession in the Arabian Gulf. He was summarily fired and exiled in 1962. Taking his place was a thirty-two-year-old American-educated lawyer who would earn the title "Mr. OPEC" and symbolize Arab oil—Sheikh Ahmed Zaki Yamani.

A COUPLE OF WILD AND CRAZY GUYS

The question whether the Mideast was stable was answered in September 1969. Col. Muammar al-Qaddafi took over Libya in a coup. His Revolutionary Command Council closed an American air base in Libya, tossed out the few Italians hanging around the desert wasteland (whose largest industry prior to the discovery of oil was selling scrap metal left over from World War II), and sold the stained-glass windows and gold crucifixes from the Catholic churches.

Qadaffi hired Abdullah Tariki as his petroleum adviser, but to handle the actual negotiations with the oil companies, he called on Abdel Salaam Ahmed Jalloud. Jalloud's methods were unorthodox to say the least. He carried a machine gun over his shoulder and laid two .45 automatics on his desk to get visitors' attention at meetings he sometimes scheduled at 2:00 A.M. When he didn't like an oil company executive's written proposal, he rolled it up in a ball and threw it in his face.

Tariki's concept that Libyan crude oil was worth more than Persian Gulf oil had merit. It had a lighter gravity (true); it was sweeter (true); and it was closer to Europe than the Persian Gulf and cut tanker costs (true). When a bulldozer "accidentally" cut the pipeline from Saudi Arabia through Syria to the Mediterranean, his point was made clear. However, he had an inflated idea that the price increase should be between 35¢ and $1 a barrel. Exxon chuckled at Libya's "compromise" of 43¢ and countered with a ridiculous offer of a 5¢

increase. Exxon could afford to stonewall Jalloud. It had a huge surplus of crude oil in the Mideast, as did all the Seven Sisters.

Jalloud expected the Seven Sisters to rebuff him, so he told the other price hawks, Algeria and Iraq, to also raise hell. Libya trained its guns on the independents without excess oil reserves. The weakest independent was Occidental Petroleum Company. The small California company depended on Libyan crude oil to meet its European supply commitments and was heavily in debt to finance its Libyan venture. It was widely known that its chairman, Armand Hammer, was disliked by the Seven Sisters for undercutting prices. And to make it enjoyable, Hammer was Jewish. Jalloud held a hammer over Hammer's head (a Libyan joke). Until Hammer agreed to a 40¢-a-barrel increase, Occidental was ordered to cut its production from 800,000 to 500,000 barrels a day. And, if he didn't agree soon, Jalloud threatened to more cuts to bankrupt Occidental.

Hammer hopped on his private jet to beg Exxon to furnish Occidental with crude oil at Exxon's production costs to stave off Libya's demands. His plea took chutzpah. A few years earlier, Hammer had committed an unpardonable sin. When Exxon's oil fields in Peru were expropriated, Hammer flew to Peru to make a deal for Exxon's oil concession. Occidental was also undercutting Exxon's crude-oil prices in Europe. Exxon told Hammer it would sell him all he needed at the market price.

Hammer caved in to Jalloud and agreed to a 30¢-a-barrel increase plus 2¢-a-barrel increase each year for five years on September 2, 1970. Then Jalloud raised another bitch—Occidental had been screwing Libya on the price for years under senile old King Idris and bribed Libyan officials to obtain the premier oil concession. To make up for Occidental's sins, the tax on crude-oil production was increased from 50 percent to 55 percent. And, by the way, Jalloud added, the new agreement is retroactive nine months earlier to January 1, 1970. Hammer and Jalloud shook hands on the contract guaranteed for five years. *As they say in New York, "If you believe that, I'll sell you the Brooklyn Bridge."*

The other independents had no choice but to agree to Libya's terms or be nationalized. One of the few exceptions was Nelson Bunker Hunt, son of H. L. Hunt, who refused to be coerced and paid the penalty of the nationalization of Hunt Oil in Libya. The Seven

Sisters couldn't afford to permit the price-cutting independents to market all of Libya's light, sweet crude oil just a short sail to Europe from across the Mediterranean, so they agreed to the terms.

During the Libyan negotiations, the other two price hawks moved quickly. Algeria jumped on the weak Eighth Sister, France's CFP, by unilaterally raising the posted price from $2.08 to $2.85. Saddam Hussein upstaged Libya and Algeria by nationalizing the American and British interests in Iraq.

When Shah Muhammad Pahlavi heard that the backward sons of camel drivers had negotiated a higher price than an Aryan king, he blew his stack. He took time out from planning the 2,500th anniversary of the Persian Empire and his coronation as *Shahanshah* ("King of Kings"), a gala that cost $250 million and was catered by Maxim's of Paris. The shah unilaterally retroactively raised Iran's crude 9¢ a barrel and increased the crude-oil tax from 50 percent to 55 percent. As expected, all the other Mideasterners raised their taxes to 55 percent.

OPEC's meeting in December 1970 turned into a celebration of its victory of obtaining a tax rate of 55 percent, although OPEC had nothing to do with the increase. It agreed that each member renegotiate new prices based on the quality of the crude oil and its location to the market as Libya had done. The crowning achievement was the decision of the gulf producers (Saudi Arabia, Iraq, Iran, Kuwait, U.A.E., and Qatar) to negotiate separately from the Mediterranean producers (Libya and Algeria). Indonesia and Venezuela sat quiet. They were already collecting a 60-percent tax and factoring the oil quality and transportation costs into the price. Nigeria, the new guy in OPEC, had been collecting a premium on its Bonny Light crude, one of the lightest and sweetest in the world, and Nigerian government officials were masters at squeezing out bribes for their personal pockets.

The American oil companies geared up to do battle with OPEC by asking the Nixon administration for support in obtaining a single negotiation. Wasn't that the purpose of OPEC? The American oil companies knew the gulf and Mediterranean producers would attempt to "leapfrog" over each other's gains at separate negotiations. Nixon offered no encouragement and his national security adviser, Henry Kissinger, claimed oil was a domestic issue. Secretary of State William P. Rogers sent Undersecretary John N. Irwin to discuss the matter with the shah and King Faisal. Irwin didn't want to offend

America's two best Mideast friends and agreed to the leapfrog after the shah and King Faisal assured America of an uninterrupted oil supply. However, they didn't mention at what price.

The 1971 gulf producers meeting in Teheran increased the gulf benchmark price 35¢. Before venturing to the next round in Tripoli, the Americans secretly agreed to create a "Libyan Safety Net" to supply each other with crude oil at a discount if Qadaffi threatened to cut a company's production or nationalize one of them. Qadaffi scared the Western oilmen without verbal rants or threats of nationalization. The Mediterranean producers increased the price from $2.55 to $3.45, a 90¢ boost.

Crude-oil prices jumped again after the U.S. dollar was devalued against gold in February 1973. Mideast gulf prices that had hovered around $1.80 for years had skyrocketed more than 60 percent, and Europe suffered an 80-percent increase from Mediterranean crude-oil increase. Meanwhile, the world reeled from the inflationary shock. In America, Nixon froze prices and wages and initiated price controls on everything.

Chapter Seventeen
The American Fiasco

POLITICIANS & OTHER SCOUNDRELS

In 1973 America was mired in the unpopular Vietnam War and faced uncontrollable inflation. Oil had been a dirty word since a Union Oil Company platform blowout off the coast of Santa Barbara, California, in January 1969. Headlines claiming three million gallons of oil spilled were accompanied by pictures of pelicans trapped in the goo and black slimy beaches and raised the public's ire against the oil companies. The press and environmentalists followed the worst-sounding scenario, rather than an oilman's measurement of 70,000 barrels. The Interior Department later calculated that the spill was closer to 675,000 gallons, but only 16,000 barrels if you are an oilman.

The antioil spill frenzy stymied the development of Alaska's 1967 North Slope oil discovery, the biggest oil strike in U.S. history. Congress did nothing to encourage domestic oil production despite warnings from the Interior Department and petroleum industry that America had reached its peak of production of 11.3 million barrels a day in 1970 and production would decline in the future. Unlike the Interior Department's previous dire predictions, this time they were right. The sure sign the country was running out of oil arrived in March 1971 when the Texas Railroad Commission announced it no longer had to enforce market-demand prorationing to maintain crude-oil prices.

It was politically correct to claim that the oil companies had plenty of oil and oppose the Trans-Alaska Pipeline. Alaska should remain pristine, and oil was nasty glop that screwed up the environment. The prize for vitriolic politics went to the ranking Republican on the House Interior Committee, John P. Saylor of Pennsylvania. Saylor, the former president of Ringling Bros. and Barnum & Bailey Circus, turned the hearings into a circus when he heard that the Trans-Alaska Pipeline had purchased Japanese steel pipe for the 789-mile pipeline instead of buying pipe from Pennsylvania steel companies at a far higher price. Saylor delayed the pipeline authorization hearings for two years.

But the biggest holdup was caused by the Democrat chairman of the Senate Interior Committee, Henry "Scoop" Jackson of Washington. Wanting the environmentalists' vote, he pushed granting the 40,000 Alaska natives 40 million acres of land for their subsistence lifestyle and give Alaska 90 percent of the federal government royalty on oil. The largess allotted 1,000 acres for every native Alaskan man, woman, and child and allowed the state of Alaska to hand out checks to its rugged independent citizens instead of paying state income taxes. In October 2002, every Alaskan received $1,540 just for being an Alaskan.

President Richard Nixon abandoned the oil-import quota system under the MOIP and instituted import fees that only served to force oil prices higher. To combat inflation, a liberal, Democrat-controlled Congress passed the Economic Stabilization Act. Then the conservative Republican president did the unthinkable—he agreed and imposed price controls. Economists, environmentalists, and politicians bitterly debated whether Big Oil was gouging the consumers, if there really was an "energy crisis," Saudi Arabia's friendship, and the need to drill for oil in Alaska. (Sound familiar? It should. It's been going on for 100 years.)

By August 1973, inflation and panic buying by Americans, Europeans, and the cash-rich Japanese pushed crude oil over the OPEC's Teheran and Tripoli prices. OPEC scheduled negotiations in October. When the oil companies arrived in Vienna, the OPEC Arabs asked, "Have you heard the good news? . . . We've invaded Israel!" The gulf states demanded a $6-a-barrel price. The oil company negotiators wet their pants. Their instructions were not to offer more than a 60¢ increase, and the gulf producers wanted a bump of $3. After a week of futile talking and it appeared that the Arabs might win the war, the Saudi Arabia, Kuwait, Iran, Iraq, U.A.E., and Qatar delegates took a plane to Kuwait and announced over the radio that the gulf price was $5.11 a barrel. On closer inspection, the price was $5.119. They had taken a page from the oil companies and added a teeny 9/10¢.

On October 19, Nixon announced $2.2 million in military aid was being flown to Israel. The next day, the pissed-off Arabs, led by our pal Saudi Arabia and the loony Libyans, called for an Arab embargo against the United States and all nations supporting Israel and a 5-percent production cutback each month until "the total evacuation of Israeli forces from all Arab territory occupied during the June 1967 war is completed and the legitimate rights of the Palestinian people are restored."

By December, panic forced an auction price of Iranian crude at $17.04 a barrel, and Nigeria flimflammed a Japanese firm into paying $22.60. Beggar European nations and Japan issued statements in support of the Arabs and Palestinians in order to obtain oil. It was time for another OPEC meeting in Tehran, however the oil companies weren't invited. America's friend, the shah, suggested a price of $11.65 effective January 1, 1974. The shah figured he needed $7 of the total for his military buildup and national budget, but offered the rational explanation that his computations were based on the cost of other forms of energy, such as coal and natural gas. OPEC agreed it was the perfect price to stifle the use and development of alternate fuels, but would not disrupt the industrial nations' economies to the extent they couldn't afford the price. In other words, greedy OPEC said the hell with the poor Third World nations. To prove they were thinking of the small nations and weren't Arab dominated, OPEC admitted tiny Gabon and Ecuador as members.[62]

Kissinger's famous shuttle diplomacy didn't stop the embargo against the United States until May 1974. By then, Nixon had secretly ordered the printing of gas-rationing stamps and handed the "energy crisis" to his underlings because he was too busy battling the Watergate scandal. Of course, Nixon and Kissinger could not be blamed for the Arab oil embargo. In masterful doublespeak, Kissinger rationalized,

---

[62] African Gabon and Latin American Ecuador had no business in OPEC. Both quit because of the high dues to maintain the OPEC bureaucracy. They just missed listing in Chart 17:1. Gabon's reserves would have ranked it thirty-first (2,499,000 thousand barrels); and Ecuador's reserves of (2,115,000 thousand barrels) would have placed it thirty-second. Together they hold less than 0.5 percent of the world's oil reserves.

207

"No one believed that military urgency prevented us from exploring the method of resupplying Israel that would least jeopardize our interests in the Arab world and the dependence of the industrial world on imported oil." (Henry, we supplied arms to their enemy!)

Between February 14, 1970, and January 1, 1974, crude-oil prices jumped almost 550 percent! Inflation crippled the United States economy and devastated the development of many Third World nations for decades. Crude oil would soar to $40 during the Iran/Iraq War in the 1980s and the Gulf War in 1991.

Unlearned Lessons & Other Foolishness

The Seven Sisters no longer controlled the world's oil supply, although they still dominated the distribution, marketing, and technology. All OPEC and Mideast oil concessions were nationalized in some fashion. The Mideast nations continue to attempt to manage the world's crude-oil production for their economic and political benefit and have used oil as a weapon of war. A glance at Chart 17:1 ranking oil reserves by nation discloses that America has few friends near the top. Iraq, Iran, and Libya, with more than 25 percent of the world's reserves, are not America's best friends; China is antagonistic to U.S. interests; and Venezuela is anti-American and its president, Hugo Chavez, is a left-wing thug. Venezuela, however, depends on the American market through its government-owned subsidiary, Citgo. Saudi Arabia, blessed with more than 25 percent of the world's oil reserves, is a question mark according to the political pundits because of the potential instability of the al-Saud monarchy and its support of terrorists. With more than 66 percent of the world's reserves in the unstable Mideast historians love to call a "tinder box," it can only be deemed unreliable. We went to war against Iraq in 1991 after it invaded Kuwait and threatened Saudi Arabia; then we removed Saddam Hussein from power in 2003.

One disturbing statistic is set out in bold in Chart 17:1—United States reserves are only 2 percent of the world total. A second factor not included should be noted in bold—**the United States consumes 26 percent of the world's oil production!** In response to the economists who point out that the United States produces more than 25 percent of the world's goods, the answer is that we won't be able to maintain the production and our high standard of living unless we have secure sources of oil or other forms of energy.

Chart 17:1—Estimated Principal World Oil
Reserves & Production

January 1, 2002
(1,000 barrels)

Rank/Nation	Reserves	Production (2001 bpd)	Notes
1 Saudi Arabia	259,250,000	6,470	OPEC/Arab/Muslim
2 Iraq	112,500,000	1,960	OPEC/Arab/Muslim
3 U.A.E.	97,800,000	1,830	OPEC/Arab/Muslim
4 Kuwait	94,000,000	1,440	OPEC/Arab/Muslim
5 Iran	89,700,000	3,130	OPEC/Muslim
6 Venezuela	77,685,000	2,830	OPEC
7 Russia	48,573,000	6,895	[1]
8 Libya	29,500,000	1,360	OPEC/Arab/Muslim
9 Mexico	26,941,000	3,100	[1]
10 China	24,000,000	3,295	
10 Nigeria	24,000,000	2,100	OPEC/Muslim-50 percent
12 United States	**22,045,000**	**5,810**	**2 percent of world's reserves**
13 Qatar	13,207,000	374	OPEC/Arab/Muslim
14 Norway	9,447,000	3,133	[1]
15 Algeria	9,200,000	820	OPEC/Arab/Muslim
16 Brazil	8,464,744	1,210	
17 Oman	5,506,000	960	[1]/Arab/Muslim
18 Kazakhstan	5,417,000	787	Muslim-50 percent
19 Angola	5,412,000	685	
20 Indonesia	5,000,000	1,200	OPEC/Muslim-87 percent
20 Neutral Zone	5,000,000	540	OPEC/Arab/Muslim [2]
22 United Kingdom	4,930,000	2,260	
23 Canada	4,858,000	2,040	
24 India	4,840,150	640	
25 Yemen	4,000,000	350	Arab/Muslim
26 Australia	3,500,000	640	
27 Malaysia	3,000,000	720	Muslim-60 percent
28 Argentina	2,973,700	760	
29 Egypt	2,947,560	755	Arab/Muslim
30 Syria	2,500,000	515	Arab/Muslim
Total World	**1,031,553,477**	**63,695**	
Total OPEC	**818,842,000**	**24,255**	**79.4 percent of Reserves**
Total Mideast	**685,592,290**	**17,872**	**66.5 percent of Reserves**

[1] Nations that often join OPEC production curtailments.
[2] The Neutral Zone is owned fifty-fifty by Saudi Arabia and Kuwait.

Oil & Gas Journal (December 24, 2001).

The United States imports 58 percent of its petroleum needs and bears much of the blame for the higher prices on the world market reflected on the New York Mercantile Exchange. Seldom mentioned, out of 11 million barrels of petroleum imported each day, 20 percent is petroleum products, including gasoline. American refineries are operating at 95-percent capacity, which is close to full capacity due to turnarounds and maintenance shutdowns, and we cannot refine our domestic needs. No new refineries have been constructed in twenty years because of the cost and environmental restraints.

To many nations, American consumers and politicians are greedy scoundrels for hogging the world's oil, a depletable invaluable world asset, and are a major factor in driving up the price. America must conserve *and* develop its oil to the extent feasible, not only for the bugaboo of "national security," but America's balance of payments. *Imported petroleum drained more than $100 billion from America's balance of payments in 2002.* It is not a question of development versus the environment or petroleum versus conservation. *American must develop all its petroleum resources, protect the environment, and conserve its use of petroleum and other energy resources . . . NOW, before it's too late!*

We have forgotten the price volatility of the 1970s, 1980s, and 1990s during the Arab embargo and years of Mideast instability. Crude oil hit $39.99 a barrel before we went to war against Saddam Hussein in 2003. The fiasco over the construction of the Trans-Alaska Pipeline was debated in Congress for six years and authorization was not passed until after the Yom Kippur War and Arab embargo in 1973. Oil cannot be turned on like your kitchen faucet. The pipeline's construction wasn't completed until June 1977, which finally allowed Alaska's North Slope oil to flow through the pipeline—nine and one-half years after its oil was discovered and far too late to help during the 1973 embargo. The North Slope oil reached its peak production of 2 million barrels a day in 1988 and, as in the case of all oil fields, began to decline. It now only produces slightly in excess of 900,000 barrels a day.[63]

Politics change swiftly in the Mideast. On New Year's Eve, December 31, 1977, President Jimmy Carter toasted the shah of Iran. "Iran under the great leadership of the shah is an island of stability in

---

[63] Energy Information Administration, Department of Energy. *www.eia.doe.gov.* (October 20, 2002).

one of the more troubled areas of the world. This is a great tribute to you, Your Majesty, and to your leadership, and to the respect, admiration, and love which your people give to you." A year later, the shah had to flee Iran, and the nation was taken over by Islamic radicals. Three years later, Ronald Reagan soundly defeated Carter for reelection by voters cringing at CNN scenes of Iranian radicals storming the American embassy in Iran and holding Americans hostage for 444 days. Americans faced long gasoline lines, $40-a-barrel crude oil, and 21-percent interest rates that destroyed the chance of a couple obtaining a mortgage on their dream house.

When Carter took office in 1976, the price of crude oil was less than $13 a barrel. When he left, it had reached $40 due to the Iranian revolution and Iraq/Iran War, an increase of 325 percent. Carter had little choice but to start phasing out Nixon's price controls that would be discontinued under Reagan. An impotent Carter could only announce a freeze of Iran's assets in the United States and order a futile embargo on Iranian oil entering the United States. The world laughed at Carter's declaring the energy crisis "the moral equivalent of war" and telling Americans to lower their thermostats to sixty-five degrees. The Ayatollah Khomeini had already announced that no Iranian oil would go to the American Satan. The United States still employs sanctions on Iran and Libya that are the equivalent of bailing out the *Titanic* with a leaking teacup. The only result of America's arrogant unilateral sanctions is to prevent American companies from obtaining concessions around the world while Russians, French, and other nations obtained Iraqi oil concessions. It should not have come as a surprise when Russia and France, which are owed billions by Iraq for arms supplied Iraq and have the choice oil concessions in Iraq, did not support the United States in is efforts to disarm Saddam Hussein of weapons of mass destruction in 2003.

It's impossible to determine when or where the next "oil crisis" will occur or if it will be caused by a rogue nation. Since September 11, 2001, Americans must be concerned about terrorists. Will it be too late because we have not developed the oil resources in Alaska or the Outer Continental Shelf off California and failed to conserve and cut down on our use of oil? California, the nation's largest gasoline consumer, banned oil exploration in its coastal waters in 1995 and is the first to bitch during an "energy crisis." When the next crisis occurs, don't believe the self-serving statements or finger pointing by politicians at congressional hearings why the price of gasoline at the pump hit $3. They will blame it on Big Oil (which isn't as big as it once was), the Arabs, and the other political party. *The scoundrels are the partisan politicians who refuse to compromise to develop and conserve the oil AND protect our environment and economy at the same time.*

PETROLEUM LIES, DAMN LIES & STATISTICS AND PUNDIT'S PROGNOSTICATIONS

Analyzing petroleum statistics is like counting worms in knee-deep mud. It's impossible to arrive at definite answers. Chart 17:1 was taken from the *Oil & Gas Journal*, a highly reputable publication. Different figures are found in *World Oil*, another respected magazine, because it includes natural gas liquids (NGLs), condensates produced with oil, and estimated processing gains. The *Oil & Gas Journal* follows the Department of Energy's Energy Information Administration method of not including NGLs, etc. In *World Oil* (February 2002), United States and Saudi Arabian production are reported 8.5 and 7.25 million barrels a day respectively. It also listed OPEC and the world production at 28.67 and 76.53 million barrels a day respectively. *World Oil* follows the Paris-based International Energy Agency practice of estimating NGLs, etc., because OPEC does not.

Reserves are often inflated, particularly by OPEC that revised its estimates to boost their quotas. Reserve estimates are classified proven, probable, or possible (the latter means "we hope its down there"). Seldom mentioned is the geologist's probability of accuracy that might range 5, 50, or 95 percent.

As for the pundits and the news media, ask where they get their figures. Most, if not all, OPEC nations cheat, which makes their figures unreliable. The petroleum industry estimates that OPEC's agreed reduction of production to raise crude-oil prices is exceeded by between 1.0 to 2.5 million barrels a day.

Read with a jaundiced eye a pundit's theory or an article complaining that gasoline prices are "up X percent from last year" or "double compared to 19XX." They generally don't tell you if it was during an economic slowdown, an OPEC cutback, one of California's so-called "energy crises," or discount day at their Texaco station.

After searching for the truth in writing this book, I no longer believe columnists, who on any given day might pontificate on a peace solution in the Mideast, the effect of oil pipelines on the sex life of the caribou and whether Al Gore lost the 2000 election because of Clinton's sexcapade with Monica Lewinsky. Alas, I recently spotted errors and bias against oil companies in a magazine

I've read since a child in the 1930s to ogle the pictures of bare-breasted native women—*National Geographic*.

Should you believe everything in this book?

NO! Check it out, and form your own opinion. Many political analysts and economists believe another major oil crisis is unlikely and rationally explain why Saudi Arabia and other Mideast oil producers cannot afford to boycott the United States or withhold their crude oil from the market for an extended period. They also believe the United States can obtain its oil requirements from Russia and other nations outside the Mideast. And I agree with them. But only to a point. No one can predict what another Saddam Hussein or the North Korea's leader with a bad haircut will do. And don't forget Iran that harbors and funds terrorists. Terrorists are well aware that America's reliance on imported oil will top 60 percent in two years, and oil terminals might be their next targets. Nixon's position on Israel and Palestine invited the 1973 Arab oil embargo. In 1975 the United Nations General Assembly passed a resolution proclaiming "Zionism is a form of racism and discrimination" by a vote of 75 to 35, with 32 abstentions, proving that nations are at the mercy of oil. War or terrorism can disrupt the unstable Mideast. The real questions are: *Where does the United States obtain its oil and at what price in dollars and in blackmail of its integrity? Remember: The world is full of scoundrels.*

CHAPTER EIGHTEEN
THE MOST DESPICABLE SCOUNDREL AWARD

WHAT'S IN A NAME?

That which we call a scoundrel by any other name would smell as rotten.[64] Born in 1898, Armand Hammer was named after the symbol of the Socialist Labor Party by his father, Dr. Julius Hammer. Julius was a founder of the U.S. Communist Labor Party and carried membership card number one. As a capitalist, Armand Hammer flew the arm-and-hammer emblem on his yacht and was labeled the "Pimp of the Politburo" by the American press corps in Moscow.

Church & Dwight Company, the manufacturer of Arm & Hammer baking soda for more than 135 years, fought Armand Hammer's takeover attempt and issued statements that he was not connected with the company. However, when Hammer was CEO of Occidental Petroleum Corporation, it held a 5.4-percent interest in the Church & Dwight Company to satisfy his egomania.

MY FRIEND LENIN

As a twenty-one-year-old, second-year Columbia medical student, Armand Hammer worked in his father's clinic even though not legally qualified nor permitted to practice medicine. Julius was often too busy running Allied Drug and Chemical Company to care for his patients. Allied Drug's primary business was illegally shipping prod-

---

[64] Stolen from William Shakespeare's *Romeo and Juliet*. Having dealt with Armand Hammer, the author altered the Bard's words for the sake of truth. After all, "Truth is truth / To the end of reck'ning." *Measure for Measure*.

ucts to Moscow through Latvia that were banned for export to Russia under U.S. law. Armand performed an illegal abortion on a woman who died, but Julius took the three-year manslaughter rap for his son. With the father in Sing Sing, the Soviets insisted Allied Drug send an agent to Moscow.

As travel to Russia required State Department approval in 1921, Harry Hammer, Armand's half-brother and acting president of Allied Drug, requested a passport for Armand to go to England, France, Norway, Sweden, and Holland to purchase wine and perfume, products Allied Drug didn't sell. Before permitting him to disembark in England, British intelligence questioned him for two days. They had been tipped off by J. Edgar Hoover, who was tracking the Red Menace. Hoover knew that Armand had been a member of the Socialist Labor Party since he was eighteen. British intelligence lost track of him during his European deal-making with his Soviet contacts, allowing him to slip into Russia through Latvia.

Lenin was waiting with bait. His New Economic Policy needed an American front man. Hammer was the first American to be awarded a Soviet commercial concession, an asbestos mine in the Urals that hadn't been operated in years and Lenin knew was worthless. The twenty-two-year-old medical school graduate with no business or mining experience was an ideal (idealist?) mark. Hammer later recalled, "If Lenin had asked me to jump out the window, I probably would have done it." Hammer handed over control of Allied Drug to the Soviets and returned to New York with $75,000 in cash for Soviet secret agents. It was the only time Armand Hammer met Lenin, but he would forever treasure Lenin's letter and autographed photo to "Comrade Armand Hammer" dated October 21, 1921, to back up his bragging that he was a "friend of Lenin."

Hammer was given many deals during the eight years in the twenties he lived in Russia. All were failures that drove the Hammer family to the brink of bankruptcy. Besides the disastrous asbestos mine concession, he lost money in furs, caviar, aircraft parts, and imported wheat. His profits, if any, had to be shared with Soviet fronts to finance spies and propaganda in the United States, including the *Daily Worker*, the Communist newspeak in America. In effect, Hammer laundered money for the Soviets and was flimflammed by them for his efforts. They even pushed the Hammer family bank in

Estonia used to launder money into bankruptcy.

The patsy's biggest claim to fame was a pencil concession the Communists awarded him in 1925 and confiscated in 1929 after Hammer had smuggled the pencil-making equipment into Russia from Germany and made it semiprofitable, if he didn't count what he lost accounting for laundered money. As the majority of pencil sales were to the slow-paying Soviet bureaucracy, he also had a cash-flow problem. After his pencil business was nationalized by Stalin, it was renamed the Sacco and Vanzetti Pencil Manufacturing Factory in honor of the anarchist murderers put to death in America in 1927 and made Communist martyrs.

After his father was released from jail, the entire Hammer family lived lavishly in Moscow by Russian standards with eight or nine servants because of the father's connections. In 1925 Armand married Olga Vadina, a nightclub singer of tearful Russian and Gypsy ballads, who presented him with his only son, Julian Armand Hammer. The Kremlin powers bailed Hammer out of insolvency, but left him with little. They had other uses for Armand in 1929.

Armand Hammer became a Russian art dealer in 1930. He set up the L'Ermitage Galleries in a run-down building on Fifty-third Street in New York to market Russian art before opening galleries in the Waldorf-Astoria and on Fifth Avenue. The Hammer Galleries sold the art through major department stores around the country, such as Lord & Taylor, Marshall Field's, and Gimbel's. But first, Hammer had to explain what he had been doing in the Communist Soviet Union for eight years and how the "capitalist" acquired Russian art. With the help of Walter Duranty, a *New York Times* Moscow correspondent his colleagues called "Stalin's apologist," Hammer "documented" his exploits in a fictional account, *The Quest of the Romanoff Treasure.* Duranty is best known for his Pulitzer Prize for documenting Stalin's five-year plans in 1932 that denied Stalin's slaughter and forced famine resulting in the death of five to ten million in the Ukraine. For years, the Ukrainians have demanded that the Pulitzer Prize be withdrawn because of its blatant lies, but the Pulitzer board and *New York Times* say it's too late.

The Hammer/Duranty fairy tale related how Hammer returned to Russia in 1921 after selling Allied Drug for more than $1 million to obtain wheat for the starving Russian peasants and, as a doctor, to fight a typhus epidemic. When Lenin heard of his humanitarian work, he offered valuable grain, tractor, fur, pencil, oil-drilling equipment, and other concessions to the idealistic doctor. And, when not toiling to save humanity and amassing a fortune, Hammer claimed he developed the hobby of collecting art treasures, including icons, paintings, priceless Fabergé eggs, and Romanoff tsar artifacts.

The media gobbled up *The Quest of the Romanoff Treasure* as gospel, and the Soviets backed him up by allowing the Hammer Galleries to show the first major exhibition of Russian art in America. The ballyhoo afforded him entry to the worlds of Marjorie Merriweather Post and Malcolm Forbes, collectors of Fabergé Easter eggs and expensive Russian trinkets only the superrich can afford to flaunt on their mantles. The notoriety allowed him to send President Franklin D. Roosevelt a Fabergé music box in 1933 after Roosevelt announced the resumption of diplomatic relations with Soviet Russia, which should have raised FDR's suspicions.

Behind the facade, few of Hammer's art objects came from Romanoff palaces the Communists had looted except for Fabergé eggs and some baubles. Several critics panned his collection as second-rate icons and paintings, lackluster silver and jewelry, *Bibles* and Torah scrolls stolen from churches and synagogues, and "knickknacks." Several "masterpieces" were discovered to be forgeries. There was no end of the supply of books from the tsar's library—the Soviets had the tsar's bookplates and printing press. The artsy set loved it, and few critics were expert on Russian art. Hammer filled the vacuum with lectures on Russian paintings and the tsar's collections. During intermission, his wife, Olga (he called Baroness von Root), entertained the suckers with Russian love songs. Fabergé items were the big sellers. The Soviets manufactured whatever he needed with the tools and equipment looted from the Fabergé plant, and Armand and his brother, Victor, affixed the original confiscated Fabergé factory stamps to trinkets in the back room of the New York store.

The faux-wealthy capitalist and art connoisseur was driven in a Rolls-Royce to his gallery and office every day. The public didn't know he was actually working on a commission from the Soviet Commissariat of Foreign Trade and his "personal collection of the riches of the late tsar" was shipped on consignment. Hammer funneled money back to Moscow through his Hammer Cooperage Company, which purchased oak staves from Russia for beer barrels to sell to breweries, including Anheuser-Busch and a Mafia-controlled Brooklyn brewery. As neither Hammer nor the Communists understood the free market system and fluctuating commodity prices, there were financial problems, and Hammer was often shortchanged by the Soviets.

Hammer's financial problems were solved with a $75,000 low-interest loan from Roosevelt's Reconstruction Finance Corporation. Hence, the RFC financed Hammer's laundering of money for Soviet espionage on America. The FBI, still watching him, was suspicious. Why was he paying far more than the market price for Russian barrel staves during the height of the Great Depression? And why were some of Hammer's barrels shipped to Mexico where they wound up being used to store and transport oil for Germany when Stalin and Hitler were pals?

HAMMERISMS

"Friends are worthless unless they can be used. When they are no longer useful, they are not worth having."

"The only reason I give is to get."

"My ideas are beyond the comprehension of ordinary mortals. The brilliance of my mind can only be described as dazzling. Even I'm impressed by it."

"I don't give a damn about environmental problems . . ." (One of Occidental Petroleum's subsidiaries was the Hooker Chemical Company that caused the infamous Love Canal environmental disaster.)

"Those who insist on telling the truth never have any future. Sometimes the only way to build a future is to build it on lies."

A Capitalist's Search for Love, Social Standing, and Political Contacts

Angela Carey Zevley was a wealthy, thirty-five-year-old divorcée socialite who drank too much. After meeting her at a cocktail party in 1938, Armand moved into her New Jersey home and started managing her business affairs. Not acceptable in New York society and interfering with his new lifestyle, his wife and son, Olga and Julian, were shipped to upstate New York for the fresh air. Soon Hammer was entertaining high society and people who could advance his interests in Angela's palatial house and on his corporate yacht. Most astounding to those who knew him, he no longer wore baggy suits that looked like he had slept in them, but donned evening dress and tailored suits.

Before long, Hammer expanded Angela's estate to more than 400 acres, and the country squire and art dealer was advising her on breeding cattle. In 1943 he divorced Olga and married Angela. Between his hectic business interests and her drinking and refusal to have children, the marriage was in name only. Angela didn't like the way he did business. He was selling her cattle and pocketing the money. Her reputation was also at stake. The American Aberdeen Angus Breeders' Association threatened to throw him out because of lawsuits over fraudulent pedigrees and injecting cattle with water to make them appear fatter and healthier. He moved quickly to settle the claims and separate his cattle operation from Angela's to avoid bad publicity. His wealthy partners and politicians he had lured into the cattle-breeding business might start asking embarrassing questions, including Senator Albert A. Gore Sr., Democrat of Tennessee.

After Angela threw him out of her house, the fifty-five-year-old "millionaire" dazzled twenty-nine-year-old Bettye Jane Murphy, a restaurant hostess, with the promise of marriage after his divorce from Angela was final, *if she bore him children*. During a romantic cruise on his yacht, he tied it up to the pier at Angela's estate and used his key to enter her house. He had bugged her phone and knew she was ill in the hospital. Hammer emerged with paintings and Angela's jewelry he said she no longer deserved and gave Bettye a trinket.

The nasty divorce battle between a socialite and millionaire art dealer hit the society pages and was read by Frances Barrett Tolman, a wealthy widow who had met Hammer at his art gallery years earlier. Frances dropped him a note of sympathy. Hammer checked her Dun and Bradstreet rating and couldn't renew their acquaintance fast enough. He needed $50,000 to bail Julian out of jail. His unstable son had been charged with murder.[65] After Hammer promised to marry Frances, she loaned him $50,000. The next day he put Bettye on a plane to Los Angeles to deliver the cash to Julian's lawyer. A few weeks later, he told a four-months-pregnant Bettye, who had agreed to have his child, that his plans had changed. He was marrying Frances, but he would set up Bettye and the child in Mexico with a home and a nice income for the rest of their lives if she and the child never revealed he

---

[65] Julian's case never went to trial. The charges were dropped for lack of evidence. The only witness was Julian's wife, who could not be forced to testify against her husband, and the Los Angeles district attorney claimed he couldn't prove Julian did not kill the man in self-defense.

was the father. Bettye Murphy, without a job and a nice Irish Catholic girl, couldn't even think of abortion. It was too late anyway.

Armand and Angela's divorce was made final on January 19, 1956. He married Frances six days later. Angela only squeezed a small cash settlement and $1,000-a-month alimony out of the millionaire. Armand's yacht, plane, art collection, and major assets were held in the names of his corporations and untouchable, a practice he would follow for the rest of his life. The "millionaire's" tax returns showed he hadn't earned more than $27,000 a year for the past five years.

On May 15, 1956, his daughter was born. He insisted Bettye name her Victoria after his grandmother. Armand visited Bettye and Victoria a few weeks later, but he only stayed for one hour. A week before he died, Hammer disinherited Bettye and Victoria by striking them from his will.

MIXING POLITICS AND BUSINESS

One of Hammer's first key political contacts was Representative James "Jimmy" Roosevelt, Democrat of California and FDR's oldest son. Hammer loaned Jimmy money when he was heavily in debt and invested in his insurance company as a silent partner. It was also an investment in a congressman. From FDR's always broke son, Elliott, Hammer bought back the Fabergé music box that Elliott inherited from his father. In 1952 Hammer invested in the Roosevelt family after the president's death by purchasing the Roosevelts' famous summer home, Campobello, from Elliott at the fire-sale price of $5,000.

President Roosevelt maintained a shield between him and his sons' leech friends. Hammer's access to FDR's White House came from a little-known Democrat senator from Utah, William H. King, whom he had met when King was a member of a congressional delegation to Moscow in the 1920s. In 1940 King arranged a meeting for Hammer to discuss his ideas for foreign aid to Great Britain with Roosevelt. There was nothing sinister or out of the ordinary about a senator requesting a meeting with the president for a wealthy political backer then or today. Hammer was a major contributor to Roosevelt's 1938 reelection campaign, including personally paying for radio commercials. He was also promoting foreign aid to Britain with full-page newspaper advertisements and contributing to pro-British aid organizations during Britain's fight for survival against Nazi

Germany. Roosevelt turned him over to his closest friend, Secretary of Commerce Harry Hopkins, who met with Hammer on several occasions. A few months later, Roosevelt announced his Lend-Lease Plan to Britain, which would be extended to Russia.

Hammer's *five-minute meeting* with Roosevelt gave him the chutzpah to claim he was "FDR's unofficial Lend-Lease consultant" for the rest of his life although he never met Roosevelt again. The question remains unanswered where Hammer obtained the money for his political contributions and the pro-British aid campaign that also helped Russia obtain Lend-Lease munitions and foodstuffs. Since the late 1930s, his companies barely eked out profits. World War II wiped out his Russian barrel staves and art imports businesses, and he personally didn't have the funds.

The capitalist's first successful venture came through Harry Hopkins when he purchased two closed distilleries during World War II. Hopkins sent him to FDR's uncle, Frederic Delano, a member of the War Production Board. The board approved Hammer's application to distill booze instead of industrial alcohol for the war effort. The Reconstruction Finance Corporation lent him the money to open a distillery in New Hampshire, even though many distilleries had closed because of wartime controls over alcohol, including the two distilleries he had bought at going-out-of-business prices. Hammer began by producing rotgut whiskey, but booze was expensive and the profits astronomical during the war, which allowed him to buy out name brands, like J. W. Dant, and form United Distillers.

As a major employer in New Hampshire, where his principal distillery was located, Hammer contributed to local politicians, regardless of political persuasion. One of his best political investments was Senator Styles Bridges, a conservative Republican and the antithesis of the liberal Democrat politicians that Hammer bragged were "in his pocket," such as Albert Gore Sr. and Jimmy Roosevelt.

THE PSEUDO OILMAN

After Hammer's honeymoon in romantic Paris and Venice with Frances, he moved into her home in Los Angeles that she and her first husband had purchased from Oleg Cassini and his actress wife, Gene Tierney, and managed her business affairs, as he had done with Angela. He also borrowed money from her to bail out of debt his

United Distillers and Hammer Galleries and took flyers with their "joint money" in diverse companies. What appeared to be the worst gamble was Occidental Petroleum Corporation. Occidental was trading on the Los Angeles Stock Exchange at 18¢ a share, it only had 600,000 outstanding shares, and it hadn't made a profit in years—an ideal company to manipulate.

On an inside tip from a member of the Federal Trade Commission, Hammer persuaded Occidental's board to diversify and invest $100,000 in a syndicate to purchase the Mutual Broadcasting System with the argument that he and Frances were each investing $53,000. The syndicate purchased Mutual Broadcasting for $650,000 and made Hammer its chairman. Hammer sold it for $2 million one year later. Within a year, the purchaser went to jail for stock fraud, and Mutual Broadcasting filed for bankruptcy.

By 1957, the man who admitted he'd never seen an oil derrick before taking over Occidental was chairman of its board. His periodic announcements that Occidental made potential oil, iron ore, and gold discoveries that never panned out raised the stock value fourfold. Occidental did hit oil, not bonanzas, but sizable strikes that made Occidental a small respectable oil company by 1961. However, Hammer was thinking of bigger plays and Mother Russia.

His political contacts couldn't help him when he decided to visit Moscow. Although a large contributor to President John F. Kennedy's 1960 campaign, he couldn't get an appointment with Kennedy or his blessing for Hammer's "trade mission." The best Senator Gore could do was get him an autographed picture of JFK (which Gore could have obtained for any Tennessee farmer or your aunt from Nashville) and a meeting with the secretary of commerce, Luther Hodges. Hodges gave Hammer a pat on the back and told him he would be glad to hear his report on Soviet business conditions when he returned. The commerce secretary winced when later handed the FBI's file on Hammer's suspicious Communist past.

Upon arriving in Moscow, Hammer was greeted by the American Embassy's economic affairs counselor (translation: CIA). The CIA operative wet his pants when Hammer insisted he set up a meeting with Anastas Mikoyan, the Soviet deputy prime minister. The CIA was unaware that Mikoyan was the former apparatchik who oversaw Hammer's concessions, art business, and money laundering more than thirty years earlier. Mikoyan sent his personal limousine for his old comrade. Two days later, Hammer's next appointment at the Kremlin was with Nikita Khrushchev, the first secretary of the Communist Party of the Soviet Union.

Khrushchev let it be known that Hammer was the Soviet's point man on foreign trade by sending Armand and Frances to London in a Aeroflot jet in which they were the only passengers. Hammer delivered Khrushchev's trade message to Secretary of Commerce Hodges. Khrushchev wanted to increase trade and the United States to issue trade credits—the good old American system of buy today and pay whenever in slave-labor goods. Hammer didn't mention that part of the trade package was for Occidental to finance and manufacture superphosphoric acid to export to Russia for conversion into phosphate fertilizers that Russia desperately needed.

Occidental's board of directors was taken aback with Hammer's grandiose scheme to purchase chemical companies capable of manufacturing superphosphoric acid to export to Russia as a base for making fertilizers, a major sulfur producer, and a phosphate mine primarily with Occidental stock. However, they had to agree. Locked in Hammer's desk were undated letters of resignation from all board members to assure their support.[66] Within eighteen months, Occidental evolved from a small oil company into primarily a chemical and fertilizer producer. Wall Street, on the hype that the brilliant Dr. Hammer was an international business whiz, sent Occidental's stock soaring. But Hammer had a problem his conceived genius and political connections couldn't solve. There wasn't an orchid's chance of blooming in a Kremlin window box during a Russian winter that he could obtain a license to export fertilizer to the Soviet bloc, and it would be many years before any White House occupant would consider export licenses for strategic materials to Russia.

President Kennedy refused Hammer's repeated requests for an appointment. Their only meeting was an accidental encounter in a White House corridor. Nevertheless, Hammer would forever claim "JFK appointed me his unofficial roving economics envoy" during their two-minute chance conversation.

---

[66] The board members' undated letters of resignation were a violation of the Security and Exchange Commission's disclosure regulations to protect the board's independence. The practice was uncovered by the SEC and the subject of a consent decree, but Hammer continued it on a selective basis.

President Lyndon Johnson avoided meeting Hammer until after he announced he would not run for reelection. Hammer proudly displayed the photo of him and LBJ in the Oval Office he received in the mail a week later. Anyone who has been part of the Washington political scene for six months would recognize the typewritten "To: Dr. Armand Hammer with best wishes," and LBJ's too, too perfect signature as the work of a White House clerk and a signature machine. Such mementos are sent out every day in response to friendly congressmen's requests, political contributors, and party hacks.

Only after Hammer contributed $25,000 for an unknown purpose to Johnson, who was not running for reelection, was Hammer invited to LBJ's Texas ranch. The ploy earned him the ear of Marvin Watson, Johnson's White House chief of staff, who Hammer made Occidental's vice president of government relations. To add a Republican to Occidental's Washington lobbying office after Richard Nixon was elected president, he hired Tim Babcock, former Republican governor of Montana and a friend of Nixon, as a vice president with Watson.

CHAPTER NINETEEN
BIG-TIME OPERATOR

LIBYA

Armand Hammer was never regarded as an oilman by the major oil companies. They considered him a promoter and not to be trusted. In 1961 Occidental's stock market value was only $10 million. There wasn't an international oilman who wasn't surprised (many chuckled) at the rumors the gadfly was planning to bid on the second round of Libyan oil concessions in 1965.

Hammer required a three-year lead time to determine whom to bribe to obtain the choice concessions. In many Mideastern and African countries, obtaining contracts and concessions requires a bidder to pay someone to find a person who can approach the right official to bribe (a friend of a friend who knows the cousin of an official or a prince). There are no guarantees any of the parties can be trusted, and bidders might have to pay "expenses" up front to prove how serious they are.

If a company is smart, it will not pay anything in advance without checking the contact's track record. Most people offering such services are sleazeballs and con men. Because oil profits cannot be determined at the onset and are hoped to be substantial, lump-sum payments are rare. Government officials and Saudi princes demanded a percentage they call "commissions" paid to Swiss bank accounts. That means you pay the *baksheesh* as a royalty for the length of the concession unless something happens to permit an oil company to weasel out of the deal. After all, bribery is immoral and illegal.

Doctor Hammer, as he insisted being called, floundered about

Europe looking for contacts and spreading cash for three years. Most middlemen scoffed at the idea that Occidental could compete. It was a dwarf compared to the Seven Sisters and the large independents operating in the Mideast. In 1965 Occidental had no major oil exploration and development experience, and a concession might cost five times the company's net worth of $45 million, *if* you believe Occidental's financial statements. The doctor had to overcome Occidental's shortcomings by bringing something unique to the table. He committed to build a fertilizer plant in Libya to make its land productive, the greater part of which lies within the barren Sahara Desert. To please King Idris, he promised to drill for water in the arid region where the king had been born. Water was a lot more important than oil to the people of the desert.

With time running out to submit a bid and aware his contacts were charlatans, Hammer looked for someone like himself—a nonoilman who could pull rabbits out of a hat. He was referred to Wendell Phillips, an American archeologist who had obtained one of the original Libyan concessions and a second concession in Oman with shell oil companies visible only on paper. Phillips introduced him to two "facilitators." The first, Hans-Albert Kunz, was a Swiss food caterer who also provided visas, permits, and introductions and "fixed things." His cohort was Kemal Zade, the owner of a Russian restaurant in Germany.

Zade contacted the brother of Omar Shelhi, a member of the royal court and King Idris's closest confidant. Shelhi laughed. Occidental didn't qualify to bid, and the crazy doctor wanted the two prime parcels next to Exxon's producing concession. Fourteen major oil companies planned to tender bids on the lands. But Shelhi changed his mind upon hearing the amount of *baksheesh*—an unheard of $2.8 million up front for obtaining the concession plus a 3-percent royalty on the price of the oil. It took Shelhi eighteen months after the bids were submitted to swing the deal. In February 1967, Occidental was awarded both concessions.

While waiting for Shelhi to pull strings in the palace, rumors of his exorbitant bribes, even by international petroleum industry standards of the time, were rampant, and Hammer could only hope they would not be uncovered. One matter that could cause serious problems was reports in the Arab press that he was Jewish and pro Israel.

He insisted Hammer was a Swedish name and joined the Community Unitarian Church of Santa Monica. For a $10,000 contribution, he received a letter from the minister attesting that the Unitarian attended church regularly.

In December 1967, Occidental struck an oil field estimated to contain three billion barrels of light, low-sulfur crude oil. Now Hammer had to make the Libyan oil field pay. Occidental was trading at more than $100 a share (up from 18¢ eleven years ago) in a soaring bull market that paid little attention to financial statements and corporate earnings. (Bull markets, like those of the late 1990s and 2000-01, should be called "Bulls——t" markets.) Occidental was cash and credit short. The $45-million company had to build a pipeline 135 miles to the Mediterranean at an estimated cost of $140 million— more than three times its net worth. Hammer made a deal with the construction giant, the Bechtel Corporation, to finance and build the pipeline out of future crude-oil sales that increased the costs to $153 million. Bechtel completed the pipeline in record time. By March 1968, Occidental's sweet, light Libyan crude oil was flowing to Europe and undercutting the Seven Sisters' prices.

Hammer, the self-proclaimed daring business genius, enjoyed Wall Street's laurels agreeing with the egomaniac's opinion of himself, although the Libyan oil field had yet to show a profit. The big-picture deal maker was never one to consider nitty-gritty costs and market fluctuations. Occidental and the other independents in Libya drove tanker charter costs up and crude-oil prices down by glutting the market. Occidental was $725 million in debt that had to be serviced. After Libyan royalties and taxes, Occidental earned 56¢ a barrel before paying the pipeline construction debt. Bechtel, experienced in building massive projects around the world, had made arrangements to assure payment. Hammer, a neophyte in the petroleum business, never worried about production and marketing costs, nor did he realize that the seemingly high prices of crude oil often meant only pennies-per-barrel profit or no cash flow until the drilling and completion costs were paid, the point oilmen call "payout." And with falling crude-oil prices, things looked bleak.

The first place Hammer looked to cut costs was the exorbitant 3-percent *baksheesh* deal he had made. Phillips's finder's fee share was .335 percent, but Phillips was too influential and couldn't be touched.

The balance went to Union Bank of Switzerland bank accounts of Kunz and Zade, who secretly transferred one-half to Omar Shelhi's Swiss bank account. Hammer told them the 2.665 percent was now based on Occidental's net after Libyan taxes and royalties, not on the crude-oil posted price that was higher than the discounted actual sales price, and they were only entitled to one-half what they had been receiving. Shelhi told him to pay up or the concession would be reviewed by the palace and subject to cancellation. Hammer paid up rather than face Shelhi's wrath.

According to Hammer, the obvious way to increase profits on a grand scale was to boost the current 600,000 barrels a day of Libyan production. Occidental geologists and petroleum engineers advised that they were producing at the maximum efficiency rate and any increase would deplete the field too fast and leave an excessive amount of crude oil unobtainable. Hammer committed an oilman's worst sin by ordering production increased to 800,000 barrels a day to pay Occidental's debts.

Another way to cut costs was to renege on his promises and renegotiate the terms of Occidental's concession. With the excuse of falling fertilizer prices, he advised the Libyan Council of Ministers that the construction of the ammonia fertilizer plant would be postponed until the market guaranteed Occidental a profit of $30 million over three years. He also delayed drilling for water in King Idris's tribal region until he was permitted to deduct the costs from the Libyan royalties and taxes. In other words, Hammer charged Libya for performing one of the conditions of Occidental's concession. The Libyan government could have drilled for the water cheaper out of the royalties and taxes. Occidental was inflating the costs on the $13-million project. Hammer never mentioned to Occidental's board of directors that the palace insiders barred Occidental from bidding on or participating in any future concessions.

About the time crude-oil production reached 800,000 barrels a day in August 1969, King Idris left on his summer vacation to Turkey along with Omar Shelhi and 400 pieces of luggage. It was a perfect time for Sub-Lt. Muammar al-Qaddafi to stage a coup and promote himself to colonel. There is no doubt that Qaddafi enjoyed putting the screws to Hammer and Occidental as described in Chapter 16.

The spelling of Qaddafi is as erratic as the man himself. The news media has transliterated it: Kadafi, Kaddafi, Khadafy, Qadhaafi, Qadhdhafi, Qathafi, Gadhafi, Gaddifi, and Ghadafy. The author follows the *New York Times* spelling. The pronunciation is simple. The first syllable is as if you are clearing your throat (Ga), and the last two syllables are pronounced "daffy." The root of his Bedouin name means "one who throws."

BUSINESS AS USUAL—HAMMER STYLE

With word of the bribes made public and Shelhi tried and sentenced to death in absentia for bribery and corruption, Hammer told Shelhi he no longer could pay him. Then he forced Kunz and Zade to reduce their *baksheesh*. The 2.665-percent payment would be based on the net receipts instead of the higher crude-oil posted price. Shelhi's one-half would be deposited in a special account in the Union Bank of Switzerland (UBS) for Hammer to use as bribes and in shady deals. When Hammer arrived back at headquarters, he did not tell Occidental's chief financial officer and controller about his private slush fund. Occidental's officers and board of directors did not learn about the UBS bank funds and similar accounts until shareholder lawsuits disclosed that Hammer had made illegal payments to officials in fourteen different foreign nations between 1969 and 1975.[67]

Hammer's penchant for secret funds, especially cash to give him a feeling of power, were the old man's aphrodisiac. Two secret off-the-books companies were OTAG, in Switzerland, and Oil Findal, in Luxembourg, both paper corporations. OTAG bought oil from an Occidental European subsidiary at 1 percent below the market price and sold it to a European utility at market price, then transferred the 1 percent to Oil Findal for deposit in another Swiss bank that would convert it to U.S. dollars and wire the cash to Los Angeles for placement in a safe-deposit box known only to Hammer and his adminis-

---

[67] It was not a crime under U.S. law to bribe a foreign government official until the passage of the Foreign Corrupt Practices Act of 1977 (FCPA). However, it was a violation of SEC regulations and a crime in the foreign country. The FCPA continues to place U.S. companies at a disadvantage in competing with foreign corporations in nations where bribery is a way of doing business. But there are ways of beating the system, although that doesn't mean you won't be caught. In 2003, Mobil Oil was indicted for funneling $67 million to the president of Kazakhstan and his oil minister.

trative assistant. The laundered money gave Hammer cash for bribes, including $3 million he spread to Venezuelan government officials to obtain an oil-service contract that was nationalized three years later.

During the 1960s and 1970s, four SEC investigations ended with Occidental being forced to sign consent decrees. The first SEC investigation involved Hammer personally writing press releases involving the discovery of "the largest iron-ore discovery in the western part of the United States" that shot up Occidental's stock. The SEC insisted that future press releases of company information be cleared with Occidental's lawyers, inside accountants, and its independent auditor, Arthur Anderson & Company. Anderson's lead auditor left two years later because of Hammer's continued chicanery. For the years 1969-1970, the SEC accused Occidental of inflating its net income by $13.8 million and releasing misleading information about its crude-oil and coal production. The shareholder suits were settled with Occidental paying $11 million. Arthur Anderson also had to contribute $1 million, an omen that the "Mr. Clean" of the accounting profession was no longer squeaky clean.

A SHAREHOLDER'S GIFT

A shareholder sent Armand Hammer a pillow embroidered: OCCIDENTAL PETROLEUM COMPANY —the Only *Fortune 500 Company Investigated by the SEC Four Times in Ten Years.*

Hammer couldn't resist the notoriety of entering the synthetic fuels development race with the likes of Exxon. He settled on the underground in-situ burning of oil shale method in the Cathedral Bluffs area of Colorado to construct a "multibillion dollar mine" in a partnership with Tenneco Incorporated. Without consulting Occidental's engineers, he told President Nixon's energy czar, William Simon, he would soon be producing oil from oil shale at a cost of $1.18 a barrel. Simon laughed after he left and said that Hammer was crazy or a con man, but whatever he was, he was getting millions in subsidies from the government. Occidental's accountants and lawyers, fearing another visit from the SEC after he publicly repeated the boast, asked Occidental's engineers to set him straight, a task not to be taken lightly. Employees who disagreed with Chairman

Hammer were generally fired the following day. Whatever was said, Hammer began upping the costs to $3 or $4 a barrel. Those who knew anything about the mining and refining of oil shale still shook their heads. He was either an optimistic nut or a con man.

Technical problems arose, as expected in the development of any new process costing billions, that served to widen the breach between Tenneco and Occidental. Hammer wasn't used to consulting his subordinates, never mind asking for the approval of a partner. After overcoming the Mine Safety and Health Administration's regulations banning open flames in underground gassy mines that were necessary to liquefy the oil shale in the mine, Hammer admitted the costs might rise to $18 or $20 a barrel. Several years later, the oil-shale mine project was abandoned. Crude oil was selling for $28 to $30 a barrel, and the best the in-situ project could do was produce oil at $44 a barrel. Occidental's write-off was around $1 or $2 billion, depending on whom you believe, assuming you can believe anyone. But, by then, Hammer was devoting his efforts to something bigger and more important.

RUSSIA

To Hammer, Nixon's Soviet détente policy meant the resurrection of his Russian fertilizer dream. It also required making political contributions to President Richard M. Nixon, a man he detested. As was his habit, he gave the 1972 Nixon campaign $100,000 in laundered cash from an off-the-books slush fund. After Nixon's Moscow summit meeting with Leonid Brezhnev, Hammer flew to Moscow. Upon his return, he announced a trade agreement that would solve America's oil and gas shortages. Not incidentally, Occidental's shares soared up 18 percent on the New York Stock Exchange. It fell to Occidental's executives to figure out to what Hammer had agreed. As it turned out, all Hammer and the Russians had done was agree to agree in the future and have their photos taken for the press.

Occidental's 1972 financial statements showed more than $2 billion in gross revenues, but only twenty-odd million in net profits. After listening to Hammer's pretentious plans, Occidental's executives thought he had lost his mind. He wanted to build several ammonia plants and a 600-mile-pipeline in Russia, a one-million-ton-a-year phosphate mine in Florida, and four tankers at a cost of more than $1 billion. Because of its lack of hard currency, Russia would pay for the fertilizer with natural gas to be delivered via a $4-billion pipeline between the interior of Siberia and Alaska. Unrelated to the fertilizer-for-gas swap was Hammer's fantasy to build a $100-million international trade center in Moscow that included a four-star hotel and Russia's first golf course. Occidental's chief financial officer faced the impossible task of telling Hammer the company couldn't afford it, ask how Occidental would earn profits, and question what Russia was putting up as its share. His question about the risk if Nixon's détente failed also went unanswered. He was fired the following morning, a risk Occidental officers faced because of their undated letters of resignation locked in Hammer's desk.

Hammer's personally negotiated final contract dropped the Siberian/Alaska gas pipeline. It had three strikes against it—the estimated cost had risen to more than $17 billion, environmentalists were holding up the Trans-Alaska Pipeline to bring oil from the Alaska North Slope and dimming the prospects of congressional approval, and no one believed it was possible to build a natural gas pipeline across the Bering Straits.

Hammer had to settle for the rejuvenation of his 1960s super-phosphoric acid and ammonia fertilizer exchange plan and his goal of a Moscow World Trade Center (the first building was to be named Hammer House). The start-up financing was solved when Nixon declared it was in the national interest to evidence détente and approved the first Export-Import Bank loans to a Communist nation. Occidental received $180 million for the fertilizer project and $35 million for the trade center. The unplanned and unexpected windfall balance was easily financed after the Yom Kippur War and Arab oil embargo. Oil prices spiraled through the clouds and provided international crude-oil producers, like Occidental, with revenues beyond their dreams . . . for a while.

The fertilizer deal was doomed from the beginning. The Russians didn't have the technical experience or facilities to handle the immense project and failed to meet construction deadlines. As when he imported barrel staves from Russia during the 1930s and made deals for his Libyan oil a few years earlier, Hammer didn't consider the free market's price fluctuations and the possibility that ammonia prices would drop down to the basement. Occidental's first superphosphoric acid deliveries were delayed until 1978. The following year the deal collapsed when Russia invaded Afghanistan and President Jimmy Carter embargoed exports to Russia. The massive billion-dollar plant only had one customer—the Soviets. Occidental's $1-billion-plus mine, plant, equipment, and tanker investments sat idle and lost tens of millions every month.

Hammer's $100,000 contribution to Carter's reelection campaign and flying to Russia and returning with Brezhnev's peace plan for Afghanistan failed to persuade Carter to lift the embargo. Brezhnev wanted five years to straighten out the pesky Afghans without U.S. interference, then Russia would pull out and leave it a better place.

Hammer feared Ronald Reagan's election. Reagan opposed détente and labeled the Soviet Union the "Evil Empire." Nevertheless, the polls in October 1980 projecting a Reagan landslide told him he had to make friends with the outspoken anticommunist conservative. Hammer paid for newspaper ads supporting Reagan. According to Reagan and the Secret Service, every time Reagan visited his Beverly Hills barbershop during the campaign, Hammer would be sitting in the next chair chatting about international trade.

The Reagan White House considered Hammer persona non grata. His phone calls to second-tier staff were not returned. Undaunted, he lavished contributions of Occidental funds on Nancy Reagan's White House redecorating plan and her favorite projects to get on the White House invitation list. But he had to read in the paper that Reagan ended the Soviet embargo that permitted Occidental to resume exporting to Russia. By then Occidental's loss on the fertilizer project had reached $400 million. The next day, he was on "Oxy One," Occidental's Boeing 727, flying to Moscow to take credit for influencing the lifting of the embargo, notwithstanding the newspaper stories and congressional endorsement that Reagan's purpose was to allow American farmers to sell grain to Russia during a Farm-Belt economic slump.

CHINA

Russia wasn't the only Communist nation Hammer attempted to use to impress the world. He became America's leading businessman in China when he announced he was building "the world's largest open pit coal mine in China" at his estimated cost of $240 million, which

Occidental engineers revised to $345 million. The mine in the barren interior required the Chinese government to construct roads, railroads, and housing for 17,000 mine workers. According to a laughing Occidental mining engineer, "They must have thought we were going to mine 15 million tons a year by pick and shovel with coolie labor. We don't need a tenth that number, but China has more manpower than it knows what to do with, and Hammer will agree with anything to make a deal."

Occidental executives couldn't complain, including Albert Gore Sr., president of Occidental's subsidiary, Island Creek Coal Company, since his defeat for reelection to the Senate. It's not known if he told Hammer that the price of coal was dropping and it would take two decades before Occidental could recover its capital investment. Possibly he didn't want to risk being fired from his $500,000-a-year position. As the mine costs escalated to $640 million in 1982, the price of coal sank lower. President Reagan's 1986 embargo of Libya forced Occidental to withdraw from its lucrative oil production and eliminated almost one-half of Occidental's total revenues.

The Egomaniac Image Maker

Hammer loved publicity more than money. His display of photos with presidents Johnson, Nixon, Carter, Reagan, and Bush; Soviet leaders Khrushchev, Brezhnev, and Gorbachev; and Chinese Chairman Deng were part of the sycophant's flamboyant style. He bragged that he was the only American to have been awarded the Soviet Union's Lenin Order of Friendship Among the Peoples, while behind his back people called him a Communist bastard and worse. Everything he did had to generate power and prestige. He portrayed himself as a lover of art, although critics panned his early collections as attempts to acquire artistic taste by volume. The Armand Hammer Museum of Art and Cultural Center, built primarily with Occidental's money, was created to show his wealth and culture. It also provided a reason to put freelance magazine writer and new mistress Martha Kaufman on Occidental's payroll. Martha traveled with him as his personal art curator and the museum's planning director. When Armand's wife, Frances, became suspicious, Martha donned a blonde wig, changed her name to Hilary Gibson, and stayed clear of Frances.

Hammer's art collection had to involve Russian art, which

brought him into contact with Soviet Minister of Culture Yekaterina Furtseva. Armand's brother, Victor, claimed that Armand and she were sexually involved and he was intrigued with the "tough cookie." There was testimony before the SEC that Hammer gave her $100,000 around the time she built an expensive summer home outside of Moscow. As Hammer traveled to Russia with briefcases crammed with cash and returned with them empty, it is probably true. Furtseva was removed from office for corruption and mysteriously died in the late 1970s.

Hammer's name had to be on everything. The Armand Hammer Museum and Cultural Center was built to house the Armand Hammer Collection. There was also the Armand Hammer Center for Cancer Biology, Armand Hammer United World College of the American West, Armand Hammer Conference on Peace and Human Rights, Armand Hammer Foundation, Armand Hammer Fund for Economic Cooperation in the Middle East, Armand Hammer Technical Center, Armand Hammer Golf Course in Los Angeles, Dr. Armand Hammer Research Fellowship, Julius and Armand Hammer Health Services Center at Columbia University, all of which were partially financed by Occidental. When Hammer purchased Leonardo da Vinci's notebook, called the Codex Leicester after the earls of Leicester who had owned it for more than 200 years, he changed its name to the Hammer Codex and established the Armand Hammer Center for Leonardo Studies at UCLA. This time Occidental had to foot the entire $6-million purchase price. And to photo his grand accomplishments, he ordered that Occidental's in-house publicity department be named Armand Hammer Productions.

One of Hammer's goals was to win the Nobel Peace Prize. His first problem was he was a convicted felon, a black mark against consideration. He had pleaded guilty to three felony counts for making a $100,000 illegal campaign contribution to Nixon's 1972 Committee to Reelect the President, bearing the appropriate acronym "CREEP." Hammer pledged $1.3 million to the Ronald Reagan Presidential Library and reminded the White House of his pledge when he sent his $100,000 pledge payments in hopes of buying a pardon. However, Reagan refused Hammer a pardon based on his blatant plea that he was innocent. (Ronnie also thought he was a Communist.) Hammer's lawyers finally persuaded the egomaniac to plead for a pardon based on compassion to a man approaching ninety. President George H. W. Bush signed his pardon after the Justice Department offered no objections.

In need of a notable world leader to nominate him for the peace prize, his first choices, former President Jimmy Carter and British Prime Minister Margaret Thatcher, declined. Prince Charles, after Hammer poured money into his pet charities to ingratiate himself, did nothing. Hammer turned to Prime Minister Menachem Begin of Israel, which took chutzpah for a man who denied he was Jewish until he was eighty. He enticed Begin by promising to drill for oil in Israel. Begin agreed to nominate Hammer, but the Nobel Peace Prize Committee thought the Dalai Lama was more deserving, so Hammer forgot about drilling for oil in Israel.

A SCOUNDREL'S LEGACY

Armand Hammer and the public thought Armand Hammer and Occidental were synonymous. Aware he was dying of cancer, during his last days he attempted to protect his "good name" and defend a $440-million lawsuit filed by the estate of his wife, Frances, for misappropriating her funds. This meant rewriting his will and transferring his assets to a living trust. He reneged on the promises to Bettye Murphy, his former mistress, and their illegitimate daughter, Victoria, by cutting them from his will. He also welshed on his promise to his only son, Julian, that he would be taken care of for life. Julian was bequeathed $250,000. Those he had to assuage to keep quiet, such as Martha Kaufman (alias Hillary Gibson) and Rosamaria Durazo, a young Mexican doctor who had traveled with him as his personal physician during his last three years, were given positions with Occidental or the Armand Hammer Foundation.

In 1990 Armand Hammer died at the age of ninety-two. The family and public thought the estate would be in the hundreds of millions, but was only $40 million. More than $27 million came from a "golden casket" clause in his Occidental employment contract, and most of that was bequeathed to the Armand Hammer Foundation to perpetuate his good name and works.

Hundreds of notables he had ingratiated himself with by supporting their charities and projects came to Armand's funeral and his postmortem bar mitzvah. Noticeably absent were his only son, Julian, and the families of his deceased brothers, Harry and Victor. Armand had pillaged their estates after they died, and there had been extended legal battles with the families. But those lawsuits were nothing compared to the claims that would eat into his estate. Dozens of Hammer's charitable promises had not been kept. To name a few: $1.5 million to the Salk Institute, $1 million to the Metropolitan Museum of Art, $640,000 to the Ronald Reagan Presidential Library, and $250,000 to the National Symphony Orchestra.

Ray Irani, the new president and CEO of Occidental, immediately reshaped the corporation by removing Hammer's bust and portrait from Occidental's headquarters. Few envied Irani's formidable task of ridding Occidental of the unprofitable ventures—the Russian fertilizer and the Chinese coal-mine boondoggles that forced a write-off of $2.5 billion ($3.2 billion in 2002). Irani eliminated Hammer's frivolities by selling the Black Angus cattle and Arabian horse-breeding subsidiaries. One holding that proved profitable was Occidental's 5.4-percent interest in Church & Dwight, the manufacturers of Arm & Hammer baking soda. Occidental was no longer in the business of pleasing Armand Hammer's ego, and Irani needed cash. The Armand Hammer Museum of Art and Cultural Center, that had been a constant drain on Occidental's cash, was turned over to UCLA, and the Codex Hammer was sold to Bill Gates of Microsoft for $32 million, who properly renamed it the Leicester Codex.

Quite different than in the past, Occidental's next annual report contained no glowing tributes to Armand Hammer or photos of him with world leaders. There was only a brief "In Memoriam, Dr. Armand Hammer." It was obvious that Occidental's management wanted to get on with Occidental's real business, clean up the mess he left behind, and forget him.

OCCIDENTAL'S LEGACY

Occidental's stock normally traded 600,000 shares daily on the New York Stock Exchange. The day after Armand Hammer died, more than 8 million shares were traded and the stock rose 10 percent. Obviously, the stock market believed Occidental was better off without him.

CHAPTER TWENTY
ENRONIANS & OTHER SCOUNDRELS

THE ENRONIANS

E nron produced more than its share of scoundrels and outright crooks. The public will never know how many. There are too many! Cases brought by investors, creditors, employees, the state of California, Securities and Exchange Commission, Federal Energy Regulatory Commission, and undeserving scoundrels inflicted with litigious paranoia will clog the courts for years—23,000 separate claims totaling $400 billion out of Enron's $15 billion assets. Creditors and the defrauded must wait until the myriad of criminal and civil courts rule before learning what really happened and the pittance left to pay their losses. Of course, the lawyers will grab their fees before everyone else.[68]

Before all the facts were clear, publishers rushed to release exposés by investigative reporters, and Enronian scoundrels were wheedling seven-figure advances to write "the inside story." Sherron Watkins, one of the three women whistle-blowers *Time* magazine named woman of the year for 2002, split a $500,000 advance with Mimi Swartz, wife of a *Houston Chronicle* editor. Robert Bryce, who admitted being a muckraker on the book jacket of his *Pipe Dreams: Greed, Ego, and Death of Enron*, titled Chapter 40 "Sherron Watkins Saves Her Own Ass." Her fellow employees describe the former Arthur Anderson auditor as "calculating" . . . "vindictive" . . . "conniving, manipulative self-promoter" . . . "poison at the well. She

---

[68] The *Houston Chronicle* reported Enron's legal fees could reach $1 billion (January 12, 2003) and $400 billion in 23,000 claims (February 21, 2003).

241

brought down people and deals to try to make herself look like a hero." In other words, she was a typical Enron vice president. Two questions to ask Watkins at her book signing: "What part did you take in the Enron Broadband Services scam?" and "Why did it take you so long to tell Ken Lay?" Before her elevation to vice president for corporate development, she helped manage off-the-books entities JEDI and Cactus and the money-loser Enron Broadband, all of which contributed to the downfall of the "Crooked E."

One thing that is certain—*the Enronians were not oilmen.* Kenneth L. Lay, Enron's founder and former CEO, is a Phi Beta Kappa Ph.D. economist. Lay merged several profitable natural gas pipelines to create the nation's largest coast-to-coast pipeline system extending more than 37,000 miles and turned it into a frenzied conglomerate built on greed and lies. Lay's handpicked president and successor as CEO, Jeffrey K. Skilling, held a Harvard MBA. Skilling's fellow aider and abettor, Chief Financial Officer Andrew S. Fastow, was an MBA from Northwestern University and, according to his rabbi, "he was a *mensch.*" His rabbi was wrong. Fastow was a *goniff.*

Enron evolved into a gigantic Ponzi scheme run by MBA and accounting executives with little or no experience running a company. They cared only about making deals and filling their pockets with bonuses and stock options. Worse, they were impressed by their self-perceived brilliance. The scoundrels obfuscated corporate earnings to hide billions in losses and debt via the shear complexity of Enron's Land of Oz fantasy financial statements while they bilked the company of hundreds of millions. Representative John Dingell, Democrat of Michigan, said, "They probably lied, too." Enronian executives covered up their incompetence and malfeasance with impudence as Enron became a trader in natural gas, electricity, fiber optics, weather derivatives, water, and 1,800 other items. They also squandered billions in baseless related stocks and foreign ventures they didn't understand in Great Britain, India, Brazil, and Argentina far out of sight of the SEC's myopic eyes.

Most Enronian culprits will never go to jail as a result of the governments' (that's plural and includes the U.S. Department of Justice and state prosecutors) practice to only go after the biggest crooks in complex cases. Second- and third-level scoundrels will be granted immunity from prosecution or receive a slap on the wrist, *if* they squeal on their bosses. The first rat to squeal was the managing director of Enron Global Finance, Michael J. Kopper, who with his domestic partner, William D. Dodson, admitted walking off with *only* $12.5 million, not including $2.6 million to pay the income tax on the illicit windfall and a $905,000 severance allowance when things went sour. Kopper copped a plea to money laundering and conspiracy to commit wire fraud and agreed to tell all at CFO Andrew Fastow's trial. Fastow is facing seventy-eight counts of mail and wire fraud, money laundering and conspiracy in which he accumulated more than $45 million in ill-gotten gains, not counting his bonuses and "alleged" insider trading. (Editors insist all misdeeds be qualified with the term "alleged" until the crooks are convicted.)

A fraud conspiracy suit filed by Enron creditors in Texas in October 2002 raised Texas lawyers' eyebrows. Only Ken Lay and eight other Enron officials were named in connection with off-the-books deals set up by the CFO. Joined with Fastow and Skilling were Enron Treasurer Ben Glison, Chief Risk Officer Richard Buy, Chief Accounting Officer Richard Causey, company attorney Kristina Mordaunt, Vice President Kathy Lynn, and Investment Director Anne Yaeger-Patel. The eight were alleged to have set up dubious partnerships to hide hundreds of millions of losses Enron incurred and were paid millions in imaginary profits from the entities.

CEO Lay was only accused of failing to pay sufficient attention to what was going on in Enron. By not being charged with conspiracy, Lay will avoid possible punitive damages. Does that mean a CEO can sleep on the job while the corporate officers defraud the shareholders and steal the corporation blind and/or stupidity are legal defenses in Texas? Maybe there is also the defense that he was too busy selling more than $100 million in Enron stock to notice that the corporation was claiming billions in revenues, but did not have enough money to pay its bills. In 2001, when Enron's phony inflated net income was reported to be $970 million, Lay permitted Enron's 200 highest paid executives to wallow like hogs in slop and be paid compensation of $1.2 billion.

While Enron's executives were being investigated, low-level employees were pitied. An estimated 14,000 lost their jobs and saw their retirement savings disappear. They claimed their $4,500 severance pay was insufficient under Enron's benefits plan. Jessie Jackson and his Rainbow/PUSH Coalition organized them with the help of the AFL-CIO to con U.S. Bankruptcy Judge Arthur Gonzalez into permitting Enron to pay the employees a severance of up to $13,500. The real question before any pity or payment to Enron employees should be: *What did the employees know about the fraud their bosses were perpetrating and did they participate in the fraud and cover-up?* No doubt many employees toiling for Enron's pipeline and electric subsidiaries, such as Portland General Electric in far-off Oregon, had no knowledge of the scams, *but many Houston Enronians did and aided and abetted in the fraud.*

The seventy-five Enron employees who participated in Skilling's setting up a phony trading floor to create the impression on visiting Wall Street stock analysts that Enron was doing a booming trading business took part in the conspiracy to defraud investors. It was a joke and common knowledge in the building during the rehearsal the day before and after the analysts left. Ha, ha . . . some of their computers they pretended to use were not even plugged in.

The electric-power traders who made phony trades to create the misleading belief of huge revenues for the purpose of defrauding investors or ran scam programs with insidious names like "Get Shorty" to increase electric prices in California are guilty of swindling consumers and shareholders. They were paid commissions and bonuses on their illicit trades. Even the accountants had to know things were going to hell at Enron Energy Services. When the retail-electric sales division lost $800 million in 2001, they covered it up by transferring it to another trading division.

There was a reason why many Houston Enronians were paid twice what employees in similar positions with other companies were earning. They were part of the scheme! Why else would "executive administrative assistants" be paid more than $100,000 a year other than to keep their mouths shut, unless they were the mistress of a top executive? (Several were.) These former Enronians shouldn't wonder why they are now earning half what they sucked out of the Enron house of marked cards.

One must feel sorry for those employees who lost most of their retirement savings in Enron stock. But the misguided employees and the press who figured the individual losses at a "million" or in the "hundreds of thousands" based on the stock market price when Enron was riding high are wrong. I had to remind several employees that they only paid a discounted rate well below the market price of

$20 a share in 1997 and under $30 during 1998 before it reached $40 in 1999. The stock skyrocketed to $90 in August 2000 and stayed around $80 until February 2001 before tumbling to pennies in November. At the close of 2000, Enron stock was at $85 a share and, of the $2.1 billion in their 401(k) plan, $1.3 billion (62 percent) was Enron stock. Contrary to most press reports, the employees could have sold the shares they paid for under their retirement plan. They were only required to hold Enron's 50-percent matching contribution until they reached fifty.

The above is not the opinion of a heartless author, but to prepare the honest employees (those not involved in the scams) for cross-examination by Skilling's lawyers. Every employee should sue Skilling for committing fraud when he announced that the stock was worth $126 in January 2001, but failed to reveal he had been selling 20,000 shares every two weeks and pocketed more than $21 million since November 2000. By now all employees have checked the SEC filings or newspapers and found that Ken Lay and Cindy Olson, the Enron vice president charged with managing their 401(k) plans, had been dumping stock. Chart 20:1—Enron Insider Traders discloses Enron officers and directors who reaped more than $1.1 billion from their stock sales. Most, if not all, should be made to disgorge their insider profits.

ENRON'S FAST FALL

On August 23, 2000, Enron's stock hit its peak at $90.75 a share. A year later, on August 30, 2001, it had dropped to $34.99. By October 31 it had plunged to $13.90. On November 5, the first credit-rating agency downgraded Enron's debt to BBB-, the lowest rating credit agencies award above junk bond status (like Harvard professors who only give their students As and Bs). On November 31, the stock sank to $0.26. On December 2, Enron filed for Chapter 11 bankruptcy.

Chart 20:1—Enron Insider Traders
October 1998 — November 2001

Name & Last Title	Proceeds $	Shares	Avg. Price $	Date Left
Lou Pai, chm. Enron Accelerator	353,712,438	5,031,105	70.30	6/01
Kenneth Lay, chm. Enron Corp.	101,346,591	1,810,793	55.97	
Rebecca Mark-Jusbasches, vice chm., dir.	79,526,787	1,410,262	56.39	8/00
Ken Harrison, chm. Portland Gen. Elect.	75,211,630	1,004,170	74.90	3/00
Kenneth Rice, pres. Enron Broadband	72,786,034	1,138,370	63.94	8/01
Jeffrey Skilling, CEO	66,924,028	1,119,958	59.76	8/01
Robert Belfer, pres. Enron Broadband	51,080,967	1,052,138	48.55	
Mark Frevert, chm. Enron North Am.	50,269,504	830,620	60.52	12/01
Stan Horton, chm. Enron Global Ser.	45,472,278	734,444	61.91	
Joseph Sutton, vice chm.	40,093,346	614,960	65.20	10/1
J. Clifford Baxter, vice chm.	35,200,208	577,436	60.96	5/01
Joseph Hirko, sr. vp.	35,168,721	473,837	74.22	6/00
Andrew Fastow, CFO	30,463,609	561,423	54.26	10/01
Richard Causey, chief accounting off.	13,329,743	197,485	67.50	2/02
James Derrick Jr., vp & gen. counsel	12,656,238	230,660	54.87	3/02
Mark Koenig, vp investor relations	9,110,466	129,153	70.54	
Cindy Olson, vp human resources	6,505,870	83,183	78.21	
Steven Kean, vp & chief of staff	5,166,414	64,932	79.57	
Richard Buy, vp & chief risk off.	4,325,309	54,872	78.82	2/02
Jeffrey McMahon, CFO	2,739,226	39,630	69.12	6/02
Mike McConnell, CEO Enron Global	2,353,431	30,960	76.02	
John Duncan, dir.	2,009,700	35,000	57.42	
Norman Blake Jr., dir.	1,705,328	21,200	80.44	
Joseph Foy, former dir.	1,639,590	31,320	52.35	
J. Mark Metts, vp corp. dev.	1,448,937	17,711	81.81	
Charles LeMaistre, dir.	841,768	17,344	48.53	
Robert Jaedicke, dir.	841,438	13,360	62.98	
Ronnie Chan, dir.	337,200	8,000	42.15	
Wendy Gramm, dir.	276,912	10,256	27.00*	
Totals	**1,102,544,671**	**17,344,584**	**63.57 average**	

Source: *Washington Times* (Jan. 15, 2002) taken from Amalgamated Bank suit against Enron. Note: Title is the last position held. *Stock sold in November 1998. See End-notes for varying figures from other sources.

FRAUD, LIES, & OTHER GREEDY DEEDS

"What Andy Fastow did was not only improper, it was terminally stupid,"

> —Vincent Kaminski, research head of Enron's Risk Assessment & Control Group, told Ken Lay before a group of Enron's top employees on October 22, 2001.

The following day, CFO Fastow blamed everything on Skilling, who had resigned in August. Lay said Fastow was doing an "outstanding job." The next morning, the board of directors learned that Fastow had "earned" $45 million in side deals. Lay had no choice but to fire Fastow for self-dealing, but announced that he was "on a leave of absence." Lay lied.

Enron's first known seeds to cover up fraud and losses were sowed in 1987, one year after Lay took over as chairman and CEO and renamed the company Enron.[69] Traders in Enron's New York office were discovered to have overstated their trading activity to inflate company revenues to boost Enron's trading prominence and increase their commissions. Lay failed to report the crime to the board of directors or SEC and covered it up. He needed to show the revenue for the Wall Street analysts. When the greedy traders continued, Enron's competitors became suspicious of the excessive volumes. If discovered, Enron's trading partners might demand that Enron cover its positions with cash, which it could not afford. Lay fired the traders and reported an $85 million loss that was actually $142 million, allowing Lay to still report a profit. Lay lied.

Like all CEOs of public corporations, Lay knew he must meet the company's projected revenue every quarter to earn bonuses and stock options. The failure to meet income expectations could send the stock price tumbling and the CEO looking for another job. Lay was paid bonuses of $3,150,000 in 1998 and $3,900,000 in 1999. In 2000, the year before Enron was flushed down Wall Street's commode, he was awarded bonuses totaling $8,220,000, not including stock options, Lay also sold $40.5 million in Enron stock in 2000.

But nothing about Enron was simple or what it appeared to be. He also transferred $8 million in Enron stock to the corporation to

---

[69] Lay's first choice for a new company name was "Enteron," but as the new stationary was being delivered, someone mentioned that it meant alimentary canal.

repay part of his "line of credit," a scam an Enron board member called "Lay's ATM approach." Stock transfers to liquidate debt did not have to be reported immediately to the SEC. Before the stock fell below $45 a share in 2001, Lay sold $37.5 million in stock and transferred $46 million in stock as payment against his line of credit. Between August 21 and 30, before the stock dropped below $35 a share, he paid another $16 million in stock against his line of credit.

On August 27 Lay e-mailed the Enron employees: "One of my highest priorities is to restore investor confidence . . . This should result in a significantly higher stock price."[70] Lay lied again.

Chart 20:1 discloses Lay sold more than $100 million in Enron shares while the company's financial infrastructure was crumbling, not including stock transfers to liquidate his line of credit that one source claimed was more than $83 million. While it does not show the profit Lay made on stock sales, it must be kept in mind that Enron insiders purchased the stock at discounted rates. With one obvious exception, Wendy Gramm, the average stock price of $63.57 indicates the insiders sold the majority of their shares before the rapid drop in prices in late 2001. Every Enron official listed on Chart 20:1 and many who are not listed should be investigated by the SEC for insider trading and made to disgorge their illegal profits.

HIDING DEBTS AND LOSSES FROM INVESTORS

Skilling planned to set up "special purpose entities" (SPE), off-the-books ventures whose debts or losses would not be reported on Enron's financial statements and SEC filings, thereby allowing Enron to meet its projected revenues. As many Enron SPEs crossed the unfathomable risky border into Alice's Wonderland, they had to be controlled by an insider, and CFO Andrew Fastow was Skilling's boy. And Michael Kopper was Fastow's boy. The SPEs took the Star Wars names of Chewco and JEDI, LJM partnerships bearing the initials of Fastow's wife and children, Southampton named after Fastow's neighborhood, and cute names like Raptors, Braveheart, and Cactus.

Chewco, set up in 1997, is the most notorious because of the blatant self-dealing and its failure to meet the SPE 3-percent ownership requirement. Kopper and William D. Dodson, a Delta Airlines employee, could only raise $125,000 and had to borrow $11 million

---

[70] *Washington Post* (July 28 & 29, 2002).

248

from Barclay's Bank to reach Chewco's 3-percent capital requirement. Not having sufficient credit, Enron guaranteed their loan. At the last minute, Barclay's had second thoughts about the shaky deal and limited the loan to $6.6 million. Fastow and Kopper merely shrugged at the failure to meet the 3-percent SPE qualification. By the time Chewco and JEDI collapsed in 2000, Koppers had been paid $2 million in management fees for his little work, part of which he claimed he had to kick back to Fastow along with part of his and Dodson's share of the $10.5 million they received on their $125,000 investment. Chewco enabled Enron to claim $405 million in dubious income during the period even though Chewco had debts of $600 million that Enron did not report.

To further inflate Enron's profits, Fastow counted the increased value of Enron's stock loaned as collateral to JEDI, which was owned by Chewco. (Yes, the deal was complicated and figures ~~never~~ lie.) On November 2, 2001, Enron's board was told the corporate books had to be restated dating back to 1997 because of Chewco's losses. Enron's income had to be reduced $586 million, and there was an additional $2.5 billion in debt, but that was just the start of Enron's unraveling.

Jeffrey McMahon, a former Enron treasurer who had been demoted by Skilling for challenging Fastow's conflict of interest, replaced Fastow as CFO. The second day on the job, he discovered that the current treasurer, Ben Glison, Enron staff attorney Kristina Mordaunt, and other Enron employees had been cut in on Skilling's LJM partnerships and had shared in Fastow's super-duper 172-to-1 rate of return to cooperate and keep their mouth's shut. Each had invested $5,800 and earned a whopping $1 million.

Chewco and the other SPEs should never have been permitted. It was an obvious conflict of interest for Fastow to represent both the partnerships and Enron. Nevertheless, the board of directors approved them at Skilling's urging, then failed to determine the accuracy of Fastow's reports. It was not as if the board didn't know better. Enron board member Robert K. Jaedicke was the ideal chairman of the board's audit committee because of his experience as a professor of accounting and dean of Stanford University's Graduate School of Business. Of interest, Chart 20:1 reveals that Jaedicke sold more than $841,438 in stock at an average price of $62.98.

Optimistic Accounting Earns Bigger Bonuses

Instead of the old-fashioned accounting method of subtracting expenses from revenue to compute profit, in 1992 Skilling conned Jaedicke into introducing a motion to the board to adopt "mark-to-market" accounting. The system allowed Enron officers to estimate the value of a deal over its projected lifetime and report it as income. This invitation to deceive was designed to add immediate profits to Enron's balance sheet and pay obscene bonuses to executives. If an accountant wearing a green eyeshade and a plastic pocket protector questioned the process, he was transferred to a less creative job. Enron's Risk Assessment and Control Group of math geniuses had computers to rubber-stamp the risky ventures . . . or else. Also of interest, Chart 20:1 discloses that Richard Buy, vice president and chief risk officer, sold more than $4.3 million in Enron stock at an average price of $78.82.

When president of Enron Trading, Skilling collected 3 percent of his division's profits, which explains his pushing for visionary accounting. Mark-to-market accounting had the absurd result of reporting $65 million revenue from a pipeline in Argentina before it was built and $100 million revenue from an English power plant before construction was completed.

Mark-to-market accounting allowed Skilling and other Enron executives to manipulate the computations and long-term price and cost estimates. A prime example was the evaluation of Enron subsidiary Mariner Energy, an offshore gas producer. Mariner's income from gas wells was immediately invested in other wells and profit estimates were made on the *gas to be discovered before the well was drilled.* When the price of natural gas dropped from $9.80 per thousand cubic feet in January 2001 to below $2 in October, Enron inflated Mariner's estimated gas reserves, former Mariner employees told a *Houston Chronicle* reporter.

Enron executive bonuses were based on the estimated value of the project, not the actual sales and expenses. This resulted in optimistic estimates, to be euphemistic, or fraudulent connivance, to be accurate. In 2000 Enron reported revenues of $979 million that included $630 million derived via Skilling's smoke-and-mirror accounting of Fastow's LJM partnerships and $296 million from a one-time tax adjustment. Nevertheless, Enron paid $750 million in bonuses to its employees for 2000, including $320 million for hitting their stock market target price.

Five months before Enron filed for bankruptcy, 139 of its top executives split $681 million in bonuses in—believe it or not—*retention bonuses*. But the hardest slap in the face to Enron's lower-level employees came on Friday, November 30, 2001—three days before Enron filed for bankruptcy—when 500 executives received $55 million in bonuses in cashier's checks so they would clear the bank after the bankruptcy filing the following Monday.

TRADING TRICKS

Trading and marketing natural gas and electricity is complex and would require a separate volume to fully explain the mechanics and risks. If you add the fraud of the electric-power generators and traders during California's 2000-2001 power crisis, you would need the help of a lawyer and economist specializing in the field to comprehend what actually occurred.[71]

Enron is but one of many electric power generators and traders from which Democrat Governor Joseph Graham "Gray" Davis Jr. sought $8.9 billion in refunds for manipulating prices.[72] In December 2002, a Federal Energy Regulatory Commission (FERC) administrative law judge (ALJ) only found $1.8 billion in overcharges out of $4 billion claimed by California during October 2000 through June 2001. That the energy suppliers had proposed paying damages of $1.2 billion was a de-facto admission of hanky-panky. The ALJ's ruling was based on complex formulas no one agrees with or understands, but it is easier than proving tens of thousands of separate transactions resulted in "unjust and unreasonable prices"—the criteria under the Federal Power Act. In March 2003, the FERC Commission realized it wasn't enough and required thirty utilities to document and justify their prices, bringing the estimated damages up to $3.3 billion, and

---

[71] *The California Energy Crisis: Lessons for a Deregulating Industry* by Will McNamara was released in April 2002, too early to reveal all the dirt, but an excellent portrayal of the facts up to that time.

[72] Other companies *alleged* to have charged the Californians "unjust and unreasonable" prices include: AES Corp., Arizona Public Ser., Avista Energy, Calpine Corp., Duke Energy, Dynegy, Mirant Corp., Nevada Power Company, Portland General Electric Company, Public Ser. Co. of Colorado, Public Ser. Co. of New Mexico, Reliant Resources, and Williams Energy Ser. According to *Webster's*, "Gray" can mean dull, dreary, or dismal.

threatened to ban such energy suppliers as BP from trading. The big surprises in those accused were the DOE's Bonneville Power Administration and the Los Angeles Department of Water and Power. So far, FERC had refused to review the $4.9 billion balance in overcharges claimed before October 2000. As the California utilities owe the power generators and traders $3 billion in unpaid bills, the Californians will appeal to the courts ad nauseam.

Separately, FERC settled with Williams Energy and Reliant Resources for purposely shutting down their California power plants to spike electricity prices in 2000. Williams was ordered to refund $8 million and Reliant $13.8 million to the state of California.

The most popular sleight-of-hand were "wash" or "round-trip" electricity trades between producers or traders, in effect selling and buying back electricity at the same price. But why buy and sell at no profit or loss? When caught, CMS Energy claimed it did it to inflate its revenue by $5.2 billion over a two year period (23 percent of its revenue). CMS's rationale sounded logical—the small company wanted to look like a big-time trader. Of course, as a new player in power marketing trading billions in revenues, CMS might incidentally attract new clients and puff up its stock value, which could explain why CMS's CEO and head of marketing were forced to resign. But it does not explain why the energy giants, like Duke Energy, Williams Energy, Reliant Resources, and Dynegy made wash trades, nor why Dynegy's CEO resigned when caught.

A likely explanation was offered by Loretta Lynch, president of the California Public Utilities Commission. She claimed that four Enron affiliates traded 10 million megawatt hours of electricity between them at ever-increasing rates to give "the illusion of an active, volatile market" in December 2000. In other words, the Enronians were raising the market price. There is no question whether Enron had the power to manipulate the market. In 2001 FERC identified twenty-four electricity marketers and generators and fifteen gas pipelines that were Enron affiliates and estimated Enron Online trading was involved as a buyer or seller in 38 percent of the natural gas and 17 percent of the electric power marketed in the U.S.

California consumers suffered seven rolling blackouts and thirty-eight curtailments of electric service during the first five months of 2001. Even Governor Davis agreed the electricity crisis was not the complete fault of the power generators and traders and admitted that California's deregulation system contained basic defects. But he had little doubt that Enron's trading strategies contributed to the inflated prices and netted Enron undeserved fees. Patrick Wood III, former chairman of the Public Utility Commission of Texas and FERC chairman since September 2001, said Enron's trading strategies involved "deliberate misrepresentations" and "exploited the flaws in California's market design." Stanford University economics professor Frank Wolak added something that FERC didn't want to admit: Enron's tactics are "standard arbitrage strategies" used by energy traders.

Enron internal memos obtained during litigation described their schemes with cute names. What is missing are the names of the "friendly" traders needed to complete some of the schemes. But they are only allegations. Enron denied the actions and claimed the memos were misinterpreted. Most lawyers agree they will be difficult to prove in court. The reader can make up his or her mind.

RICOCHET

Enron purchases cheap power in California under price caps and sells it to a "friendly" out-of-state buyer, who sells it back at a higher price not subject to price caps. Enron "ships" it back to California and sells it at an uncontrolled, even-higher price. (What are friends for?)

FAT BOY

Enron traders speculate that California utilities underestimated the next day's demand for electricity with the California PX (power exchange). Enron was right the vast majority of the time. It does not take a genius to know the utilities will attempt to hold down the price by lowering the projected demand. Enron schedules to send more power over the grid than its customers require, a violation of the rules many traders ignore. When the demand exceeds the utilities' estimates, Enron sells its "extra" electricity on the spot market at top dollar.

Enron's defense is that it merely overestimated and the utilities underestimated. It delivered the electricity when needed and helped avoid a shortfall, all to the benefit of the consumers.

GET SHORTY

Enron agrees to provide standby generation and transmission services the following day for a fee if and when the state power grid requires. Enron plans to purchase the services if requested, which is contrary to the agreement requiring it to identify the sources. It purchases the rights to the services early the next day when prices are cheap and submits a false statement of its source.

LOAD SHIFT (TRADING PLACES)

Enron deliberately overestimates the power demand in Northern California to create a fear of congestion and raise the price in the north at the same time it underestimates the demand in Southern California. Enron earns a fee to shift the load to the south from the north to alleviate the make-believe congestion.

This is a variation of the old "inc-ing" strategy (short for load increasing) to earn fees for not sending power a company never intended to send.

DEATH STAR

Enron schedules to import electricity on California's southern border and transport it to the north. As the transmission lines are booked, it receives a fee to transmit the power in another direction and relieve the congestion. If it sends any to northern California, which it seldom does, it sends it outside the California grid.

In October 2002, Timothy N. Belden, Enron's chief trader on the West Coast pleaded guilty to one count of conspiracy to commit wire fraud to drive up California's electricity prices. As part of the thirty-five-year-old Belden's plea bargain, he agreed to turn over $2.1 million in salary and bonuses earned in 2001, "which represents the portion tied to the fraud." As he earned $5.5 million in salary and bonuses during 2001, what great things did he do for the other $3.4 million that the feds don't know about? Belden is facing up to five years in prison and a $250,000 fine, so maybe he will tell the jury why he scheduled 2,900 megawatts of power over a 1,500 megawatt interconnection. Another question for Belden that will bring smiles to the jury: "Did you receive a bonus for the $570 million of electricity sold to Pacific Gas & Electric, which is bankrupt and might never pay?"

ENRONIAN & CALIFORNIA QUOTES

"They can do all these sham transactions because no one's ever seen a kilowatt hour."

> —S. David Freeman, chairman, California Consumer Power & Conservation Financing Authority

"I do not recall," he said nineteen times. "I am not an accountant," he said seven times.

> —Enron CEO and Harvard MBA Jeffrey K. Skilling's testimony before a congressional committee on February 26, 2002. He couldn't recall receiving a $5.6 million bonus or selling $66 million of Enron stock less than two years earlier.

APPENDIX A
INFLATION INDEX
WITH ANALYSIS AND SNIDE COMMENTS

During the 1850s, Samuel Kier sold 30,000 half-pint bottles of "medicinal" Rock Oil annually for $1 each. Today it would be the equivalent of charging $22 and grossing $660,000 a year. To obtain the current value of money during the last 150-odd years, the Columbia University's Web site was consulted at www.cjr.org/resources/inflator.asp. The current equivalents added a flavor of the times when oil was selling at 10¢ or $1 a barrel and offered a perception of what a dollar was worth and the consequences of the Civil War and inflation on the early oil industry.

For ready reference, the values are listed by Part and Chapter and the years are in **bold** type. The amounts are computed to the value of a dollar in 2002, sometimes referred to as "today" or enclosed in parenthesis.

Warning: Don't forget the counsel of Mark Twain: "There are lies, damn lies, and statistics." The inflation index is extrapolated for the dollar value of all goods and services, not specific commodities. For example, the $6.50 average price of crude oil in **1865** during the Civil War inflation equates to $71.44 in 2002. However, in September of 2002, the price of West Texas Intermediate crude oil, the benchmark price on the New York Mercantile Exchange, fluctuated between $28 and $30 a barrel. But even that price range was considered $4 high because of United States-Iraq tensions, according to *Oil & Gas Journal* (Sept. 9, 2002). Thanks to improved technology and efficient transportation systems, today petroleum beats the inflation curve or gasoline would be more than $5 a gallon at the pump.

Part One — Early Oilmen

Chapter 1 — One dollar during **1859-60** equals $21.74 in 2002. Thus Drake's $1,000 annual salary would be worth $21,740 today, and Uncle Billy's $2.50 daily wage would be the equivalent of $50.35.

The $20,000 Drake lost speculating in oil stocks in **1866** is valued at $225,000 today. Drake's **1873** annual pension of $1,500 would pay him $22,395 in 2002.

Chapter 2 — Mining claims under the General Mining Law of 1872 are issued for $5 per acre on lode claims and $2.50 on placer claims. In **1872** $2.50 would equal $36.76 today, but the law is still on the books. Today you can obtain a federal placer land patent on a "valuable mineral discovery" for $2.50 an acre. Although crude oil has not been covered by the 1872 act since 1920, placer minerals, including gold, are still open to claimants whose minimum claims are generally of 20 acres. Damn it, $50 for 20 acres is a giveaway of the nation's public lands the Congress should eliminate.

Chart 2:1 — Annual Crude Oil Production and Average Price Per Barrel in Oil Regions 1862-1873 fails to paint the entire picture unless the Civil War (1861-65) inflation and the postwar recession are taken into account. Drake's first crude-oil sales in August and September **1859** at $30 a barrel would be the equivalent of $652 today. The price dropped to $20 in January **1860** and ended the year at $4, the equivalent of $435 and $87 today. Overproduction in **1861** caused erratic price fluctuations from a high of $10 down to 10¢ a barrel. Today that would translate to a plunge from $204.10 to $2.04 a barrel. Between 1860 and 1861 inflation jumped 6.1 percent then soared another 14.9 percent during 1862. By the end of the war in **1865**, the inflation based on 1860 dollars reached 49.4 percent and crude oil was selling for $6.50 a barrel, which equals $71.44 today, but only $4.35 in 1860 dollars.

The Pithole town lot that sold for $2 million in **1865** would carry a price tag of $22 million today. Its $4.37 auction sale price in **1878** would be $78.05 today.

Part Two — Rockefeller & Standard Oil

Chapter 3 — In **1855** sixteen-year-old John D. Rockefeller worked for $300 a year, the equivalent of $6,600 in 2002 and below today's minimum wage of $10,500. By **1859,** he was earning $600 a year, equal to $13,050 today. Rockefeller's **1860** $2,000 investment was substantial for a nineteen-year-old and would equal $43,500 today. The **1863** $4,000 investment by Rockefeller and his partner is tantamount to $58,500 today, but pales by the $72,500 the twenty-six-year-old book-keeper borrowed to buy out his partner in **1865**, which would equal $797,000 today.

Standard Oil Company of Ohio's **1870** $1-million capitalization would be on the books at $13,700,000 today. Unlike today's corporate promoters, Rockefeller was a firm believer in cash, hard assets, and no frills or perks. The thirty-year-old oilman's 2,667 shares would make him a millionaire today with a worth of $3,653,790 on paper, not including his interest in the partnership of Rockefeller, Andrews & Flagler. The records are not clear how Standard Oil of Ohio raised its capital to $3.5 million in **1872** that would be in excess of $51 million in 2002.

Chapter 4 — The **1872** "Treaty of Titusville" shows the price volatility of crude oil during the petroleum industry's first price-fixing attempt (2002 value in brackets). The producers insisted crude oil should be $5 a barrel ($73.55) when the market price was $3.25 ($47.80). Rockefeller baited the producers by promising to pay $4 ($58.84) and raising the price 25¢ per barrel for every 1¢ increase in the New York per gallon wholesale price of kerosine *if* they enforced production quotas. Rockefeller knew they would cheat (like OPEC today). Overproduction lured by promises of higher prices drove the price down to $2 ($29.42) in less than a month. The New York kerosine price averaged 23.6¢ ($3.47) a gallon in **1872** and fell to 17.9¢ ($2.67) in **1873** along with the price of crude oil that averaged $1.80 ($26.87). By comparison, in mid-September 2002, the New York wholesale price of kerosine hovered around $0.95 a gallon, well below the inflator index.

Chart 4:1—Annual Average Crude Oil Prices, Production & Inventory in the Appalachian Fields 1874-1884 involved a mild depression that resulted in a devaluation of 16.4 percent, one-half of which came between 1874 and 1875. The highest annual average price was $2.58 in **1876** ($43); and the lowest was in **1882** at $0.78 ($13.68). In 1884 the average crude price was $0.84 ($15.27). The drop in crude prices after 1877 was exacerbated by Standard Oil's "Empire War" with the Pennsylvania Railroad.

Rockefeller's buyout of Empire's assets for $3.4 million in **1878** would equal $60.7 million in 2002. Rockefeller personally borrowed $1.25 million to swing the deal that would be $22.3 million today. The **1878** average crude price of $1.20 ($21.43 today) is a reminder that averages can be misleading, as the price dipped to $0.70, 41.6 percent below the average, which today would equal $12.50.

Standard Oil strangled its competitors with its $0.64-per-barrel transportation advantage in **1878** that would amount to $11.43 today, almost the price crude oil was at its low of $0.70 ($12.50) a barrel. Emblematic of its power, while cutting prices, Standard Oil declared a $60-per-share dividend (on closely held $100-par-value stock). The equivalent of $1,071.60 today, it earned Rockefeller $160,020, which would be $2,857,957 today.

Chapter 5 — In **1907** the state of Texas fined Standard Oil's subsidiary, Waters-Pierce, $1,623,000, the equivalent of $32,460,000 in 2002.

In **1888** the Lima field sour crude oil was a bargain at $0.15 a barrel that would equal $2.83 today. The smelly gunk was only one-fifth to one-sixth the sweet crude-oil prices in Pennsylvania that ranged from $0.75 to $0.90 a barrel, which would equate to $14.15 to $16.98 today.

In **1902** the Hogg-Swayne Syndicate sold 1/24 acre plots at Spindletop for $50,000, around $1 million today. If square, the plot would be 42.5 by 42.5 feet. Equal to $1.2 million an acre in 1902, it would equal $24 million an acre today.

Rockefeller's $32-million donation to the Negro educational fund in **1907** would be worth $640 million today. Judge Landis's $29,240,000 fine of Standard Oil of Indiana was the largest levied against a corporation until then and would be substantial by today's standards without taking inflation into consideration. Its 2002 equivalent is $584,800,000.

The $100,000 Rogers and Archbold political contributions to President Roosevelt in **1904** is the equivalent of $2 million today, but was an astounding contribution in 1904, especially from the Standard Oil Trust to the "Trustbuster."

The $666-million estimated value of Standard Oil at the 1911 dissolution would be the equivalent of $13.3 billion today. However, Exxon-Mobil's assets were worth $143.17 billion in 2002, according to the *Oil & Gas Journal. (See Chart 3:1.)*

The estimated wealth of the six Standard Oil directors in **1914** is open to question. Rockefeller's stated $1-billion worth would be $17.9 billion today, but by then he had transferred much of his wealth to John D. Junior and made tens of millions in charitable contributions.

PART THREE — TEAPOT DOME

Chapter 7 — The **1921** "$50 Million Oil Deal" would be worth $505 million today. Oil at $1.50 a barrel is the equivalent of $15.15 in 2002, which means the corporate presidents skimming 25¢ a barrel from their companies would have netted $2.525 a barrel today. The navy's estimated $200-million cost to build oil storage depots around the world would be budgeted by the Pentagon today at slightly more than $2 billion—petty cash to today's Pentagon admirals.

Secretary of the Interior Albert Fall made history when he took the $100,000 bribe in a little black bag in **1922** that would equal $1,075,000 today. The $269,000 in Liberty Bonds and cash Harry Sinclair gave Fall in **1922** would be worth $2,891,750 today. Fifth-grade math students should be able to calculate, if a **1922** dollar is comparable to $10.75 in 2002, Harry Sinclair's $400-million net worth would be $4.3 billion today. I leave it to readers to figure the value of the hush money Sinclair paid to Leo Stack and the millions he raised in stock deals. The estimated inside-trader profits of $30 million would be $322.5 million in 2002, making Martha Stewart's accused hanky-panky seem like petty larceny.

Chapter 8 — Harry Sinclair's **1923** promise to spend $115 million to develop the Russian oil fields would be around $1.2 billion today. It was almost as big a pipe dream as the Russians believing he could float a $250-million loan on Wall Street, a mere $2.6 billion today when one considers the tens of billions in international bailout loans by the World Bank and International Monetary Fund.

On the political side, Democrat Edward Doheny admitted spreading $100,000 between both political parties in **1920**, which would be handing out $900,000 in 2002 and top Enron's political contributions. In **1925**, when the House of Representatives appropriated $100,000 for the Teapot Dome investigation, they would find it insufficient. Although it would be slightly in excess of $1 million today, everyone knows today's Congress would spend at least ten times that.

Chapter 9 — In **1927** the Supreme Court ruled that Pan American

Petroleum and Transport was not entitled to the $7,350,814.11 it incurred in constructing the 1.5 million barrels of storage tanks at Pearl Harbor, which would equal $75,787,000 in 2002 according to the inflation index. But to actually construct the tankage today, the cost would be in excess of $160 million because of modern safety and environmental standards. Pan American's payment to the navy for the oil of $34,981,449.62 would equal $360,658,745.58 today to be precise. Sinclair's Mammoth Oil refund to the navy for the oil was $12,156.246.66, the equivalent of $125,330,903.06 today.

PART 4 — INTERNATIONAL SKULLDUGGERY

Chapter 10 — William D'Arcy's **1901** £20,000 payment for the concession covering five-sixths of Iran would be $2.6 million today.

Marcus Samuel turned down Standard Oil's offer of $40 million for Shell Transport and Trading around **1897.** An astronomical price at the time, it would equal around $880 million today. But that is insignificant to the multibillion dollar mergers and buyouts of the last few years, such as BP's takeover of Amoco in 2000 valued at $55 billion and Exxon's 1998 merger with Mobil worth $86.4 billion.

Winston's Churchill's **1914** purchase of 51 percent of Anglo-Persian for £2.2 million for the British government would be valued at around $235 million today.

Chapter 12 — Walter Teagle of Standard Oil of New Jersey called it a "billion-dollar error" when he turned down Frank Holmes's **1927** offer of the Bahrain concession for $50,000, which equals $515,500 today. It was small change to Standard Oil of New Jersey then and still is at today's equivalent to a corporation with assets of $143 billion and 2001 revenues of $213 billion.

Standard Oil of California's (Chevron) **1933** upfront payment for the Saudi Arabian oil concession was £35,000 in gold ($175,000), the equivalent of $2,430,750 today. As £30,000 was a loan and £5,000 an advance royalty, Chevron could recoup the entire amount—thus it paid *nothing.* The £20,000 ($100,000) loan due six months later and £100,000 ($500,000) loan when oil was discovered were also recoupable, so the fact that Chevron's total payment of $775,000 is worth $10,764,750 today is moot.

In **1948,** when the first independent oil companies obtained Mideast oil concessions in the Saudi Arabia/Kuwait Neutral Zone with up-front payments of $7.5 million by Aminoil (plus a $1-million yacht for Emir Al-Sabah) and Getty Oil's $9.5- million payment, it was considered ruinous by the Seven Sisters. Today it would amount to Aminoil shelling out cash of $56 million and giving the emir a $7.5-million yacht and Getty paying $70 million. Unknown to Ibn Saud, Getty had instructed his agent to pay as high as $10.5 million, equal to $78.3 million today. Getty's agent returned home with amoebic dysentery and received a bonus of $1,200 for his efforts from the tightwad multimillionaire. Its $8,950 equivalent today would barely cover his medical bills.

It wasn't only the millions paid by the independents that concerned the Seven Sisters, they thought the royalties were outlandish and disclosed how badly they were screwing the Mideasterners. The following chart shows the royalties paid based on the average price paid of $1.80 a barrel for the benchmark crude oil (Arabian Light 34° API f.o.b. Ras Tanura, Saudi Arabia) during 1948-1953, including Aminoil's partial royalty paid on profits estimated at $0.075 (based on **1948** prices):

Concession Royalties	Per Barrel	Percent Royalty	2002 Value
Getty Oil to Saudi Arabia	$0.55	30.56	$4.10
Aminoil to Kuwait	$0.425	23.61	$3.17
Aramco to Saudi Arabia	$0.33	18.33	$2.46
IPC and BP to Iraq and Iran	$0.165	9.67	$1.23
Gulf and Anglo-Persian to Kuwait	$0.15	8.33	$1.12

The $1.80-per-barrel crude-oil price in **1948** equals $13.43 in 2002, but on September 13, 2002, Saudi Light 34° API was quoted at $26.20. During 1948-1953 the price of East Texas 39-40° API sweet crude was also constant at $2.65 a barrel, the equivalent of $19.77 today. However, East Texas crude oil was quoted at $29.25 on September 20, 2002. *Oil & Gas Journal* (September 30, 2002). The current market-driven comparisons are convincing evidence that the Seven Sisters controlled the world oil prices during the period.

The standard royalty in the United States has been 12.5 percent free of production costs since the 1860s, but it is often larger during an oil boom or on highly potentially productive oil leases. In the Mideast, the Seven Sisters deducted production costs in computing

263

the royalty. Based on a 12.5-percent royalty and the $1.80-a-barrel crude price, which the Seven Sisters kept low, it would amount to $0.225 per barrel, $1.68 today. J. Paul Getty was right when he said the Mideasterners were being screwed. No doubt Emir Al-Sabah of Kuwait and King Ibn Saud wondered how Getty and Aminoil could afford to pay higher royalties than the Seven Sisters, especially considering the crude oil in the Neutral Zone is inferior heavy gunk. Ibn Saud moved fast when he heard about American corporate taxes of 48 percent and Venezuela was taxing oil-company profits. Saudi Arabia set a tax rate of 50 percent in 1950, and soon the rest of the Mideast followed. The American oil companies agreed. The Revenue Act of 1918 contained a "foreign tax credits" provision that permitted the oil companies to offset the foreign taxes against their U.S. taxes.

When George Getty died in **1930,** he left an estate undervalued at $10 million for tax purposes that would equal $107.5 million today. Most of the estate value was the George F. Getty Incorporated oil company that was probably worth double the total estate valuation. J. Paul Getty's one-third of the company he inherited was likely worth $7 million, $75 million today. When *Forbes* magazine declared Getty a billionaire in **1957,** it reported he was worth $1.6 billion, $10.5 billion today.

PART FIVE — THE BLACK GIANT

Chapters 13-15 — Dad Joiner's $25 Rusk County Oil Syndicate "oil play" was unusual and complex, but not difficult to analyze. In **1927** drilling a well to 3,550 feet cost between $20,000 to $25,000 ($205,000 to $260,000 in 2002). Each certificate entitled the holder to a 25/75,000 interest (1/3,000) plus an undivided 1/500 interest in 500 acres of additional oil lands. This indicates Dad set a value of $75,000 on the deal with a maximum of 500 certificates that could raise up to $12,500 or one-half the well costs. Dad retained 5/6 of the interest in the well and was committed to raise the remaining costs, including paying for Daisy's lease, Doc Lloyd's interest, and raising any additional funds required. (The math is a $75,000 value set by Dad, less $12,500 or 5/6 of the value.) This explains how Dad could give Walter Tucker a 1/4 interest in the well on the condition he sold 1/8 and gave Dad the proceeds of $900 ($9,280 today). Dad hoped to make a profit out of his 5/6 interest that he didn't sell.

A big *IF* was *IF* he could raise all the money. He didn't (or pocketed it), and the first well was not completed when the drill "got stuck in the hole." The same problems arose in drilling the second well, and it appeared as if they might repeat on the Daisy Bradford No. 3. In **1930** Dad sold $100 certificates that would have a face value of $1,075 today. The $100 certificate was based on a 1/300 interest in 80 acres surrounding the well and a bonus of four acres in an additional 320 acres. This indicates he estimated the costs at $30,000.

Was Dad's math bad on the bonus acreage or was he planning to only sell eighty certificates to raise $8,000 for the drilling costs and keep a 220/300 interest for himself, raising the difference by other means? Don't forget that your fourth-grade math teacher insisted you reduce fractions to their common denominator, so Dad was responsible for 11/15. And keep in mind Dad had already peddled an untold number of certificates from two $25-a-share syndicates and sold one lease eleven times to raise money. We'll never know how much because of the 300-odd lawsuits claiming that he oversold the venture by 350 percent. Another thing you must consider, Dad had living expenses and lots of widows to woo during the three-and-one-half years.

Dad sold his interest to H. L. Hunt for $1,335,000 in 1930, the equivalent of $14,430,000 today. As Hunt only paid $30,000 up front and the balance from crude-oil sales, his borrowed "down payment" would have been $333,500 in 2002. Hunt's payment to Wilford of $25,000 ($268,750 today) to persuade Dad to sell his interest and the secret payment to Foster of $20,000 ($215,000 today) to let him know if the nearby well was a producer were not paid for several months. Hunt was broke.

In the beginning of the Great Depression, a **1930** dollar would be valued at $10.75 in 2002. Thus the $100-bill tip to the bellhop to flush out Dad would be worth $1,075 today. A 2002 dollar was worth $11.90 in **1931,** a deflation of 10.7 percent. By **1935,** the dollar would be valued at $13.16, down 22.4 percent from 1930.

Annual averages of oil prices are not only misleading because of price fluctuations during a year, they are deceptive due to variations in the quality of the crude oil in the diverse oil fields. No two oil fields contain identical crude oils, and their price is based on the value and quantities of the products they can be refined into, such as gasoline and jet fuel. The following shows the *average* per-barrel crude-oil price by state (not by oil field) in **1930, 1931, and 1935**, according to the API's *Petroleum Facts and Figures* (1950):

265

State	1930	2002	1931	2002	1935	2002
Pennsylvania	2.61	28.06	1.98	23.56	2.14	28.16
California	1.20	12.90	0.72	8.57	0.82	10.79
Illinois	1.59	17.09	0.89	10.59	1.11	14.61
Texas	1.04	11.18	0.66	7.85	1.00	13.16
National average	1.19	12.79	0.65	7.74	0.97	12.77

The above reflects Pennsylvania's high-quality sweet crude oil valuable for lubricants and its proximity to markets in the Northeast. Illinois crude was near the Midwest markets and refineries. California crude is primarily heavy, and the state was (and still is) isolated from the rest of the country by the lack of pipelines over the Rocky Mountains. Texas's tremendous production, as well as Oklahoma's (not shown), dragged the national average price down. Texas's **1931** state average is misleading. In January 1931, Humble Oil cut the East Texas price from $1.30 to $1.15 a barrel. In March through May, Humble slashed prices to $0.67, then $0.35, and finally to $0.10. The effect of the Humble's control was catastrophic. In five months, the crude-oil price fell like a lead balloon from $1.30 to 10¢, a 92-percent drop. In 2002 it would be the equivalent of the price falling from $15.47 to $1.19.

East Texas oil-boom price comparisons in **1930** make little sense unless you know if they are before or after Dad Joiner struck oil. Ed Laster, the driller, was earning $6 a day ($64.50 today) and his crew was making $3 a day ($32.25) before the oil strike. The wages for the unskilled laborer improved little afterward because of the hordes of unemployed migrating to East Texas. Farmers were no longer interested in cotton selling at 8¢ a pound ($0.86). Before Dad's gusher, they couldn't sell their land for $30 ($322.50 today) an acre. Afterward, they were signing oil leases for $400 an acre ($4,300), and, if they held on to the land for a few months, leases went for between $5,000 and $15,000 an acre ($53,750 to $161,250), plus promises of royalties of 1/8 to 1/4 on the price of oil. Thus the landowners felt the pain with the independent oilmen when Humble Oil cut the price of crude oil from $1.30 to 10¢ a barrel—their 1/8 royalty dropped from 16.25¢ to 1.25¢ a barrel ($1.93 to $0.15). When 20,000-barrel-a day gushers were curtailed to 75 barrels a day or were shut in by the Texas Railroad Commission, it cut deep into their earnings or eliminated all royalty income.

In **1930** the national average price of gasoline was 18¢ ($1.94 today), including an average 2¢ state tax. The actual national average on September 18, 2002, was $1.446 for regular (87 octane), including 40.6¢ in taxes (18.4¢ federal and a 22.2¢ state average). But averages are misleading. Less than one-half the states taxed gasoline at the time, and by **1931** independents were selling Eastex gasoline at 11¢ a gallon, $1.309 today, while the national average changed little. On September, 18, 2002, the average price of regular gasoline in Los Angeles was $1.801 due to California's environmental requirements and a state tax of 31.9¢. At the same time, the average price of regular gasoline in Houston was $1.32, including a 20¢ state tax. *Oil & Gas Journal* (September 30, 2002).

A six-ounce, 5¢ (59.5¢ today) Coca-Cola sold for 10¢ in East Texas during **1931,** the same price as East Texas crude oil and equal to $1.19 in 2002. Today I can get a twelve-ounce can of Coke at my Amoco station for 75¢, but only 25¢ if I buy a twelve-pack at my local Safeway. Credit for beating the inflation index must also be given to Pepsi Cola. Pepsi came out with "twelve full ounces, that's a lot, and twice as much for a nickel, too," according to Pepsi's jingle.

The erratic crude-oil prices during the Depression impacted everyone in East Texas until the goal of "dollar oil" was reached. Credit for the achievement is shared by the relatively fair, but far from perfect, Texas Railroad Commission prorationing regulations, the realization that conservation was necessary to protect the East Texas oil field from depletion before its time and leaving much of its oil unrecoverable in the ground, and the 1934 tariff on imported crude oil of 21¢ a barrel and $1.05 on petroleum products to protect the petroleum industry. The crude-oil national average price in **1934** was $0.99 ($13.38) and the 21¢ tariff was 21.2 percent ($2.84).

PART SIX — MODERN SCOUNDRELS

Chapters 16 & 17 — In **1959** Venezuela faced the loss of 1.1 million barrels a day in exports to the United States under the Mandatory Oil Import Program. At $2.80 a barrel ($17.39 today), Venezuelan Oficina crude oil was slightly below the U.S. average price for an equivalent crude oil of $2.90 ($18). East Texas 39° API sweet crude was posted at $3.25 ($20.18). It was an economic disaster to President Betancourt's new government that counted on crude-oil exports to the U.S. to contribute $600 million to its annual budget, more than $3.7 billion today. Venezuela's proximity to the Texas and Louisiana Gulf ports gave it a 10¢-tanker-cost advantage over Mideast crudes, but it could not offset the Mideast average f.o.b. price of $1.80 ($11.18). (Saudi light was posted at $1.90 ($11.80), Iranian light at $1.81 ($11.24), and the heavier Kuwait crudes at $1.67 ($10.37).) Venezuelan heavy crude had to make up for the loss of its U.S. market in the lower-priced European market that was closer to the lighter and sweeter Mideast crude oil. Another disadvantage was Venezuela's production costs were 80¢ ($4.97) a barrel compared to 10¢ to 20¢ ($0.62-$1.24) in the Mideast. No wonder Pérez Alfonzo wanted to make a deal for economic prorationing à la the Texas Railroad Commission with his new Mideast friends.

Exxon's **1959** unannounced 7-percent cut in Saudi light from $1.90 to $1.76 is best described as an unannounced 7-percent cut in the Saudi Arabian government's annual budget by an American oil company of approximately $27 million, equal to $167.7 million today. (Saudi Arabia produced 1.1 million barrels a day in 1959, compared to its current output of more than 8 million barrels a day.)

Libya squeezed Occidental in **1970** with an increase in the posted price of 30¢ ($1.395 in 2002) plus a 2¢ (9.3¢)-a-barrel annual increase over five years and a 5-percent increase in taxes of 4.2¢ (21¢). Regardless of the actual price Occidental charged below the posted price to undercut the Seven Sisters' price, its royalty and taxes were computed on the posted price.

Aware the weak CFP had been selling its Algerian crude oil below the posted price and undercutting the Seven Sisters, Algeria unilaterally raised CFP's posted price from $2.08 ($9.67) to $2.85 ($13.25).

In **1971** the gulf producers boosted their price by 35¢ ($1.55) plus a gravity adjustment on the various crude oils of up to 2¢ (8.9¢). Libya "leapfrogged" its 40° API sweet crude 90¢ from $2.55 ($11.32) a barrel to $3.45 ($15.32), with the Libyan government increasing its take from $1.38 ($6.13) a barrel to $2.02 ($8.97), which was what the game was all about—the Mideast governments increasing their revenue. The following chart depicts the posted prices and government revenues from November 14, 1970 to January 1, 1974 for the benchmark Saudi Arabian 34° API light crude with the 2002 equivalent values in parenthesis:[73]

---

[73] Cooper, Brian, ed. *OPEC Oil Report*. London: Petroleum Economist, 1977.

Effective Date	Posted Price $	Government Revenue
14 November 1970	1.80 (8.37)	0.98 (4.56)
15 February 1971	2.18 (9.68)	1.27 (5.64)
20 January 1972	2.48 (10.69)	1.45 (6.25)
1 June 1973	3.90 (15.87)	1.82 (7.41)
16 October 1973	5.12 (20.84)	3.45 (14.04)
1 January 1974	11.65 (42.64)	9.31 (34.07)

The Arab boycott and OPEC price increases of 1971 through 1974 caused a worldwide recession and inflation. Not surprisingly, OPEC claimed it "contributed but insignificantly to the high rates of inflation" at its Algiers meeting in March 1975.[74] During the Iranian revolution and Iran/Iraq War, the spot price hit $40 in **1979** ($99.20) and remained in the neighborhood of $32 ($58) for several years before dropping to around $28 ($47) in **1985**.

Falling prices also cause economic disruptions. In **1986** Saudi Arabia, tired of being the swing producer and its fellow OPEC members cheating on their quotas, let loose its production and generated a price crash to $10 ($16.40) in April before it bottomed at $8 ($13.12) in August. The downward spiral prompted President Ronald Reagan to send Vice President George Bush, the Connecticut-born Texas oilman, to Saudi Arabia to discuss its disastrous oil policy. American oil companies and banks were hurting. More than 300,000 oil-industry workers were laid off, and banks who had loaned money to the oil industry held billions in uncollectible loans. During the next months, a consensus developed between oil-producing and oil-consuming nations that a New York Mercantile Exchange price of $18 ($29.52) a barrel would strike a nice balance, but the market-driven price stayed $2 to $3 below the target until Saddam Hussein decided to invade Kuwait in 1990 and all hell broke loose.

The price peaked on the day of Desert Storm's first air strike in January **1991**—the NYMEX price hit $40 ($52.80). The next day it dropped faster than an Iraqi soldier diving for cover to $20 ($26.40) as oilmen and traders watched both their NYMEX computers and smart bombs hit their targets on CNN. *Crude-oil prices were now led by the NYMEX and London's International Petroleum Exchange markets based on reactions to perceptions of future demand and availability.*

---

[74] *OPEC General Information and Chronology.* Vienna: OPEC, 1994, p. 27.

Chapter 18 — In **1921** Armand Hammer returned from Russia with $75,000 in cash for Soviet secret agents that would be equal to $757,500 in 2002. When **1935** rolled around, Hammer borrowed $75,000 from the Reconstruction Finance Corporation to finance his art galleries that were laundering money for Soviet spies, which would be borrowing the equivalent of $987,000 in 2002.

The $50,000 Frances Tolman lent Hammer in **1955** would be worth $335,000 today. Hammer's tax returns showing he made less than $27,000 during the last five years indicate his income would be in the range of $180,000 to $195,000 today.

Victor, Armand Hammer's brother, was the source of Armand's purchase price of the Roosevelts' Campobello estate from Elliott for $5,000 in **1952,** which would be the equivalent of $34,000 today. The FBI reported in Hammer's file that the price was $12,000 ($81,600), but the FBI was probably in error. Perpetually broke Elliott had purchased Campobello from his father's estate for $12,000. When Elliott told his mother, she was pissed off that he had sold their summer home—a national shrine—and it is believed he told her the price was $12,000 so she wouldn't know how hard up he was. Hammer contributed Campobello to the American and Canadian governments in 1961 in an effort to ingratiate himself with President Kennedy, gain support for his Russian fertilizer project, and earn a tax write-off.

When Hammer invested in Occidental Petroleum Corporation in **1956,** it was trading at 18¢ a share ($1.19 in 2002) and only had 600,000 outstanding shares. Thus its total stock equity was $100,800 ($715,000), although its book value was only $34,000 ($225,000). The corporation borrowed $100,000 ($662,000) to invest in the Mutual Broadcasting Company in what turned out to be a stock scam, although Hammer was not implicated. Occidental's $100,000 investment earned $308,000 ($1,975,000) when it was sold in **1957.** Armand's and Frances's $53,000 ($351,000) individual gambles each swelled to $163,000 ($1,045,000).

Chapter 19 — Occidental's market value of $10 million in **1961** would be the equivalent of $60.2 million today. By **1965,** Occidental's inflated net worth rose to $45 million, the equivalent of $257 million today. But Occidental has come a long way. In 2001 the *Oil & Gas Journal* ranked it the fifth-largest U.S. petroleum company with assets of $17.85 billion. (*See Chart 6:3.*)

Hammer's payment of $2.8 million *baksheesh* was an enormous bribe in **1967** and would equal $15.15 million today. The $10,000 contribution to a Unitarian church to falsely claim he wasn't Jewish and guarantee an afterlife in hell is the equivalent of $54,100 today.

The Libyan pipeline cost of $153 million in **1968** would be equal to $792.5 million today. Occidental's $725-million total debt would be a staggering $3.75 billion today. Libya was Occidental's only major cash cow, and oilmen calculate the payout of wells and oil fields in barrels of oil. To Hammer's chagrin, Occidental was only netting 56¢ a barrel ($2.90) before paying off Bechtel's pipeline construction costs. At the rate of 600,000 barrels a day of current production, the debt would take more than five-and-one-half years to pay the total debt and reach payout before showing a profit and paying the Occidental's shareholders a dividend. The fastest way to pay off the debt was to increase the oil production to 800,000 barrels a day. So what if overproduction depleted the oil field before its time and left millions of barrels of oil unrecovered? While Hammer was cutting costs, he charged Libya for the water wells he promised to drill as part of the concession terms—they could afford the $13-million cost ($67.3 million today).

The 3-percent *baksheesh* was a big drain on Hammer's calculations in **1969** and had to be cut. At $1.80 a barrel and 600,000 barrels a day, it cost Occidental $32,400 a day, the equivalent of $158,760 today.

The $3 million in bribes Hammer spread around in Venezuela in **1970** would be the equivalent of almost $14 million today. The SEC finding that Occidental inflated its income by $13.8 million during **1969** and **1970** is petty larceny by today's standards and would only amount to $65.9 million in 2002. The shareholder suit settlement of $11 million is also only worth $51.2 million today. Of interest, Arthur Anderson of Enron infamy had to pay $1 million ($4.65 million).

Around **1983,** when Occidental's oil shale mining project was abandoned, crude-oil prices were about $32 ($57) and the estimated cost of producing a barrel of oil from oil shale was $44 ($80). There are no accurate reports of Occidental's write-off, but it was more than $1 billion ($1.8 billion today).

Hammer advocating a pipeline across Siberia and the Bering Straits to Alaska then to the Lower Forty-eight drew ridicule from engineers and financiers. Its estimated cost of more than $17 billion in **1972** would be more than $73 billion today. His $1-billion fertilizer project ($4.3 billion) and $100-million Moscow Trade Center ($431 million) received loans of $180 million and $35 million for each project respectively from the Export-Import Bank ($732.6 million and $142.5 million today) because of Nixon's and Kissinger's craving for détente.

In **1981** Hammer signed a coal-mine deal with the Chinese government committing Occidental to invest $240 million ($456 million) when he actually needed $345 million ($652 million). By **1982** the costs had risen to $640 million ($1.2 billion), and he was asking the Chinese to guarantee Occidental's investment.

Hammer's purchase of the Codex Leicester that Occidental paid for and he renamed the Hammer Codex (the egomaniac had to put his name first) actually cost $5,280,000 plus a 10-percent commission in **1980**, which today equals $12,719,500. (It was bought after Hammer's death by Microsoft's Bill Gates for $32 million, so it wasn't a bad deal.)

The size of the scoundrel's estate in **1992** surprised everyone—it was only $40 million ($51.6 million today), $27 million ($34.8 million) of which came in a "golden casket" from Occidental upon his death. Wall Street pundits and business associates thought Hammer's estate would be in the hundreds of millions. What didn't surprise those who knew him was that he owed millions, especially to charities that had bestowed honors on him and were no longer useful to the scoundrel.

ENDNOTES

Mea culpa! I admit writing a 142-page legal oil treatise for the American Bar Association containing 745 footnotes (an average of 5.25 footnotes per page). After nitpicking by a swarm of ABA-anointed law clerks, the number swelled to 817 and was sprinkled with "id."—*idem,* Latin for the previous citation. With haggling, I managed to reduce the number to 786. I have read books containing thousands of footnotes, confirming my theory that the number is directly proportionate to the writer's pomposity or attempt to prove scholarship. While citations are necessary to reference authority for stated facts and credit the original author's work, they should not detract from reading by infesting the pages like ants on a picnic blanket.

I opted for endnotes under chapter and some section headings and limited the footnotes to cite court cases, facilitate clarification, and cut down on thumbing to the small print in the back. As the end product is a composite digest of lengthy and detailed works and required separating fact from fiction and myth to arrive at my irreverent analysis, I decided broad references are more helpful to readers interested in confirmation or comparison. While searching for what actually happened, at times there were four or more books spread on my desk that required I pick the facts from one and laugh at the biased misinformation in others.

Endnotes also provide the opportunity to praise some sources and offer snide remarks to forewarn the unwary reader, as some authors are bias *scoundrels* with an ax to grind or oil company apologists.

PART ONE: EARLY OILMEN

PART 1

Lockwood, John. "Booth's oil-field venture goes bust," *Washington Times*. March 1, 2003, p. C-1.

CHAPTER 1 THE FIRST OILMEN
—Ancient Oil History

Anderson, Robert O. *Fundamentals of the Petroleum Industry*. Norman: Univ. of Oklahoma Press, 1984, pp. 4-6, 15, 20. [Excellent readable overview of the oil industry.]

Casson, Lionel. "Imagine a Time When Oil Was Only a Nuisance," *Scientific American*. August, 1991, pp. 108-112.

Tait, Samuel W. Jr. *The Wildcatters: An Informal History of Oil-Hunting in America*. Princeton: Princeton Univ. Press, 1946, p. 47.

Williamson, Harold F., and Arnold R. Daum. *The American Petroleum Industry*. Vol. 1, *The Age of Illumination, 1859-1899*. Evanston: Northwestern Univ. Press, 1959, pp. 4-12. [Biased pro-petroleum industry and Rockefeller, but contains excellent endnotes and references to early works and is the most detailed treatise on the petroleum industry in its infancy.]

—The Early Americans

Anderson, *Fundamentals*, p. 122.

Casson, "Imagine a Time," *Scientific American*, p. 112.

Tait, *The Wildcatters*, pp. 7-8, 17-18.

Williamson, *Age of Illumination*, pp. 15-23, 94.

—The First Oilmen

Knowles, Ruth Sheldon. *The Greatest Gamblers*. Norman: Univ. of Oklahoma Press, 1978, pp. 5-9.

Tait, *The Wildcatters*, pp. 3-4, 9-17.

Williamson, *Age of Illumination*, pp. 23, 67-81.

Yergin, Daniel. *The Prize: The Epic Quest for Oil, Money, and Power*. New York: Simon & Schuster, 1991, pp. 26-29. [The excellent and well-written history of the oil industry through 1990, won a Pulitzer Prize in 1991, but doesn't expose the scoundrels.]

Chapter 2 Seeds of Chaos
—The Oil Regions
Tarbell, Ida Minerva. *The History of the Standard Oil Company.* New York: Macmillan, 1904. Reprinted by Norton in 1969 in condensed version, p. 12. [A Muckraker's diatribe, but reveals Standard Oil's many abuses. Separating her *National Inquirer*-style exposés from the facts is difficult.] References are to the condensed version unless noted by volume number, as librarians frown on my habit of fluorescent yellow highlighting in rare books.

Williamson, *Age of Illumination*, p. 97.

—The Rule of Capture
Anderson, *Fundamentals*, pp. 28-29.

Kuntz, Eugene O., and John S. Lowe, Owen S. Anderson, Ernest E. Smith, David E. Pierce. *Oil and Gas Law.* 3rd ed. St. Paul: West, 1998, pp. 9-14.

Williamson, *Age of Illumination*, pp. 758-762.

—Barrels & Transportation
Tarbell, *History,* pp. 6-8.

Williamson, *Age of Illumination*, pp. 82-86, 107, 164-185.

Yergin, *The Prize,* p. 788 (barrel size).

—Oil Prices and Production
The Derrick's Hand-Book of Petroleum: A Complete Chronological and Statistical Review of Petroleum Developments from 1859 to 1898. Vol. I. Oil City: Derrick Pub. Co., 1898, pp. 704-712.

Henry, J.T. *The Early and Later History of Petroleum with Authentic Facts in Regard to its Development in Western Pennsylvania.* Philadelphia: J.B. Rodgers, 1873, pp. 5, 13-14.

Tait, *The Wildcatters,* p. 23 (J.W. Sherman Well).

Tarbell, *History,* pp. 6-11.

Williamson, *Age of Illumination,* pp. 118, 120-126, 371-374, 381-383.

Yergin, *The Prize,* pp. 29-34.

—Refiners
Gale, Thomas A. *The Wonder of the 19th Century! Rock Oil, in Pennsylvania and Elsewhere.* Erie: Sloan and Griffeth, 1860, pp. 40-41.

Gesner, Abraham. *A Practical Treatise on Coal, Petroleum, and Other Distilled Oils.* 2d ed. Ed. George W. Gesner. New York: Balliére, 1865, pp. 128-129.

Williamson, *Age of Illumination,* pp. 45, 108-111, 287-295.

Yergin, *The Prize,* pp. 22-23.

—**The Seeds of Chaos Sprouted Confusion**

Chernow, Ron. *Titan: The Life of John D. Rockefeller, Sr.* New York: Random House, 1998, p. 153. ("angel of mercy"). [A well-written and fairly balanced biography.]

Nevins, Allen. *John D. Rockefeller, the Heroic age of American Enterprise.* Vol. I. New York: Charles Scribner & Sons, 1940, p. 373. [Rockefeller's Pulitzer Prize winning apologist could not get a reputable house like Scribner's to publish the tripe today.]

—**Booms, Burns, & Busts**

Anderson, *Fundamentals,* p. 23 (Pennsylvania State Geologist quote).

Henry, *Early History,* pp. 232-33.

Williamson, *Age of Illumination,* pp. 112-113, 120-126.

Yergin, *The Prize,* pp. 29-34.

PART TWO: ROCKEFELLER & STANDARD OIL

Chernow, *Titan,* p. 325 (hymn).

CHAPTER 3 BOOKKEEPER TO OIL BARON
—**Warning**

Camden, Johnson Newlon, "The Standard Oil Company," *North American Review,* (February, 1883), pp. 181-190.

Chernow, *Titan,* p. 341 (*Nation* quote).

Tarbell, Ida Minerva. "John D. Rockefeller, A Character Study," *McClure's,* XXV (1905), pp. 227-249, 386-398; "Commercial Machiavellianism," *McClure's* XXVI (1905), pp. 453-463. [Her nasty personal attack on Rockefeller shows her bitterness.]

Williamson, Harold F., and Ralph L. Andreano, Arnold R. Daum, Gilbert C. Klose. *The American Petroleum Industry.* Vol. 2. *The Age of Energy, 1899-1959.* Evanston: Northwestern Univ. Press, 1963, pp. 16-17. [Biased pro-petroleum industry, but contains informative data.]

—The Baptist Bookkeeper's Bloodlines

Chernow, *Titan*, pp. 7-11, 28, 37-8, 42-5, 60.

O'Conner, Richard. *The Oil Barons.* Boston: Little Brown, 1968, pp. 24-25. [Weak on documentation and perpetuates a few myths.]

Tarbell, *History*, pp. 23-24.

Yergin, *The Prize*, pp. 35-37.

—The Oil Business

Chamberlain, John. *The Enterprising Americans.* New York: Harper & Row, 1961, p. 149.

Chernow, *Titan*, pp. 60, 63-72, 76-79, 87-88, 100-108.

Tarbell, *History*, pp. 24-26.

Williamson, *Age of Illumination*, pp. 301-302.

—Divisions and Self-interests

Williamson, *Age of Illumination*, pp. 194-201, 287-294, 297-300.

—The South Improvement Company

Chernow, *Titan*, pp. 134-142.

Nevins, *John D. Rockefeller*, Vol. I, p. 324.

O'Conner, *Oil Barons*, pp. 30-32.

Solberg, Carl. *Oil Power.* New York: Mason Charter, 1976, pp. 34-36. [Critical and well-documented analysis of the oil industry and oil-men.]

Tarbell, *History*, pp. 29-37.

Williamson, *Age of Illumination*, pp. 346-352.

CHAPTER 4 THE OCTOPUS SPREADS ITS TENTACLES
—The Cleveland Massacre

Chernow, *Titan*, pp. 142-147, 445-447.

Solberg, *Oil Power*, pp. 35-36.

Tarbell, *History*, pp. 32-33, 41-42, 79-82; Vol. I, pp. 201-207.

Williamson, *Age of Illumination*, pp. 352-356.

—The Treaty of Titusville

Chernow, *Titan*, pp. 157-160, 110 (Flagler's plaque).

Tarbell, *History*, pp. 46-55.

Williamson, *Age of Illumination*, pp. 356-360.

—Rockefeller's Plan

Chernow, *Titan*, pp. 161-171, 204.

Tarbell, *History*, pp. 62-70.

Williamson, *Age of Illumination*, pp. 366-367, 416-429.

—The Pennsylvania Railroad's Last Stand

Chernow, *Titan*, pp. 171-172, 200-203.

O'Conner, *Oil Barons*, pp. 37-38.

Tarbell, *History*, pp. 74-77.

Williamson, *Age of Illumination*, pp. 422-426.

—Pipelines—The Final Loop in the Noose

Chernow, *Titan*, pp. 197-200, 207-215.

O'Conner, *Oil Barons*, pp. 39-41.

Tarbell, *History*, pp. 100-109.

Williamson, *Age of Illumination*, pp. 383-388, 397-402, 412-416, 432, 440-456.

Wolbert, George S., Jr. *U.S. Oil Pipelines*. Washington: American Petroleum Institute, 1979, pp. 2, 5-6.

CHAPTER 5 THE BIGGER, THE BETTER, & THE BADDEST

—Legal Skirmishes

Chernow, *Titan*, pp. 211-214.

O'Conner, *Oil Barons*, pp. 44-47.

Tarbell, *History*, pp. 90-93.

Williamson, *Age of Illumination*, pp. 430-437.

—The Standard Oil Trust

Chernow, *Titan*, pp. 224-229, 331-333.

Henderson, Wayne, and Scott Benjamin. *Standard Oil: The First 125 Years*. Osceola, Wisconsin: Motorbooks International, 1996, p. 11. [Slick public relations flack for Standard Oil.]

Williamson, *Age of Illumination*, pp. 468-470, 709-715.

Yergin, *The Prize*, pp. 44-47.

—Stretching Its Tentacles
Chernow, *Titan*, pp. 255-256, 284-288.

Clark, James A., and Michel T. Halbouty. *Spindletop.* New York: Random House, 1952, pp. 108-109, 161-168.

Day, James M. *The Black Giant.* Austin: Eakin Press, 2003, pp. ——— ——— [Buy it. The author needs the money.]

Henderson, *The First 125 Years,* pp. 8-9.

Solberg, *Oil Power,* pp. 56-59.

Weaver, Jacqueline Lang. *Unitization of Oil and Gas Fields in Texas.* Washington: Resources for the Future, 1986, pp. 52, 394. [Excellent treatise and background on Texas oil and gas law.]

Williamson, *Age of Illumination,* pp. 476, 541-545, 688-689, 714-715.

Yergin, *The Prize,* pp. 83-92.

—Trustbusters and Blusters
Chamberlain, *The Enterprising Americans,* pp. 163-184.

Chernow, *Titan,* pp. 376, 426 (citing *The World* (10/12/98)), 429, 539-544, 545 (Mark Twain quote), 661, 662.

Fox, William F., Jr. *Federal Regulation of Energy.* Colorado Springs: Shepard's/McGraw-Hill, 1983, pp. 280-284, 299.

O'Conner, *Oil Barons,* pp. 15-19.

Williamson, *Age of Energy,* pp. 8-9, 104-105.

Wolbert, *U.S. Oil Pipelines,* pp. 251-252.

CHAPTER 6 THE BUSTED TRUST

The Standard Oil dissolution was extracted from the Supreme Court's decision in *Standard Oil Company of New Jersey v. United States,* 221 U.S. 1 (1911), and the Circuit Court of the United States for the Eastern District of Missouri case of the same name at 173 Fed. 177. The reuniting and major mergers and 2002 status in Chart 6:1 and Chart 6:2 are from Henderson, *Standard Oil: The First 125 Years,* Anderson, *Fundamentals,* and the Securities Data Co.

Anderson, *Fundamentals,* p. 27.

Chernow, *Titan,* pp. 555-558

Cushman, Clare, Ed. *The Supreme Court Justices.* Washington: The Supreme Court Historical Society-Congressional Quarterly, 1993, p. 274 (Chief Justice White).

Henderson, *The First 125 Years,* pp. 11-17, 125-126.

Phillips, Kevin. *Wealth and Democracy.* New York: Broadway, 2002, p. 50.

Tussing, Arlon R., and Connie C. Barlow. *The Natural Gas Industry: Evolution, Structure and Economics.* Cambridge: Ballinger, 1984, pp. 32, 96-98, 205-208. [A must read to understand the basics of the natural gas industry.]

Williamson, *Age of Energy,* pp. 12-14.

PART THREE: TEAPOT DOME

Part Three was drawn largely from *Teapot Dome* by Werner and Starr, written in the investigative reporter style digging for dirt, but well after the fact and without a bibliography, and *Teapot Dome: Oil and Politics in the 1920's* by Noggle, a scholarly professorial work emphasizing politics. The intrigue and background was supplemented by O'Conner's *The Oil Barons*. The facts and elements of the oil leases and chicanery were taken from the Supreme Court's decisions in *Pan American Petroleum and Transport v. United States*, 273 U.S. 476 (1927); and *Mammoth Oil Co. v. United States*, 276 U.S. 1 (1927). Other sources are included below.

Cushman, *The Supreme Court Justices,* p. 310 (Chief Justice Hughes), 369 (Justice Roberts).

Knowles, *The Greatest Gamblers,* pp. 81-82, 203-219 (Doheny background).

Noggle, Burl. *Teapot Dome: Oil and Politics in the 1920's.* Baton Rouge: Louisiana State Univ. Press, 1962, passim.

O'Conner, *Oil Barons,* pp. 241-263.

Solberg, *Oil Power,* pp. 80-102.

Werner, M.R., and John Starr. *Teapot Dome.* New York: Viking Press, 1959, passim.

Wood, Harold W., Jr. "Pinchot and Mather: How the Forest Service and Park Service Got That Way," *Not Man Apart.* (December, 1976) (Pinchot).

Yergin, *The Prize*, pp. 211-218.

Part Four: International Skulduggery

Part Four was written with Blair's *The Control of Oil*, Sampson's *The Seven Sisters*, Yergin's *The Prize*, congressional reports, and the author's *What Every American Should Know About the Mid East and Oil* open on my desk as I pecked on my word processor trying to ascertain what really happened. Blair's *The Control of Oil* was largely taken from *The International Petroleum Cartel*, Staff Report of the Federal Trade Commission, Senate Small Business Committee Subcommittee, 82nd Cong., 2nd Sess., 1952, which he directed and co-authored. It reads like an indictment of the oil companies and eventually was the basis of an antitrust suit against the Seven Sisters that never amounted to anything. Blair heavily cited the Senate Subcommittee on Multinational Corporations, Committee of Foreign Relations *Hearings on Multinational Petroleum Corporations and Foreign Policy*, 93rd Cong. 2nd Sess., 1974. On the other side of the spectrum are Sampson's *The Seven Sisters*, a British journalist's view, and Yergin's *The Prize*, an American economist's view, both of which lean towards the defense of the oil industries of Britain and the United States. There are many other views cited in *What Every American Should Know About the Mid East and Oil*. For example, Mostafa Elm presents the Iranian side of Anglo-Persian's skulduggery in Iran in *Oil, Power, and Principle* that is closer to the truth than Western histories. The irreverent opinions are mine, as are the choice of quotes, such as selecting Sampson's quote on page 13 of Gulbenkian, "Oil friendships are greasy." Yergin's quote on page 202 is, "Oil friendships are very slippery."

Chart 11:1 "Should Anyone Believe the Interior Department's Dire Predictions?" sources are the House Committee on Interstate and Foreign Commerce, *Presidential Energy Program, Hearings before the Subcommittee on Energy and Power on the Implications of the President's Proposals in the Energy Independence Act of 1975*, 94th Cong. 1st Sess., 1975, p. 643; U.S. Geological Survey, *Papers on the Conservation of Mineral Sources*. Washington: Government Printing Office, 1909, p. 45; U.S. Geological Survey, "The Oil Supply in the United States," *Bulletin of the American Association of Petroleum Geologists*. (January-February 1922, p. 45; and Williamson, *Age of Energy*, pp. 16, 302, 810. Other sources are noted below:

Blair, John M. *The Control of Oil.* New York: Pantheon Books, 1976, pp. 29-76, 152-159 ("window dressing").

Day, James M. *What Every American Should Know About the Mid East and Oil.* Carson City: Bridger House, 1998, pp. 49-77, 108-118. [Buy it and read the author's irreverent account that offends everyone involved in the Mid East. He needs the money.]

Elm, Mostafa. *Oil, Power, and Principle: Iran's Oil Nationalization and its Aftermath.* Syracuse: Syracuse Univ. Press, 1992, pp. 7-19, 144, 315-321. [A relatively accurate account of how the British and the Seven Sisters screwed Iran with the help of the American government.]

Ferguson, Niall. *The House of Rothschild.* New York: Viking, 1999, p. 355 (Rothschild interests in Baku).

Jacoby, Neil H. *International Oil.* New York: Macmillan, 1974, pp. 25-31.

Jones, Peter Ellis. *Oil: A Practical Guide to the Economics of World Petroleum.* Cambridge, England: Woodhead-Faulkner, 1988, pp. 11-12. (Russia and Far East.)

Lacy, Robert. *The Kingdom: Arabia and the House of Saud.* New York: Harcourt Brace Jovanovich, 1981, pp. 128-130, 233-234, 258, 309 (Philby). [A must read for those desiring to understand Saudi Arabia.]

Sampson, Anthony. *The Seven Sisters.* New York: Viking Penguin, 1975, pp. 56-102, 107-182.

Yergin, *The Prize,* pp. 115-164, 184-206, 220-221 (Doherty "barbarian"), 260-269, 280-301, 410-416.

Washington Times. April 28, 2002. (Senator Ted Stevens "liars.")

Weaver, *Unitization,* p. 382 n1 (Doherty and API).

Williamson, *Age of Energy,* pp. 316-321, 504, 531, 736-744.

PART FIVE: THE BLACK GIANT

Part Five is a digest of my *The Black Giant,* much of which was derived from James Clark's and Michel Halbouty's *The Last Boom,* H. L. Hunt's *H. L. Hunt Early Days,* Hurt's *Texas Rich,* Weaver's *Unitization of Oil and Gas Fields in Texas,* and Blair's *The Control of Oil.* Other sources are noted below.

Clark, James M., and Michel T. Halbouty. *The Last Boom*. New York: Random House, 1972, *passim*. [By two gentlemen insiders who didn't want to offend anyone, but covers the events in detail.]

Clark, *Spindletop,* pp. 108-109, 128-134, 139, 143-146.

Hunt, H. L. *Early Days*. Dallas: Parade Press, 1973, *passim*.

Hurt, Harry III. *Texas Rich: The Hunt Dynasty From the Early Oil Days Through the Silver Crash*. New York: Norton, 1981, pp. 70-121.

Larson, Henrietta M., and Kenneth W. Porter. *History of Humble Oil and Refining: A Study in Industrial Growth*. New York: Harper Brothers, 1959, p. 45. [Standard Oil public relations newspeak.]

Yergin, *The Prize,* pp. 93-94, 220-222, 244-259.

PART SIX: MODERN SCOUNDRELS

Lenzner, Robert. *The Great Getty*. New York: Crown, 1985, p. 123. (Getty quote.)

Hunt v. Mobil Oil, 550 F.2d. 68, 73. (2nd Cir. 1977) (Qaddafi quote).

Yergin, *The Prize,* p. 525. (Pérez Alfonzo quote.)

CHAPTER 16 OPEC & CHAPTER 17 THE AMERICAN FIASCO

The chapters were taken from my *What Every American Should Know About the Mid East and Oil*. Much of the material relied upon came from Skeet's excellent *OPEC: Twenty-Five Years of Prices and Politics*, Yergin's *The Prize,* Sampson's *Seven Sisters,* Anderson's *Fiasco,* and Organization of Petroleum Exporting Countries' *OPEC General Information & Chronology 1960-1994*. The section entitled **Unlearned Lessons** is my personal ranting, but is supported by Stobaugh and Yergin's excellent *Energy Futures*. Other sources are noted below.

Anderson, Jack, with James Boyd. *Fiasco*. New York: Times Books, 1983, pp. 111-159.

Kissinger, Henry A. *Years of Upheaval*. London: Weidenfeld & Nicolson, 1982, p. 515 (quote).

Organization of Petroleum Exporting Countries. *OPEC General Information & Chronology 1960-1994*. Vienna: OPEC, 1994, *passim*.

Skeet, Ian. *OPEC: Twenty-Five Years of Prices and Politics*. Cambridge England: Cambridge Univ., 1988, *passim*. [Well-documented unbiased history of OPEC.]

Stobaugh, Robert, and Daniel Yergin. *Energy Futures: Report of the Energy Project at the Harvard Business School.* New York: Random House, 1979, pp. 5, 17, 24-29. [It is heartwarming to find economists' analysis and predictions that hold up after twenty years.]

Terzain, Pierre. *OPEC: The Inside Story.* London: Zed Books, 1985, p. 21 ("the masses" and "importance of oil.") [A left-wing diatribe of misinformation.]

Wall Street Journal, April 27, 1988 (TRC & Nance).

Weaver, *Unitization,* p. 395 n 84. (Humble pipeline profits.)

CHAPTER 18 THE MOST DESPICABLE SCOUNDREL AWARD & CHAPTER 19 BIG-TIME OPERATOR

The chapters relied heavily on Edward Jay Epstein's marvelous hatchet job, *Dossier: The Secret History of Armand Hammer,* and Carl Blumay's and Henry Edward's exposé *The Dark Side of Power: The Real Armand Hammer.* Weinberg's *Armand Hammer: The Untold Story* was also revealing. I paid little heed to the pseudo autobiography, *Hammer,* by Armand Hammer with Neil Lyndon, and Robert G. Considine's *The Remarkable Life of Dr. Armand Hammer,* so neither earned space in the Bibliography.

Blumay, Carl, with Henry Edwards. *The Dark Side of Power: The Real Armand Hammer.* New York: Simon & Schuster, 1992, *passim.* [It delves into Hammer's mind, but Blumay believed too much of what Hammer and his brother, Victor, told him.]

Epstein, Edward Jay. *Dossier: The Secret History of Armand Hammer.* New York: Random House, 1996, *passim.* [Well-documented and looks in the dark crevices that Hammer hid so well.]

Weinberg, Steve. *Armand Hammer: The Untold Story.* London: Abacus, 1992, *passim.* [I enjoyed it. Weinberg didn't like Armand Hammer any more than I did.]

Woodward, Bob. *Veil: The Secret Wars of the CIA, 1981-1987.* New York: Simon & Schuster, 1987, p. 40 (Hammer and Reagan in the barber shop).

Washington Times. Duranty (Mar. 29, 2003); Mobil/Kazakhstan (Mar. 17, 2003).

CHAPTER 20 ENRONIANS & OTHER SCOUNDRELS

Newspaper clippings in my files covering the Enron collapse and scandal fill two four-inch thick notebooks. My library shelves hold a half-dozen Enron exposés and "inside stories." The most complete press coverage was by the *Houston Chronicle* and the *Wall Street Journal*. There is also an excellent five-part series in the *Washington Post* by Peter Behr and April Witt. Unfortunately, the sources and this chapter were written before the ending and everyone wants to know: Which of the scoundrels went to jail and how much of their ill-gotten gain was disgorged and paid to those the scoundrels deceived?

The most informative books covering Enron's rise and collapse are *Enron: The Rise and Fall* by Loren Fox, a professional analysis by an experienced business reporter and editor, and *Pipe Dreams: Greed, Ego, and the Death of Enron* by Robert Bryce, an admitted muckraker with a penchant to look behind the scenes and under rocks. Both are enjoyable reading. Mimi Swartz and Sherron Watkin's collaboration on *Power Failure: The Inside Story of the Collapse of Enron* showed good insight into the characters, but no one believes that Sherron the Shark was that innocent. Other sources are noted below:

Bryce, Robert. *Pipe Dreams: Greed, Ego, and the Death of Enron.* New York: Public Affairs, 2002, *passim.*

Cruver, Brian. *Anatomy of Greed: The Unshredded Truth from an Enron Insider.* New York: Carroll & Graf, 2002. [Written by one of the smart men who proved he was a jerk. It was on the $2.95 bargain counter six months after its release.]

Fox, Loren. *Enron: The Rise and Fall.* Hoboken: John Wiley & Sons, 2002, *passim.*

Fusaro, Peter C., and Ross M. Miller. *What Went Wrong at Enron.* Hoboken: John Wiley & Sons, 2002, pp. 86, 88-90 (Enron-Qwest sham trades). [Scant on details in a rush to be the first expose published.]

McLean, Bethany. "Why Enron Went Bust," *Fortune.* December 24, 2001, *passim.*

McNamara, Will. *The California Energy Crisis: Lessons for a Deregulating Industry.* Tulsa: PennWell, 2002, pp. 32-35, 51-58.

Swartz, Mimi, and Sherron Watkins. *Power Failure: The Inside Story on the Collapse of Enron.* New York: Doubleday, 2003, not much.

285

Houston Chronicle: Enron owed $570 million by California (Nov. 8, 2001); Enron's restated earnings for back years (Nov. 9, 2001); Jesse Jackson (Nov. 13, 2001); Enron inflated gas assets (Sept. 21, 2002); Arthur Anderson (Oct. 16, 2002); Belden and electric trading tricks (Oct. 17 & 18, 2002); Tom Fowler, "The Pride and Fall of Enron," *passim* (Oct. 19, 2002); Enron employee losses (Oct. 23, 2002); Lay stock sales (Oct. 24, 2002); Enron books (Dec. 7, 2002); $1.8 billion overcharges (Dec. 12, 2002); Lawyers fees (Jan. 14, 2003); Lay's ATM approach (Jan. 16, 2003). Data on Enron directors, stock trades, and Enron 2001 Annual Report via houstonchronicle.com.

New York Times: Top gas and electricity marketers (Nov. 10, 2001).

Wall Street Journal: Watkins's letter to Lay (Jan. 16, 2002); Skilling testimony (Feb. 27. 2002); Lay background and history of Enron & golf with Clinton (Apr. 26, 2002); Lynch quote (Apr. 12, 2002); Kopper guilty plea (Aug. 21, 2002); Special purpose entities (Sept. 30, 2002); Fastow charged (Oct. 3, 2002); $1.8 billion overcharges (Dec. 13, 2002); FERC ruling (Mar. 24, 2003).

Washington Post: Insider trading (Dec. 6, 2001, Jan. 7, 2002); Lay bonuses (Feb. 3, 2002); Skilling testimony (recollection) Feb. 27, 2002; Executive bonuses (Mar. 2, 2002, June 19, 2002); employees (Mar. 3, 2002); Enron electric trading/Wood, Wolak, and Freeman quotes (May 7, 2002); Wash transactions (May 9, 2002); Peter Behr and April Witt five-part series (July 28-Aug. 1, 2002), *passim*; Fastow (Oct. 3, 2002); Belden trading (Oct. 18, 2002); Reliant Resources $13.8 million penalty (Feb. 1, 2003).

Washington Times: Insider trading (Jan. 15, 2002); Executive bonuses for hitting stock target (Mar. 2, 2002).

INDEX